Milton and the Line of Vision

Bust of Milton. *Collection of G. William Stuart, Jr., and John Homer Loetterle.*

MILTON
and the Line of Vision

EDITED BY

Joseph Anthony Wittreich, Jr.

THE UNIVERSITY
OF WISCONSIN
PRESS

Published 1975
The University of Wisconsin Press
Box 1379, Madison, Wisconsin 53701

The University of Wisconsin Press, Ltd.
70 Great Russell Street, London

First printing

Printed in the United States of America

For LC CIP information see the colophon

ISBN 0-299-06910-9

All hangs harmoniously together. The same word that . . . tells of the way to a sonship condition, lays open, at the same time, the prospect of a sonship inheritance.

—Patrick Fairbairn

Criticism is the art of knowing the hidden roads that go from poem to poem.

Milton is the central problem in any theory or history of poetic influence in English . . .

—Harold Bloom

X

Contents

Illustrations

Preface

. . . the similarity [that exists between two poets] should not be the kind that obtains between a portrait and a sitter . . . , but rather . . . the kind that obtains between a son and a father. . . . there may often be a great difference between their individual features, [but there is also] that similarity that reminds us of the father as soon as we see the son. . . . We shall therefore make use of another man's inner quality and tone, but avoid his words. For the one kind of similarity is hidden and the other protrudes; the one creates poets, the other apes.

—Francesco Petrarca

The formal study of Milton's influence on English poetry began with John Good's premises that "the influence of Milton was powerfully felt upon all the multiplied forms and phases of eighteenth century life" and that "by far the mightiest element of this Miltonic influence came, directly or indirectly, . . . from *Paradise Lost*." Good's own intention of examining Milton's influence "in all its comprehensiveness, and multiplicity," was quickly surpassed by Raymond Dexter Havens's exploration of "all the available English poetry written between 1660 and 1837 regardless of its esthetic value or historical importance." Undiscriminating in his explorations, however, Havens managed only to yield up a model of poetic influence which led T. S. Eliot to conclude that Milton had been a bad influence—could only be a bad influence—on his successors. Eliot's conclusion, together with the credence F. R. Leavis lent to it, has fostered the recent proposal that Milton, though himself unburdened by the past, was a source of unremitting anxiety for all those poets who came under his sway: weak poets could only submit to the figure from whom strong poets, like Blake, were compelled to swerve.

xiii

Indeed, it is Blake's squaring off against Milton that provides
this heavily psychologized theory of influence with its historical
model of how poets subsequent to Milton related to one another—a model that is said to find its mythic source in the enmity
existing between God and Satan in *Paradise Lost* and that finds an
unacknowledged theoretical context in an essay on Milton in
which De Quincey, pondering the problem of influence, writes of
Samuel Butler that "like many other original minds, there is little
doubt that he quelled and repressed, by his own excellence, other
minds of the same cast. Mere despair of excelling him . . . drove
back others who pressed into the arena." On the other hand, "in
that mode of power which *he* wielded," says De Quincey, *Milton*
was able to act upon other poets; rather than stifling their talents,
he animated them.

This collection of essays pursues De Quincey's perception rather
than later perversions of it, and from him it takes the question
that stands behind each of its essays:

"Who and what is Milton?" That is to say, what is the place he fills in his own
vernacular literature? what station does he hold in universal literature?

That question these essays answer by locating Milton at the center
of a tradition of English poetry—the line of vision, not the line of
wit—that encompasses, among others, Chaucer, Sidney, and Spenser, the major Romantics, and many moderns.* A collection of
essays, this volume is also, by design, a collective essay in criticism.

*I do not mean to suggest that these two traditions do not converge. Recent criticism
shows otherwise. Having identified George Chapman with the visionary tradition of
poetry, Raymond B. Waddington proceeds to comment illuminatingly on Donne: "The
two *Anniversaries* are the conspicuous exception to his [Donne's] antigeneric bent" and
are an occasion, says Waddington, when this poet situates himself in the visionary
tradition, "assum[ing] the persona of biblical prophet, first an Old Testament prophet
of law and then a New Testament prophet of grace" (*The Mind's Empire: Myth and
Form in George Chapman's Narrative Poems* [Baltimore and London: Johns Hopkins
Univ. Press, 1974], pp. 11, 16). Moreover, in an Ohio State University dissertation
(1973), "Dryden and the Prophetic Mode: An Examination of His Poetic Theory and
Practice in the Light of Seventeenth-Century Concepts of Prophecy," Thomas Francis
Woods points to Dryden's lines from "To Robert Howard"—". . . let me take your
Mantle up, and I/ Will venture in your right to prophesy" (101–2)—by way of suggesting
that prophetic devices are employed by Dryden not only in some of his lyrics but in his
satires and heroic dramas as well. Finally, Maureen Mulvihill, in a University of Wisconsin
dissertation now in progress, makes a similar argument for some of Pope's poetry,
especially *Windsor Forest* and *The Dunciad*, where prophetic elements are both notable
and meaningful.

Individual essays examine a variety of poetic relationships—some entered into by Milton with his predecessors and some entered into with Milton by his successors. Not all relationships, Milton's own or others' with Milton, are here explored. Milton's encounter with Shakespeare is a notable omission: already drawn into focus by Angus Fletcher, this relationship, immensely involved, requires a book. The relationship between Milton and eighteenth-century poetry, already the subject of two books, has here been neglected, as have the Victorians' encounters with Milton, previously studied by James Nelson. Moreover, my own essay breaks with the pattern of the others, attempting to throw up a bridge that unites the first half of this volume with the last and, from this bridge, to survey the minute particulars of the tradition to which all these poets, in and through Milton, are allied.

That tradition (one is tempted to call it *the Milton tradition*) is more exactly the tradition of prophecy. Prophecy is a way of seeing and a way of writing; that is, it is a system of aesthetics. But prophecy is also a way of relating: it postulates a theory of influence and provides a paradigm for intrapoetic relationships that is mapped out by various commentators on the Book of Revelation, but by none of them so eloquently as by Blake in *Milton*. At the center of Blake's poem is the notion that the tradition of prophecy, paralleled by the line of visionary poets, is, in the words of Patrick Fairbairn, "a chain composed of many links, each running into others before and after it." The interconnectedness of the tradition requires that the poet-prophet give to his precursors the same diligent study that Daniel gave to Jeremiah and that John of Patmos gave to Daniel. The involvement of these biblical prophets with one another is replicated by the relationship Spenser strikes with Chaucer, Milton with Spenser (and Sidney), Blake and the other Romantics with Milton, and Yeats or Stevens, as well as many other moderns, with both Milton and Blake. Moreover, the interrelationships, often noted, between the Book of Revelation and other prophecy (especially Daniel's) are archetypal for those that exist between *The Canterbury Tales* and *The Faerie Queene,* between *The Faerie Queene* and *Paradise Lost,* between Milton's epics and those of Blake, and between Blake's epics and the lyric-epic vision of Yeats or the epical novels of Joyce.

Isolated from the visionary line, the prophet is speechless;

touching it, he becomes articulate, even to the point of engaging (as Milton does with Spenser, and Blake with Milton) in corrective criticism. This corrective function is validated by the fact that, while prophets communicate with one another, they all derive their vision from Christ; they are all ministers of the Word. But prophets are also human, possessing infirmities that occasionally disfigure their visions. The first obligation of the prophet is to explicate the vision that serves as a gateway into his own; and explication involves correction, sometimes of the visionary himself, but more often of a body of commentary that has perverted his vision. Once correction is accomplished, interpretation can commence. But whatever its initial purpose—correction or simply interpretation—new prophecy locks into old; and, in consequence, visionary art, whether it be exemplified by biblical prophecy or the poetry of one of the figures under discussion in this volume, is marked by what the Cambridge Platonist, Henry More, calls a "multifarious Allusivenesse" that establishes continuity between prophecies and among prophets. Allusion establishes context, and through context the seals that would hide a new vision are opened. Or, to make the same point differently: prophecy is a mode of reflection; and reflection on it, as Abraham Heschel remarks, "gives way to communion with the prophets." Such communion Milton sought with his predecessors and, in turn, his successors have sought with him.

Most of the essays in this volume, but not all, postulate a theory of influence that resembles the one I have outlined here. The notable exception is the first essay, by Donald Howard, which derives from Chaucer's *The House of Fame* an idea of influence "as a grab bag of verbal tidbits." But then Professor Howard is dealing with a poet whose position among the other poets represented in this volume is unique and whose conception of his predecessors is correspondingly different from Spenser's or Milton's: Chaucer is, after all, "the *first* major *English* poet in the *English* literary tradition as we know it and as Milton knew it," and his lot was to initiate "a *new* tradition," one that was necessarily "based on *continental* models" (italics added). Insofar as Chaucer's successors turned to continental models (and most of them, at one time or another, did), they, too, assumed an attitude like his toward their sources. (One thinks of Milton, who, as much as he belittled

Homer and Virgil or, for that matter, the Church Fathers, stole whatever he wanted from them.) Yet, unlike Chaucer, his successors, beginning with Spenser, had a vernacular tradition in which to ensconce themselves; and their attitudes toward existing models in that tradition is notably different from that taken by Chaucer toward his continental models. Within the English literary tradition, Chaucer's uniqueness can be defined simply: his position is anomalous, whereas that of his successors is roughly analogous. Chaucer, as Professor Howard observes, initiates a literary tradition that shifts the accent to the ideational content of poetry and that makes of the poem "a world unto itself"—the poem, like the world, possessing a multiplicity of structures and being an aggregate of forms, its structures, its forms, existing not so that they may be just "seen" but so that they may be "experienced." Here, in Chaucer's poetry, are the "elements . . . of an aesthetic" that poets like Spenser and Milton appropriate into a system of aesthetics and develop within its context. And here in Chaucer's poetry, too, is an understanding of poetic influence that relates it to phases of "consciousness" and that views it as mental process.

Chaucer's idea of poetic influence as a "grab bag" may be accepted only conditionally by his successors, but his understanding of influence as a psychological process, involving "the shared consciousness of poets," is fully embraced by them. Such an understanding is implicit both in Kathleen Williams's idea of "a community of poets" and in what S. K. Heninger happily calls "the poetics of making." Yet, as Professor Williams observes, poets not only assert continuity with tradition, they are involved in a "dialectic" relationship with it. Two aspects of poetic influence, then—the continuous and the dialectical—are explored by the essays that compose the last half of this volume. Those by Jackie DiSalvo and Stuart Curran probe the contrasting visions of Milton, on the one hand, and of Blake, Byron, and the Shelleys, on the other. And Professor Curran, by introducing into his essay Shelley's celebrated conception of the great poem that "all poets, like the co-operating thoughts of one great mind, have built up since the beginning of the world," links his own essay with those by James Rieger and Joan Webber—essays that find in the "landscape of disillusionment," which beset Romantic England no less than modern America, a path, sometimes heroically traveled, leading back to Milton and from him upward to "the pinnacle" of vision and outward into a "world without end."

By exploring a set of major relationships—every one of them consequential—the essays in this collection are designed to inspire the study of others; and, as a collective essay in criticism, these essays generate a model of poetic influence that, deriving from prophetic tradition, finds its mythic prototype in *Paradise Lost*—in the relationship of the Father and the Son, the Father shining "Most glorious ... Substantially express'd," "without cloud/ Made visible," in his son. Like the eternal son, the poetic son enables us to behold "visibly" what is there "invisibly" in the poetic father; and like the eternal son of *Paradise Regained*, he provides "glimpses of his Father's glory." Such a poetics of influence is not, of course, new. In the nineteenth century, Christopher Wordsworth understood it well, tracing it to the Book of Revelation where, he explains, "one part is ... blended with another" and the whole piece is "woven with the prophecies of the Old Testament," forming "a compact whole with them." This very process, authenticated by scriptural prophecy and nobly articulated by both Petrarch and Shelley, is operative in English poetry. The same lesson in the poetics of influence that these poets would teach to fellow artists is the one that Spenser taught to Milton, that Milton schooled Blake in, and that Blake, in *Milton*, delivered to future generations of artists—to those, that is, with the eyes to see and the ears to hear.

My debts here are legion, and they are owed in the main to those who have labored to contribute to this volume. Others, however, have assisted me along the way: both Kathy Reynolds and Barbara Hornick, who typed portions of the manuscript; Richard Ide, Donald Rowe, Andrew Weiner, Les Tannenbaum and Camille Slights, who read portions of it; and especially William Gibson and Merton Sealts, who read this manuscript in its entirety. There are also those anonymous readers who commented judiciously on the manuscript and thus helped to perfect it into the state it has here achieved. Were it not for the kind permissions supplied by the Folger Shakespeare Library and the Henry E. Huntington Library, this book would not be so handsomely adorned. And, as everyone who passes through these libraries must, I owe special thanks to their Attendant Spirits, O. B. Hardison and James Thorpe, who, though they never taught me virtue (nor did they try), otherwise aided this "wand'ring Passenger."

J. A. W.

1 July 1974
Henry E. Huntington Library
San Marino, California

The lighter tones of the preceding paragraph proved, in retrospect, to be but a dalliance before the sad task that follows. One of this book's contributors did not live to see her essay in print. She did, however, read two of the essays, Tim Heninger's and my own; and, by the circumstance of my spending the summer of 1974 in California, it was with her, more than any other contributor, that I shared the excitement of putting this book together, and it was to her that I first communicated the happy news that it had been accepted for publication. That was on the nineteenth of November, and Kit was delighted—so much so that she determined to make a few last-minute revisions on her essay. It is one of life's ironies that, returning to Madison after a long Christmas holiday, I found a letter awaiting me: it was dated "Thursday, 5 December" (the day of Kit's death). That letter contained the several last-minute revisions that have now been incorporated into Professor Williams's essay. It is my desire—and the desire of the other contributors—that this book be dedicated to the memory of Kathleen Williams. Some of us loved her. All of us appreciated her, as one is wont to do those who are charming, gracious, inspiring. Spenser said it best: "Another Grace she well deserues to be,/ In whom so many Graces gathered are."

J. A. W.

CITATIONS

All quotations from Milton, both his prose and his poetry, accord with the Columbia Milton (hereafter *CM*), *The Works of John Milton*, ed. Frank Allen Patterson et al., 18 vols. (New York: Columbia Univ. Press, 1931–38), and quotations from the Bible follow the King James Authorized Version. The following standard abbreviations have been used: *PL* for *Paradise Lost*, *PR* for *Paradise Regained*, and *FQ* for *The Faerie Queene*. In all cases, citations are given parenthetically within the text of individual essays.

Milton and the Line of Vision

Flying Through Space: Chaucer and Milton

DONALD R. HOWARD

Suppose they could have met, Chaucer and Milton: what would they have talked about? One can't imagine they would have had much temperamental affinity, and their views on politics and religion would not have made for compatibility. They couldn't have talked business: both were civil servants, but Chaucer was a lifetime professional trained for such a career, Milton only for a time a learned hanger-on in a revolutionary government. And Milton would have talked rings around Chaucer about the classics or the ancients. They might have talked about women and marriage, interests they shared; but Chaucer would have been more respectful of "great ladies" and would not have been prepared for Milton's views about divorce. In the end I imagine they would have talked about traveling on the continent and flying through space.

They would surely have talked about Italy. Milton remarks in *Mansus* (34) that Chaucer too (he uses Spenser's pastoral nickname Tityrus) went to the Italian shores. Actually Chaucer went twice, possibly three times, always on business. Judging from echoes and influences in his poems, he knew Dante's works from the trip of 1372–73, Petrarch's and Boccaccio's from the later trip of 1378; by then the two Italian humanists were dead, hence more famous. There is not a scrap of evidence that Chaucer met either, though it used to be a favorite fancy of Chaucerians that he did. Quite by accident, Chaucer saw Italian humanism in its earliest moment and guessed something important was happening; Milton went to Italy expressly for the grand tour and saw Italian humanism at the end of its great tradition. It is axiomatic that we cannot begin to understand Milton without understanding the quality of that humanism. But it is not enough to call it classical humanism or Christian humanism; it was a specifically English humanism, an English reaction to Italian trends and to Italy itself. Chaucer, who traveled to Italy and was influenced by Italian poets, was the first Englishman to experience it. And Chaucer's most important influence on English writers was on Spenser.

Looking back at English literature from Milton's point of view, Chaucer and Spenser were two wells of English undefiled—Spenser by far the more important. Yet Chaucer and Milton, despite the centuries between them, and the intermediary Spenser, could have talked like contemporaries about Italian writers, especially Dante. Both engaged themselves with Dante but in different ways. Milton wrote a poem comparable to *The Divine Comedy* and, like Dante, felt Virgil in the background. "When Milton chose Virgil as one of his epic models," says Irene Samuel, "he had the precedent of Dante in putting the model to the use of his own 'sacred song' and then going beyond it. Dante too soars above the mount up which the ancient poet guides him, and his flight may have encouraged Milton to renounce his earlier Spenserian and Tassonian projects."[1] Chaucer, on the other hand, wrote nothing comparable to *The Divine Comedy*. He declined to, in the very work which is always reckoned "Dantean," *The House of Fame*. Lydgate, in what Kittredge called a maddening phrase, had said Chaucer wrote "Daunt in English"—it isn't clear whether he meant *The House of Fame* or another poem, or was speaking in general; possibly he did not, being Lydgate, know what he meant. He could have meant the noble closing of *Troilus and Criseyde* where the hero looks down from the spheres upon "this litel spot of erthe" (V.1815),[2] for there is an unmistakable debt to Dante there. And *The House of Fame* imitates Dante. Apart from these two places, I find no other where Chaucer gets anyone off the earth in the Dantean manner. In the *Knight's Tale*, when Arcite dies, Chaucer humorously bids him adieu and omits the soul-journey of his source:

1. *Dante and Milton: The* Commedia *and* Paradise Lost (Ithaca, N.Y.: Cornell Univ. Press, 1966), p. 66.

2. All the Chaucer quotations are from *The Works of Geoffrey Chaucer*, ed. F. N. Robinson, 2d ed. (Boston: Houghton Mifflin, 1957).

His spirit chaunged hous and wente ther,
As I cam nevere, I kan nat tellen wher.
Therfore I stynte, I nam no divinistre;
Of soules fynde I nat in this registre,
Ne me ne list thilke opinions to telle
Of hem, though that they writen wher they dwelle.
Arcite is coold, ther Mars his soule gye!
Now wol I speken forth of Emelye.
 Shrighte Emelye . . .

(I.2809–17)

Chaucer, unlike Dante and Milton, was earth-bound. The idea of a poetical flight into space—into the Ptolemaic sky, into eschatological realms, into chaos and old night or the limbo of vanities—did not suit his bent. He found his limbo of vanities on the way to Canterbury, his chaos in human experience. True, in *The House of Fame* he imitates Dante; the eagle, his Virgil, is drawn from the *Commedia.* But the eagle is *funny,* a smug pedant and a compulsive talker. And the flight through space is *absurd:* it leads to a realm of hot air which has risen up by "kyndely enclynyng" to Fame's house, something between a crazyhouse and a casino, where reputations are passed about like poker chips; and to the nearby House of Rumor, a whirling wicker basket in which "tydynges" are passed "fro mouth to mouth," ever increasing—some true, some false—until they pass out a window or through a crack to the House of Fame. It is a wildly humorous fancy, and like all great humorous works of art profoundly serious.

The House of Fame is the greatest statement in the English language about the nature of poetic influence. It represents poetic influence as a grab bag of verbal tidbits ("tydynges") which may be lies or truths filtered to posterity by capricious Fame; their content can be exaggerated or distorted, the value put upon them just or unjust, their meaning understood or misunderstood. Yet despite this unsettling circumstance the fame of former civilizations rests upon the poet's shoulders (1429–1519). The poem asks what poems are made of. It begins with an account of the *Aeneid,* then proceeds to the imitation of Dante. Virgil influenced Dante, Dante influenced Chaucer—very simple: poems are made of other poems. Then the Dantean eagle arrives and we get down to basics: poems are made of language. The professorial eagle turns linguist and asks what language is made of. He takes the traditional view

that speech is prior to writing, and when he then asks what is
speech he turns to phonology—"spech is soun" (762). He doesn't
say "words" or "grammatica," for the assumption is that language
would not exist without the vocal organs, and on this assumption
he turns from phonology to physics and asks what *sound* is. Again,
the answer is simple: it is broken air (765). He uses the analogy of
a stone dropped in a pond to explain sound waves and, reminding
us that air is the lightest element, introduces the medieval equivalent of the law of gravity, the doctrine of "kyndely enclynyng," to
let us know that sound goes *up*. This is why the eagle and the poet
are in the sky, where the houses of Fame and Rumor are. And
once there, the poet in his invocation to Apollo wishes that "Here
art poetical be shewed" (1095)—not to display his skill, but to
show "sentence" (1100) and to show what "in myn hed ymarked
ys" (1103).

What is this imaginary celestial realm? It is the upper part not of
the macrocosm but of the microcosm: it is *mind*. Not one mind or
mind in the abstract, but an intellectual, literary, and aesthetic
tradition, seen diachronically—a part of the history of consciousness. That is after all where literary influence happens. And
Chaucer had a valid insight when he saw that this happening is a
jumble of component influences, altogether unpredictable and
uncontrollable, yet capable of being intuited. In this mentalistic
and linguistic realm there are two "houses." The House of Rumor
is the place where "tydynges" are passed by word of mouth—
remembered and communicated, but in the process distorted,
exaggerated. Some, but not all, escape to the House of Fame,
where prestige is assigned or not assigned to them, justly or
unjustly, and where each is given a name and a duration (2110–
17). There are many ramifications we cannot go into—for example, mixed up with "tydynges" is pure sound (what Northrop Frye
called "babble"[3]), and also chance, for "Aventure," we are told, is
the mother of "tydynges" (1982f.); chance is mixed up with
prestige too, for "Fortune" is the sister of Fame (1547). But there
is one ramification that we cannot ignore: the House of Fame is
built upon ice, "a feble fundament" (1132). On the ice are
engraved the names of famous people, and except on the north

3. *Anatomy of Criticism* (Princeton: Princeton Univ. Press, 1957), p. 275; it translates *melos*, as "doodle" translates *opsis*—I am not sure that the latter figures in *The
House of Fame*.

side, in the shade of the castle of Fame, the names are melting:
"But men seyn, 'What may ever laste?' " (1147). The image allows
for the possibility that a whole tradition, or a whole side of a
tradition, may pass away forever without any chance of a rediscovery or rebirth.

Chaucer is the first major English poet in the English literary
tradition as we know it and as Milton knew it. He initiated a new
tradition based on continental models, and his influence on poets
of the fifteenth and sixteenth centuries largely shaped that tradition. So it is an arresting fact that very early in his career he made
a statement about poetic influence. And it is in this work, *The
House of Fame,* that Chaucer parts company with Dante. We can
see him especially at the end of Book I catch Dante's manner,
then in Book II reverse himself and parody his Tuscan master.
"Had Chaucer been able to sustain this note," says John Fisher,
"he would have been a different poet. But we prefer to have him
Chaucer, as he evidently preferred to be"—for he then rejects the
mystical way out of the wasteland, "employing the homely
touches and incongruities of sound and situation of which he was
already such a master," and turns Dante's divine messenger into a
Disney-like figure who "spak/ In mannes vois, and seyde 'Awak!' "
(555–56).[4]

Chaucer's influence on Milton, compared with Dante's or Virgil's, seems *de minimis.* Milton did not feel Chaucer as a burden.
Chaucer's influence did not cause him anxiety. Milton conceived
of Chaucer as he wanted to—selectively, with the misunderstand-
ings and projections of his time and his persuasion. It is no reason
for us to condescend to Milton, for we read Chaucer in the same
selective way. Until recently the earthy, realistic Chaucer and then
the genial, ironic one were *our* Chaucers, which meant ignoring or
demoting his religious writings like the *Parson's Tale* or pathetic
stories like the *Clerk's Tale.* More recently the gloomy Chaucer[5]
has enjoyed a certain vogue, and there is even a fringe group of

4. *John Gower: Moral Philosopher and Friend of Chaucer* (New York: New York
Univ. Press, 1964), p. 211.

5. See Morton W. Bloomfield, "The Gloomy Chaucer," in *Veins of Humor,* ed. Harry
Levin, Harvard English Studies, No. 3 (Cambridge, Mass.: Harvard Univ. Press, 1972), pp.
57–68. Bloomfield splendidly concludes that "Chaucer passes into a metauniverse in
which laughter becomes gloom and gloom laughter. . . . True negative capability arises
from an objective love" (68).

nostalgia freaks who think all his poems are religious allegories. The Chaucer of the future is being planned even now at the meetings of the Mediaeval Academy and the Modern Language Association. The "real" Chaucer, to borrow a phrase of his own, might as well be one thing as another, but I wouldn't object if someone said the real Chaucer is this continually shifting historical entity.

Milton always speaks of Chaucer with reverence. In *Of Reformation*, he calls him "our renowned Chaucer," and in *Animadversions*, "our learned Chaucer" (*CM*, III, i, 59, 111). He was especially fond of the spurious *Plowman's Tale* that appeared in sixteenth- and seventeenth-century editions of Chaucer, a work closer to Langland in spirit. He alludes, in *Of Reformation*, to "our Chaucer's Plowman" and quotes the tale once to prove that Chaucer's political and religious ideas were like his own: "this, besides *Petrarch*, whom I have cited, our *Chaucer* also hath observ'd, and gives from hence a caution to *England* to beware of her *Bishops* in time, for that their ends, and aymes are no more friendly to *Monarchy* then the Popes" (*CM*, III, i, 28, 44). (The anonymous author of the *Plowman's Tale* probably would have been as puzzled by this as Chaucer would have been.) It sounds as though Milton read Chaucer in the second edition of Speght (1602);[6] like earlier editions it contained the non-Chaucerian *Plowman's Tale*, and it was the great seventeenth-century edition of Chaucer, reissued in 1687. Its title evidently gave Milton the "our": *The Workes of our Antient and Learned English Poet, Geffrey Chavcer, newly Printed*—the 1687 edition had it *Ancient, Learned & Excellent*. The Renaissance enthusiasm for a native poet writing in the vernacular, the awe of what is ancient, and the love of learning all get into this title—it is very "humanistic" and pretty well suggests the psychological fix with which our Milton would have approached his Chaucer.

The Speght edition contains nearly all Chaucer's works plus a number of apocryphal ones and a few poems by such as Gower and Lydgate. How much of this did Milton read? In the Commonplace Book he mentions the Wife of Bath three times, the *Merchant's Tale*, the *Physician's Tale*, and *The Romaunt of the Rose*.

6. See *Complete Prose Works of John Milton*, ed. Don M. Wolfe et al., 8 vols. (New Haven and London: Yale Univ. Press, 1953–), I, 402, n. 31.

There appear to be some "echoes" of *The House of Fame* in some of his Latin poems and one in line 8 of *Il Penseroso;* these are indexed in the Columbia Milton and I expect are genuine (the alleged echo from *The Former Age* in line 64 of *Natura non pati senium* might come from Boethius, as *The Former Age* does). And there is the famous allusion to the *Squire's Tale* in *Il Penseroso,* 109–15. I do not find any hard evidence that Milton had read *Troilus and Criseyde* or *The Book of the Duchess* or *The Parliament of Fowls,* but he may have read these, along with the *General Prologue* and the *Man of Law's Tale.*[7] One would suppose that he at least glanced through the *Parson's Tale,* which in the Speght edition comes just after the spurious *Plowman's Tale.* It's no surprise that Milton was drawn to the tales which Eleanor Prescott Hammond named the Marriage Group (and which Kittredge renamed "Chaucer's discussion of marriage"). Milton noted in the Commonplace Book that the *Wife's Prologue* and the *Merchant's Tale* treat the "discommodities of marriage," a subject about which Milton, like the Wife, was expert in all his age. (It surprises me that he did not extoll or even mention the *Clerk's Tale* of the patient Griselda, with its initial encomium to Petrarch; perhaps he did not care for the Clerk's ironical envoy—and too, the Clerk was an Oxford man.) From these allusions and echoes it looks as if Milton skipped over the "courtly" side of Chaucer—the *Troilus,* the *Knight's Tale,* the *Franklin's Tale*—and picked what suited his interests: writings about religion which could not be reckoned popish, writings about the discommodities of marriage, the "Dantean" *House of Fame.*

Still, Milton might have read many of Chaucer's works without ever mentioning them or being influenced by them. There is one thing we do know: Milton saw Chaucer through Spenser's eyes. It is more than possible that he read Chaucer as "background" to Spenser and admired "our Chaucer" because Spenser did. So it would seem, anyway, from the allusion in *Il Penseroso:*

> Or call up him that left half told
> The story of *Cambuscan* bold,
> Of *Camball,* and of *Algarsife,*
> And who had *Canace* to wife,

7. See ibid., 667, nn. 13–15, and 716, n. 28.

That own'd the vertuous Ring and Glass,
And of the wondrous Hors of Brass,
On which the *Tartar* King did ride . . .

(109—15)

Spenser's adaptation of the unfinished *Squire's Tale* surely prompted this passage. Spenser had supposed, as readers did until the twentieth century, that Chaucer began a long episodic romance with an interlaced structure and meant to finish it. If he had done so it would have gone on with episodes involving not just the magic ring, but the magic mirror and the magic brass horse (plus the magic sword which Milton fails to mention). If Chaucer had finished the *Squire's Tale* he would have ended up with a work about as long as *The Canterbury Tales* itself—and it would have been the kind of work he was revolting against. For we now know that in the *Squire's Tale* he was ridiculing the kind of structure which he and some contemporaries had turned away from, which Malory was to simplify, Tasso to attack, Cervantes to parody;[8] like Boccaccio, Chaucer turned to discrete tales, eschewed *entrelacement*. But no one understood until the last few decades that the unfinished *Squire's Tale* is funny—that it is full of absurdities and exaggerated, parodic touches, that the Squire spends half his time apologizing for his deficiency in rhetoric, repeats himself ridiculously, and in one place spends eight lines (401—8) making the point that he has gotten to the point. It is not as broad a parody as *Sir Thopas* nor as grand a one as *Don Quixote*, yet a parody. It satirizes a literary form and a kind of literary structure, and satirizes the knightly or courtly or romantic mentality which took pleasure in such fantastical, meandering tales. The consensus is now that Chaucer never meant to finish it any more than he meant to finish *Sir Thopas*.

So it is one of the ironies of literary history that Spenser was drawn to the tale in which Chaucer expressed his impatience for the genre Spenser admired. Spenser meant to revive interlaced structure, reintroduce the romance matters (at least the "matter of Britain"), and add layer-cake allegory—something medieval too but not found in medieval romances nor really even in medieval

8. On this literary movement, and on Tasso's attack in the *Discorsi del poema eroico* (1594), see William W. Ryding, *Structure in Medieval Narrative* (The Hague and Paris: Mouton, 1971), esp. pp. 9–18, 154–61.

literature so much as in literary theory, for example, in Dante's letter to Can Grande.[9] Milton took these ideas seriously, as any reader of Spenser must; in his discipleship he planned an epic about Arthur. Chaucer would have raised an eyebrow at that, for he never mentions Arthurian stories without ridicule and was skeptical about what he called "storial thyng that toucheth gentillesse," skeptical enough to make fun of it even (though gently) in the *Knight's Tale*. But then, Milton chose not to write an Arthuriad, and in making that choice he made his own small revolt against the romance mode.

We must not be too amused by Spenser's estimate of the *Squire's Tale*. It happens there is a further irony which vindicates his instincts: while Chaucer opposed interlaced structure and made fun of it in the *Squire's Tale*, he did not escape it.

English-speaking readers know about interlaced structure chiefly from Spenser and from Malory (though Malory tried to unravel the interlace of his sources). Recently Eugène Vinaver and others have given us some insight into what interlaced structure really was—what kind of experience and taste it involved.[10] The interlace was a form with no beginning, no end, in which everything was related to everything else; it was a thematic rather than a fictional mode, and had a kind of unity which a modern reader may have trouble perceiving. Yet it is not wholly foreign to us; critics like Vinaver and Per Nykrog sometimes suggest that we would do better to approach such works with the novels of a writer like Robbe-Grillet in mind: it would be a more usable anachronism than if we approached them with Tolstoy in mind.

9. There is, of course, allegory aplenty in medieval literature, but it is difficult to find four discrete levels consciously put into a medieval poem by its author and readily perceived by a reader. *The Divine Comedy*, Morton Bloomfield once remarked in a public address, cannot have four levels, for the anagogical level deals with eschatology and the poem treats eschatology on the literal level. A persuasive case for *Piers Plowman* was made by D. W. Robertson, Jr., and Bernard F. Huppé, Piers Plowman *and Scriptural Tradition* (Princeton: Princeton Univ. Press, 1951), yet there is much overlapping and uncertainty about the levels. I have had my say about these matters in *The Three Temptations* (Princeton: Princeton Univ. Press, 1966), esp. Chap. 1. Multilevel allegory intentionally cultivated by poets was, rather, a Renaissance phenomenon, though poets like Spenser felt it to be medieval. The fashion has been chronicled by Don Cameron Allen, *Mysteriously Meant: The Rediscovery of Pagan Symbolism and Allegorical Interpretation in the Renaissance* (Baltimore and London: Johns Hopkins Press, 1970).

10. Eugène Vinaver, *The Rise of Romance* (New York and Oxford: Oxford Univ. Press, 1971); Per Nykrog, "Two Creators of Narrative Form in Twelfth Century France: Gautier D'Arras—Chrétien de Troyes," *Speculum*, 48 (1973), 258–76.

Certain soap-operas and comic strips might be usable too. Did Chaucer never write anything that uses this kind of narrative structure? His works all seem to have a clear line of development, a climactic or dramatic structure, a beginning, middle, and end—at least an intended end. *The Canterbury Tales* has a beginning (the *General Prologue*) and an end (the *Parson's Prologue* and *Tale*), but the big, complicated middle, the series of tales, has some missing parts. Critics have struggled endlessly to uncover its form or structure. Approach it with straight realism in mind and you divide it up into days of the journey. Approach it with allegory in mind and you look for a thematic schema like the seven deadly sins. Approach it with drama and "the human comedy" in mind and you look for ways the tales reflect the pilgrims' personalities and involve conflicts among them. Approach it with the tales uppermost in mind and you parcel them into genres. Each is a valid approach and has had valid, though not always important, results. In the end the series of tales is an elusive structure in which various themes recur, treated variously, from various viewpoints, in various modes and genres, with various degrees of "poetic closure," various tones and degrees of irony, of seriousness, of morality. Structures appear within structures, interruptions within series. As a fictional mode it is a mishmash, yet a delightful one, a world unto itself. The metaphor imposed by its beginning and end, the pilgrimage of human life, puts definitive parentheses around that world. But inside those parentheses everything *does* seem to lead to everything else. We come away from it with the feeling that it is of a piece but cannot explain that feeling. Perhaps the microcosmic society introduced in the *General Prologue* imposes a central point of reference which produces such a feeling. But it is more than that—ideas, situations, problems keep cropping up. Where in medieval literature had there been anything like this? The dream-vision, perhaps. But the great dream-visions, like the *Roman* or *Piers Plowman,* though complicated and digressive, have a line of development which can be traced point for point—one thing leads to another, not everything to everything else. The only thing like it in medieval literature was the interlace of the continental romances.[11]

11. Vinaver, *The Rise of Romance,* Chap. V, associates this kind of narrative structure with the "ribbon" or "endless knot" design so often found in medieval

But the structure of the tales in *The Canterbury Tales* is only *like* the romance interlace. Both involve a thematic mode, but the "themes" of the romances are recurring characters and situations, on-going stories—not ideas, problems, ways of behaving; not questions about love, marriage, domestic harmony, chivalric conduct, chastity, perfection, and so on. In the romances the content of ideas, such as it is, was secondary and implicit. In *The Canterbury Tales* it is brought into the foreground; the recurrence of characters and situations is pushed into the background—yet vestigially present, for example, in the omnipresent Host, in the Narrator, in the Pardoner's interruption of the Wife, in the Friar's and Summoner's contretemps before the Wife's tale (which sets up their two tales to follow hers), in the joke played on the drunken Cook in the *Manciple's Prologue.* Chaucer chose to relate *ideas* in an interlace while keeping the tales and their tellers discrete.

I say "ideas," using a Renaissance word Chaucer wouldn't have known; he might have said "thoughts," "questiouns," "sentences"—or "tydynges." At the end of his flight through space in *The House of Fame,* when he arrives at the House of Rumor, "tydynges" are what he finds:

> And, Lord, this hous in alle tymes,
> Was ful of shipmen and pilgrimes,
> With scrippes bret-ful of lesinges,
> Entremedled with tydynges . . .
> (2121–24)

The "tydynges" are mixed with lies ("lesinges"), and they come especially from pilgrims! A curious house indeed, and the house is made as "wonderlych," he says, as "Domus Dedaly,/ That Laboryntus cleped ys" (1920–22). The labyrinth or maze called "Domus Dedaly" was a visual design to be found on the floors or walls of cathedrals and churches, and it was used in doing penance as a substitute pilgrimage—the penitent would crawl about it on his knees or trace it tediously with a finger. It was said to symbolize

manuscript decoration, especially in initial capitals. Vinaver's illustrations are extremely suggestive. The analogy between narrative forms and visual designs has been pursued extensively by John Leyerle in several papers not yet published. His aim is to uncover fundamental ways in which medieval men organized experience, and he would claim that the interlace has antecedents going back well before the twelfth-century romances; see his "The Interlace Structure of *Beowulf,*" *University of Toronto Quarterly,* 37 (1967), 1–17.

the many difficulties on the road of life: its destination at the
center was the Heavenly Jerusalem, the true destination of the
Canterbury pilgrimage according to the Parson in his prologue.
John Leyerle has suggested that this passage in *The House of Fame*
is the germ of *The Canterbury Tales*. Precisely how it is so is
bound to be one major debate in future Chaucer criticism.[12]

The world of "tydynges," then, looked to Chaucer—in the
mind's eye—like a labyrinth. As a visual design the labyrinth was
like the interlace, but not the same. The interlace is an "endless
knot" or "ribbon" which has no beginning or end or center and is
yet a satisfying and "unified" visual design. The labyrinth does
have a beginning, is a complex road with many dead ends, and has
its end at its center; it is tactile as well as visual, is meant to be
experienced rather than merely seen. Such a convoluted design, in
which the parts seem interrelated, turning forever back upon
themselves, leading everywhere and nowhere, yet having a satisfying unity, a point of departure, and a destination—such a design
seems to me as close as we can come to a visual counterpart for
the design of *The Canterbury Tales*. And such a design was one
that Spenser fastened upon; Angus Fletcher and others have called
attention to this labyrinthine structure in *The Faerie Queene*,
without noting its provenience in medieval churches or its association with the pilgrimage. Spenser, who had it from "Renaissance"
writers, Ariosto and Tasso, might have sensed it in medieval
Chaucer. And Spenser added to his narrative interlace and labyrinthine structure precisely what Chaucer added, ideas. He kept the
recurring characters and interrupted story-lines of romance but
turned them into allegory so that the narrative was imbued,
perhaps overburdened, with ideas. How much Spenser got this

12. Leyerle, "Chaucer's Windy Eagle," *University of Toronto Quarterly*, 40 (1971),
247–61, esp. 259f. On medieval cathedral labyrinths as substitute pilgrimages, and on
the use of the terms *domus Daedali* and *chemin de Jerusalem* to describe them and the
terms "heaven" or "Jerusalem" to denote their center, see W. H. Matthews, *Mazes and
Labyrinths: Their History and Development* (1922; reprint ed., New York: Dover,
1970), Chap. IX. Matthews quotes (p. 57) the legend inscribed next the labyrinth in the
church of San Savino at Piacenza: "*Hunc mundum tipice laberinthus denotat iste . . .*"
See also *Dictionnaire d'Archéologie Chrétienne et de Liturgie*, ed. F. Cabrol and H.
Leclercq (Paris, 1928), VIII, 973–82. The most notable labyrinth still in existence is the
large circular one on the floor of Chartres cathedral. I am indebted to Christian K.
Zacher for useful instruction on this subject. The problem figures in my book, *The Idea
of the Canterbury Tales* (Berkeley and Los Angeles: Univ. of California Press, 1975).

design from reading Chaucer we cannot know. That is the sort of circumstance one is dealing with when "literary tradition" is being traced: it is very like a labyrinth itself—one knows where it starts out and ends up but one is never sure how one got there.

Did Milton inherit from Chaucer and Spenser the interlaced thematic structure, and the labyrinth design with its beginning, its tangled procedure, and its destination at the center? Perhaps. But when in *Paradise Lost* he chose the fall of man as his topic, the choice itself did everything for him. The characters were, for Milton, real historical figures, the story was history or *Heilsgeschichte*, yet those characters and that story had "tydynges" inextricably associated with them, the greatest tidings man could know. The subject itself imbued the poem with ideas, for one cannot write about Satan as a historical figure without writing about evil, nor about Adam without writing about the fall. The Christian mythology, like any other, is a complex of ideas, and it cannot be treated in a sophisticated way without a complexity which itself seems like an interlace or labyrinth. The result in Milton is that *Paradise Lost*, like most great poems, including Chaucer's, is not "generically pure": it invokes a multiplicity of genres to represent a variegated universe, one that humans can see only from multiple perspectives. The interlace and the labyrinth were ways of accommodating into a meaningful scheme the diverse particularities and perspectives of "the world," and Chaucer and Spenser were writing about the world. They were concerned with worldly things like politics and moral conduct—Chaucer most notably in the two prose treatises of *The Canterbury Tales* (the *Melibee* and the *Parson's Tale*), Spenser in two levels of his allegory. The interlace, the labyrinth, the pilgrimage are all journeys through the world; Milton chose to soar above the world, to write about the universe. But he still focused upon the world, and to the extent that he did so he owed to Chaucer and Spenser certain debts. Aside from all the sources, analogues, echoes, and borrowings that can be tabulated, he shared with his predecessors the elements—at least some elements—of an aesthetic. That is at base what a literary tradition is, and "influence" only operates within such traditions. Milton's great inheritance from Chaucer and Spenser was the "mentalistic" quality of his epic—its tendency to traffic in mental space, to be a landscape of the mind. This is not a quality we usually associate with Chaucer. With the *Troilus* and individual Canterbury tales in mind we think of him as a dramatic, novelistic poet. Yet if we think of *The House of Fame* and the grand overall design of *The Canterbury Tales,* we find him at home in mental space, in the world of dreams and ideas. This does not make him any the less earthbound: the inner world he explored is the world of particular, mundane experience. Even when abstract phases of that world attracted his attention, phases as elusive as tradition and fame, they were explained by a comic bird who spoke "In mannes vois, and seyde 'Awak!' "

So in part Milton shared with his two great English predecessors the labyrinthine structure, the focus upon the world and the tendency to represent that world by mixing genres and introducing multiple perspectives. The labyrinth places the end or destination at the center of the design. In a literary work this can mean that the ending of the work is the central focal-point about which all that goes before has been interwoven. In *The Canterbury Tales,* the sight of Canterbury from a distance, and the Parson's meditation about the true way on "thilke parfit glorious pilgrymage/ That highte Jerusalem celestial" is the middle of the *literal* journey to and back from Canterbury; it is the central focal-point from which all that has gone before must finally be weighed—and there are impressive reasons for saying that Chaucer did not ever intend to depict the return journey. In *Paradise Lost,* though we are permitted to soar up to heaven, fall through space, descend into hell, the heart or center of the work is what happens on earth. It is figured not as a pilgrimage but as a battle. And the ending of *Paradise Lost,* the expulsion from the Garden, is the central point in the temporal events recounted—on the one side of it the creation and the fall, on the other side the redemption and the last judgment: at the end of the poem the battle is only half fought.

Paradise Lost, then, centers not upon the creation of the earth but upon the beginning of that realm of human activity known as the world, the realm of activity for which it was proper to practice contempt. In medieval ideas of the "ages" of the world the first age began with Adam.[13] The prelapsarian state was not "of the

13. George Boas, *Essays on Primitivism and Related Ideas in the Middle Ages* (1948; reprint ed., New York: Octagon Books, 1966), pp. 177–85. For an extended treatment

world"; in it there was nothing to hold in contempt, neither the corruption of nature, nor the weakness of the flesh, nor the evils of the social order.

Yet even the prelapsarian scenes in *Paradise Lost* have one aspect which puts them in the tradition of Chaucer, makes them seem worldly, even earthy, and gives them something in common with the *Merchant's Tale* or the Wife of Bath on the "discommodities of marriage": that aspect which permits us to linger over details for their own sake because those details make us participate in the daily lives of the characters. It is what Erich Auerbach [14] called *creatural* realism, the realism which fastens upon the domestic realm, upon the events of the everyday, and particularly upon the interaction between a man and wife. Auerbach found this realism occurring first in medieval literature in the twelfth-century *Mystère d'Adam* and demonstrated it by analyzing the speeches of Adam and Eve during the temptation. It is reasonable that "creatural" realism should crop up in those speeches, no less in Milton than in the twelfth-century liturgical drama, for creatural realism as we know it in a fallen world began at that precise moment. Yet the figure of Adam was the example par excellence of what Auerbach called *figural* realism—that realism which comes about through mental and intellectual associations and equations. Adam retains that figural character in Milton and indeed to the present day: the figure of Adam summons up the idea of the fall, but summons up too what the fall prefigures—that other garden Gethsemane, those other three temptations, that other "tree" the Cross. This fundamental typological correspondence between the fall and the redemption was central to Auerbach's conception of creatural realism because it was central to what he called Christian anthropology, which "emphasizes man's subjection to suffering and transitoriness."[15] One hardly needs to add that this typological correspondence was also central to Milton's choice of poetic themes.

The element of creatural realism in *Paradise Lost*—which from an English point of view can be reckoned a "Chaucerian" ele-

---

of this and related ideas, see James Dean. "The World Grows Old: The Significance of a Medieval Idea" (Ph.D. diss., Johns Hopkins, 1971).

14. *Mimesis: The Representation of Reality in Western Literature*, tr. Willard Trask (1953; reprint ed., Garden City, N.Y.: Doubleday, 1957), pp. 124–51, 226–29.

15. Ibid., p. 218.

ment—is easy to ignore; all the grandeur of Milton's deity, angelology, and eschatology draws our attention away from it. This must have been what made Dr. Johnson say that the want of human interest is always felt, but for once he was wrong. There is a very considerable amount of human interest in *Paradise Lost,* enough to make some readers since Johnson's time view it as a blemish or an embarrassment. The Romantics, for example, turning to Milton as a visionary poet, found the human interest not visionary enough. Adam asking about the angels' love-life, the angels themselves humanized with sexuality and digestive systems, Eve seeing her image in the mirror-surface of a pool, the couple keeping busy clipping and pruning their primordial garden, Eve proposing to go off on her own and Adam reluctantly granting her request—it is a side of the poem which in the hands of a less skillful bard could have become ludicrous. As it is, it's amusing and delightful, and always proportionable and under control, because it is there for a purpose.

That purpose is to let us see what life was like *from day to day* in the primeval world. Milton had to do this in order to make it seem real. Hence he gives us a sense of effulgent vegetation, the rhythm of animal life, the stately passing of day and night—

> Now came still Evening on, and Twilight gray
> Had in her sober Liverie all things clad;
> Silence accompanied, for Beast and Bird,
> They to thir grassie Couch, these to thir Nests
> Were slunk, all but the wakeful Nightingale . . .
> (IV.598–602)

He makes us aware that Adam and Eve had to be *doing* something, and he makes it clear that it was "daily work" like our own:

> Man hath his daily work of body or mind
> Appointed, which declares his Dignitie,
> And the regard of Heav'n on all his waies;
> While other Animals unactive range,
> And of thir doings God takes no account.
> (IV.618–22)

Nor does he hesitate to describe that daily work:

> On to thir mornings rural work they haste
> Among sweet dewes and flours; where any row

> Of Fruit-trees overwoodie reachd too farr
> Thir pamperd boughes, and needed hands to check
> Fruitless imbraces: or they led the Vine
> To wed her Elm . . .
>
> (V.211–16)

That our first parents talk to each other in measured cadence and in a totally rational way is of course not domestic or creatural realism as we know it, and requires of the postlapsarian reader a willing, perhaps a grudging, suspension of disbelief; but it is one of Milton's finest feats of imagination—to have surmised what it would be like to live from day to day, to work, talk, sleep, and love, to be that fundamental unit of domesticity, a married couple, before original sin. And there is "psychological" realism: Milton lets us see into their minds, their thoughts. He gives us a sense of Adam's innocent curiosity and uxoriousness, of Eve's innocent self-love as she sees her image, her innocent independence, his innocent permissiveness. We see a mistake taking shape as no mistake has since—without a tinge of human orneriness in it. The element of creatural realism intrudes (unrealistically) into the prelapsarian scenes in order to make us see how the *possibility* of evil was there—not theoretically but palpably, observably there—in a world where there was no evil.

How central this element is to the concerns of the poem we can only see when it takes the form of *real* creatural realism, the kind we know (as the Wife of Bath did) by experience—that of a fallen world. Eve, at once upon eating the fruit, "Intent now wholly on her taste" (IX.786), tastes something extraordinary, "whether true/ Or fansied so"—the experience, if the truth be known, of any gourmet. "Jocond and boon," she apostrophizes first the tree and then, like the Wife of Bath,

> Experience, next to thee I owe,
> Best guide; not following thee, I had remaind
> In ignorance . . .
>
> (807–9)

It crosses her mind that she might keep the odds of knowledge in her power (820) without sharing it; but the thought that God might do her in and Adam be wedded to another Eve—incipient jealousy, bane of courtly lovers—detains her. So with Adam. Together they

> . . . swim in mirth and fansie that they feel
> Divinitie within them breeding wings
> Wherewith to scorne the Earth . . .
>   (1009–11)

It is the beginning of all delusion and shares something with Troilus's expectation of "heaven's bliss" and January's thought that in marriage he will have his heaven on earth. And Adam's tone changes—he speaks as one who leers: "*Eve*, now I see thou art exact of taste,/ And elegant . . ." (1017–18). In the remaining lines of Book IX Milton includes a compendium of human feelings in the fallen state—the overindulgent sexuality, "of thir mutual guilt the Seale," followed by a sleep which "Oppress'd them, wearied with thir amorous play" (1045), a "grosser sleep/ Bred of unkindly fumes, with conscious dreams/ Encumberd" (1049–51); their shame; their guilt; their passions—"Anger, Hate,/ Mistrust, Suspicion, Discord" (1123–24). All of which degenerates into their mutual accusations, the first domestic squabble and all very familiar: "Would thou hadst heark'nd to my words" (1134), he begins. "Too facil then thou didst not much gainsay" (1158), she replies. "I warn'd thee" (1171), he counters,

> Thus it shall befall
> Him who to worth in Women overtrusting
> Lets her will rule; restraint she will not brook,
> And left to her self, if evil thence ensue,
> Shee first his weak indulgence will accuse.
>   (1182–86)

It is quite a lot like *The Canterbury Tales*. "Neither self-condemning," concludes Milton, "And of thir vain contest appeer'd no end."

This picture of quotidian domestic life after the fall reveals things about the human condition which are going to result in the Wife's demonstration-lecture on the discommodities of marriage, the Merchant's bitter antifeminism—his cynical picture of May cuckolding January in his own enclosed garden (and in a tree at that)—but, too, the Clerk's nostalgic tale of a patient wife, the Franklin's ambitious plan for mutual concession. As a part of human experience, the horrors of domestic life have always existed and always will. Milton got at the root of it better than Chaucer did, but he could not have done this as he did without the benefit of Chaucer's influence on English literary tradition.

And there is the problem. You cannot say this realism is a "Chaucerian" element in Milton; yet you cannot say it isn't. "Influence" has always been a major concept in literary history, and since Eliot "tradition" a magic word. When we find something like this domestic, creatural realism in Miton, we recognize its conventions—mundane detail, dialogue, soliloquy, projected thought—and can sense its provenience. And while we can say that it was part of English literary tradition because of Chaucer's influence, we can *not* say that without Chaucer it would never have gotten there. The probabilities are high that it would have gotten there in another way—from the miracle plays, from Boccaccio, from Jean de Meun; perhaps not quite the same, yet there. The tradition is as it is, and we owe some part of it to "our Chaucer," as Milton acknowledged. Literary influence and literary tradition seem to operate by their own logic, and we sense this operation in a poem or a poet but cannot state its rules, cannot be sure there *are* rules.

Perhaps in our own century a whole side of the tradition has melted away and we can only recapture it as antiquarians. It is true enough that nowadays if you write a poem which has anything like a thought in it or any resemblance to a mental landscape, nine out of ten people will tell you it isn't poetry; still, there are a few signs that this obsession, having found its place in the sun, is melting too. Besides, we still read Chaucer and Milton, and read them with pleasure and with feeling, so we have not altogether lost the tradition in which they were writing. The attempt to recapture that tradition by building a house of filecards has not, however, been a success. For several generations scholars have been recording poetic debts and influences and uncovering allusions and allegories, and the sum total of this industry is impressive. But what we have not uncovered is the *process* which makes influence work. We have instead given it the label "tradition" and said to ourselves, "Well done thou good and faithful servant." This is understandable, though, because to find out where tradition happens we have to look in the most inaccessible place—not "the background," not "the text itself," not language, not history, but *inside the poet's mind.*

And how are we to look there? Only through a glass darkly by
examining the shared consciousness of poets, the shared language
and experience which let them read and partly understand each
other, and which lets us do so. The undertaking does not require a
"methodology"; it requires an intellectual affinity, an act of
empathy, a *feel*. It is not unreasonable to expect a responsive
reader to have a *feel* for the poets he reads. When scholars began
to study the history of ideas, or later stylistics, or when "phe-
nomenological" criticism focused upon the poet's world and "in-
tersubjectivity," it looked as though critics had got hold of such a
feel, a way to cultivate such a feel. But the fate of all such
movements is to go out of style before they have faced any major
issues. Their adherents flee in terror at the smell of success and
mope off to rethink their positions. To go on is to risk being
"derivative." Then too, when we begin to see into a poet's mind
we suppose we are practicing some form of literary psychoanalysis, and this makes people nervous just at that point when
they realize that psychoanalysis, like criticism, isn't a science but
an art. How much easier to suppose tradition just works auto-
matically like the Oedipal conflict or the collective unconscious.

So it is curious that in all our awe of literary tradition, while we
have been puzzling over what makes it tick, an imaginative exploration of literary tradition has been lying before us all the time
in the tradition itself—by "our" Chaucer, the putative "father of
our English poetry." *The House of Fame* is among his first
important poems, perhaps his first.[16] It stands at the beginning of
our tradition. And what it tells us about tradition, not everyone
will want to hear. For it tells us that the world inside the poet's
mind is—if one could only find the right modern simile—like the
stock market. What happens in it is unpredictable, indeed absurd;
there is no rightness or justice or logic to the process going on, yet
it is a process. It is swayed by fads and trends—*names* are impor-

16. *The House of Fame* is normally dated in the mid to late 1370s, after the Italian
voyage of 1372–73 and, assuming lines 652–60 refer to the poet's job as Controller of
Customs, after the appointment was made in 1374. It is normally assumed that *The
Book of the Duchess* is an earlier work, written soon after the death of the Duchess
Blanche in 1369. Recently, however, Edward Condren has argued that *The Book of the
Duchess* may have been written for one of the anniversaries of her death in the late
1370s—see "The Historical Context of the *Book of the Duchess*: A New Hypothesis,"
Chaucer Review, 5 (1970), 195–212.

tant, and some have more glamor than others; but all that glamor and all those names have an unpredictable life expectancy, and any one of them, or a whole sector, or the whole structure may tumble at any moment or slowly dissolve. The structure looks like, and is, a gorgeous edifice, but it is built on ice. People are involved in Fame's house as well as speeches, poets as well as poems: every speech, we learn, when it comes to that palace, "wexeth lyk the same wight/ Which that the word in erthe spak" (1076f.). But the reputation each speaker gets—rather, each image of a speaker—has absolutely nothing to do with his deeds, as the reputation of a tiding has nothing to do with its content of truth. Traditions, oral and written, hold up the past, but those traditions are made in a random, inexplicable process which has no rules, no justice, no certitude. And it will all pass away in the end. Yet at the heart of the matter, at the end of the poem, is "a man of greet auctoritee." That is all. If we want to know more about him, we have to use Chaucer's methods, stated at the beginning of the poem: reading and dreaming. By them we can fly through the space within our heads, where eagles talk.

Milton, Greatest Spenserian

KATHLEEN WILLIAMS

For the nineteenth century and part of the twentieth, the "Spenserian" poets were Spenserian in the sense that the Scottish Chaucerians were Chaucerian: that is, they were a group of writers who followed with various degrees of faithfulness and of ability certain forms and stylistic habits characteristic of their chosen master. Giles and Phineas Fletcher, William Browne: they leave us with the impression that the influence of Spenser on his successors had effects almost as dispiriting as that of Milton on the diction of the less accomplished long poems of the eighteenth century. In both cases the reasons for our discomfort are similar, that what used once to be thought of as a Spenserian or Miltonic poem was one which recognizably tried to form its style on the highly idiosyncratic diction of *The Shepheardes Calender, The Faerie Queene, Il Penseroso,* or *Paradise Lost,* all styles developed, with great exactness, for a particular and unrepeatable purpose. The Fletchers gain an additional fame by mediating in some small way between Spenser and Milton, and the "Spenserians" do produce occasional pieces of some charm or even, in the case of Giles Fletcher, a certain clumsy power. But what strikes one most is their inability to respond in their own work to the essential qualities of Spenser's. Their use of pastoral is trivial compared with his, their allegory crude.

Yet it is plain enough that, outside the small group of what used to constitute the Spenserians, Spenser's can be a stimulating influence. Drayton develops in his own way Spenser's distinctive use of pastoral to explore the relation of poetry to the worlds of fact and vision. Especially in the lovely and moving *Muzes Elizium* Dray-

25

ton's pastoral statement of poetic value is wholly in the tradition of the *Calender* and the legend *Of Courtesy*, though it copies neither and indeed is reminiscent of pre-Spenserian poems as well. Of this last, Spenser, who liked to think of himself as one link in a long chain of tradition, would wholly approve. Similarly in the eighteenth century the important Miltonic poets are the poets who, like Pope, make their own metaphoric use of the Miltonic themes and manner. The *Dunciad*, with its magnificent prophetic evocation in a literary context of creation and uncreation, could only have been written by a poet whose response to Milton was profound, going far beyond observation of his stylistic habit or his syntax to the vision that these were formed to express.

There are other examples, of course, before Pope and after. My intention here is merely to refer, in relation particularly to Milton and Spenser, to a poetic line, a community of poets extending through time and engaging, as often as not, in a kind of dialectic with the tradition of which they so strongly feel themselves a part. This is far more of course than what, at one time, was commonly meant by "influence." These are strong, original poetic minds for whom the achievement of one's great predecessors is something to work upon as one works upon the very conventions of poetry, the "kinds," the myths. One might, for example, make a case for saying that all epics, even pre-Christian ones, are likewise in some way and to some degree anti-epics, and that when Spenser for certain specific purposes shapes the adventures of his knights, especially the Knight of Temperance, to point to the limitations of the heroic ideal and of heroic poetry, his practice becomes part of that tradition which is made up not of a number of examples of a genre known as epic, but of a number of sharply differing actual poems which make the idea of the epic genre part of their material. "The epic" develops through the interplay of each new individual, even idiosyncratic, epic poem with what its predecessors have established; Spenserian romance-epic contributes to its successors as it is incorporated and changed through the insights of later members of the tradition.

Thus Spenser himself, and the Italian writers of romance-epic, worked upon the idea of the epic and the practice of others. Spenser's meditations upon Ariosto and Tasso, or his reworking of Odysseus's voyage, are well-known examples, but more to our present purpose is his use of the *Squire's Tale*. Here Chaucer's heroine and her brother become the center of a story which, beginning from the charm and wisdom of the marriageable Canacee, "as fresh as morning rose" (*FQ* IV.iii.51),[1] moves easily to map out the nature of concord and its dependence upon the prior existence of discord in affairs human and cosmic. Spenser draws attention rather insistently to what he has done here, as part of a proud claim to be (as indeed he is) the heir of his great English predecessor. It is here in the fourth book of *The Faerie Queene,* the legend *Of Friendship,* that Spenser makes his most famous reference to "Dan Chaucer, well of English undefyled," and devotes two humble yet increasingly exalted stanzas to the praise of the earlier poet and to his own claim to inherit.

> Then pardon, O most sacred happie spirit,
> That I thy labours lost may thus revive,
> And steale from thee the meede of thy due merit,
> That none durst ever whilest thou wast alive,
> And, being dead, in vaine yet many strive:
> Ne dare I like, but through infusion sweete
> Of thine owne spirit, which doth in me survive,
> I follow here the footing of thy feete,
> That with thy meaning so I may the rather meete.
> (*FQ* IV.ii.34; see also 32–33)

The meaning Spenser meets with is one that draws Chaucer too into the line of cosmic visionary poets, in which the learned Ovid joins hands with the Orphic wisdom of those heroic singers in the halls of the princes who are reverently described for us by Homer.

And as for Spenser, so for Milton, as consciously and as proudly the next inheritor—and hence also the next fully informed and licensed critic—of the tradition and of its individual representatives. He says nothing so plain about his own descent from Spenser as does Spenser about the surviving spirit of Chaucer, but the terms in which he writes of his predecessor in the famous passage in *Areopagitica* can leave no doubt of his understanding of that descent, even without the evidence of his poetry. Milton's reading goes to the heart of the sage and serious poet, taking what is of particular interest to himself, the heir of the past, the current representative of the great English poets. He too, like Spenser,

1. All references to Spenser's poems are to *The Complete Poetical Works of Spenser,* ed. R. E. Neil Dodge (Boston and New York: Houghton Mifflin, 1936).

follows "the footing of thy feete" (one of the minor things
Spenser and Milton have in common is a fondness for puns). But
he too, like Spenser, presses into the master's tracks the mark of
his own characteristic step. Thus his absorption of Spenser's sense
of the limitations of the heroic forms is the basis for his own more
radical criticism in *Paradise Lost* and *Paradise Regained;* the Bower
of Bliss, with its adaptation of the Odyssean Circe story, lies
behind *Comus.* It is perhaps to be expected that the examples of
Milton's use of Spenserian epic which come most readily to mind
are from the legend *Of Temperance.* The fact is itself suggestive of
Milton's relation to the epic world of *The Faerie Queene.* But his
comprehension of Spenser's way with pastoral is equally complete.
Lycidas, that seemingly ultimate and unsurpassable summation of
what pastoral can do, is richer than the *Calender,* but its materials,
more dispersed, more tentative in the process of being worked
through, are all there in the earlier poem. Without it, *Lycidas*
could not be what it is.

That there are certain large differences between these two poets
is as clear, of course, as their connection. If it were not so, Milton
would have been the less a true Spenserian poet and the more a
"Spenserian." A tradition depends for its life upon the vitality and
independence of its individual members. Northrop Frye's formulation, given of course with more explanation and justification than
can be given here, is that Spenser is like those conservative poets
whose "total body of work, from tentative beginning to disciplined end, reflects the organic evolution of the forms they use.
. . . Spenser . . . begins with experiment but moves toward the
single convention of the Spenserian stanza, and his work unfolds
logically from the allegorical emblems contributed in his nonage
to van der Noodt's *Theatre* to the great pageants of *The Faerie
Queene.*" Milton is said to possess a "radical or revolutionary
temperament" which is "also found among the greatest creators,
and which contrasts with the conservative one."[2]

This would seem to be true as a general statement, which is
what its writer intended. It does not mean, however, that Milton
inherits nothing and hands on nothing, or that Spenser develops
nothing and criticizes nothing, from the past. Spenser, in his quiet

2. *The Return of Eden: Five Essays on Milton's Epics* (Toronto: Univ. of Toronto
Press, 1965), pp. 89–90.

way, looks doubtfully enough at some aspects of the tradition he
has himself done so much to form into its existing shape; *Paradise
Lost* is, as Frye says, "a profoundly anti-romantic and anti-heroic
poem,"[3] but it is not, so to say, a non-epic, and it is not unrelated
to Spenser any more than it is unrelated to Homer. Even *Paradise
Regained,* so radical in form that there is no general agreement on
what genre it belongs to, has organic relationship not only to
Spenser's legend *Of Temperance* in particular, but in general to the
cyropaedic[4] interests of the major poems, including the epic, of
Renaissance England. Milton, revolutionary as he is, never makes
so radical a criticism, so all-embracing, almost devouring, a use of
Spenserian epic as Blake does, in *Milton,* of Miltonic epic; the
varying relations of all these poets to the work of their predecessors does not mean that any one of them is not firmly and
consciously in the same clear tradition. On the contrary, indeed.

I have spoken of it, so far, as an epic tradition, given that epic
is, as Pope might say, essentially Nature rather than Homer, not a
skeleton to be covered over carefully by each succeeding poet, but
a series of living and developing poems. Chaucer might well be
seen, by a critic like Sidney or by ourselves, as approximating in
his own terms to the epic intention. The epic may go on to absorb
the cyropaedic and the encyclopaedic, the romantic, the idyllic,
and to comment on all these and on the heroic itself by placing
them within its own bounds, as it does in Spenser and Milton.

All these aspects are subsumed under the prophetic, which is
inevitably interlinked with the educative, and it is in their relation
as poets of the prophetic, and hence cyropaedic, epic that I should
like chiefly to consider the two poets. *The Faerie Queene* aims "to
fashion a gentleman or noble person in vertuous and gentle discipline" (*A Letter of the Authors*), and *Paradise Lost* has been said
by Northrop Frye to contain, in the conversation of Adam with
Raphael, "the education of Adam,"[5] and has been finely shown
by Stanley Fish[6] to be in a very real and lively sense, and a very

3. Ibid., p. 28.
4. The epithet is adapted, again, from Frye, who writes in *The Return of Eden* (pp.
9–12) of the ways in which what he calls the cyropaedia, or the manual of royal
discipline, and the encyclopaedic influence Renaissance epic.
5. Ibid., p. 12.
6. Stanley E. Fish, *Surprised by Sin: The Reader in* Paradise Lost (London and
Melbourne: Macmillan; New York: St. Martin's Press, 1967).

strenuous sense, the education of the reader. Spenser's "gentleman or noble person" is also the reader; and though the educational methods, if one might put it so, of the two poems differ, yet the final intention is the same. We, and Adam, and the noble person, and Guyon, are to learn not so much a set of facts as how to form a set of values. The noble discipline is educative in Sidney's sense; poetry is "this purifying of art, this enriching of memorie, enabling of judgement, and enlarging of conceit."[7] It teaches us understanding, the power to see clearly, to make distinctions between matters not readily distinguishable, to choose, or, in another characteristically Miltonic phrase, to see and know, and so to act. The instructiveness of poetry has much to do with seeing clearly,[8] and the poet, the first teacher of civilization, has much in common with the prophet or visionary, as we may see in the archetypal figure of Orpheus the wise prophetic seer, and also in the Old Testament prophets (though Sidney makes a careful and, for his purposes in the *Defence of Poesy,* wholly proper distinction between the *vates* and the "right poet"). Much very interesting work has been devoted in recent years to examining the idea of the prophetic and visionary in the Renaissance and its relation to poetry, especially the poetry of Spenser. Particularly important are recent books by Angus Fletcher and Michael Murrin.[9]

We may enter a little way into the difficult and complicated terrain explored by Professors Murrin and Fletcher by making a model of one way in which the prophetic acts as the educative, a model provided by the operations of prophetic vision within the fictions of our two poets. In *Paradise Lost* Adam is given two revelations, one by Raphael of the past and present and one by Michael of the future. The reader is in a similar situation with regard to the poem itself. Like Adam we, faced with the whole prophetic structure, have to learn how humanly, virtuously, discriminatingly (the adverbs are so many virtual synonyms), to

7. *The Defence of Poesie,* ed. Albert Feuillerat (Cambridge: Univ. Press, 1923), p. 11.

8. I have discussed this matter in relation to Spenser in "Vision and Rhetoric: The Poet's Voice in *The Faerie Queene,*" *ELH,* 36 (1969), 131–44, and in "Spenser and the Metaphor of Sight," forthcoming in *Rice University Studies.*

9. See Fletcher's *The Prophetic Moment: An Essay on Spenser* (Chicago: Univ. of Chicago Press, 1971) and Murrin's *The Veil of Allegory: Some Notes toward a Theory of Allegorical Rhetoric in the English Renaissance* (Chicago: Univ. of Chicago Press, 1967).

respond to what we are shown. If we are wrong in our first response, the poem (like Raphael, Michael, or God) will show us, sooner or later, our error. In Faeryland or Eden, we may make these initial errors with less disastrous consequences than would threaten us in our daily experience, and it is the poet's hope, as it is the hope of Raphael or Michael in relation to the revelations within the poem, that such experiences of corrected error in the protected world of poetry may help us to manage better in the world of practical endeavor.

Spenser perhaps spells this out for us more clearly, in the sixth book of *The Faerie Queene,* where we have a series of more and more protected, special, and meaningful places, increasingly complete versions of what Angus Fletcher calls the temple set at the center of the labyrinth. The most labyrinthine of labyrinths exists outside *The Faerie Queene*; it is our perplexed and perplexing world. Within the poem, the experience of the characters is still labyrinthine enough, as we see in the opening canto where Red Crosse and Una lose their way almost as soon as they appear, and their attempts to find a path "like to lead the labyrinth about" only lead them further into densest forest and to Error itself in the heart of the wandering wood; to them no templar clarity but a more total "perplexitie."

The wandering wood is omnipresent in some form: Arthur astray in the dark passionate forest, confused about the identity of his Faerie Queene and about the truth of the vision or dream in which she has appeared to him; Florimell in the changing seas and in the power of another prophet, Proteus the shape-changer. Yet for the reader, the poem's labyrinth comes to seem more like what Pope calls the world when it is seen with the eye of instructed wisdom, a maze, which as is the nature of mazes is "not without a plan" and is constructed not merely to mislead or to test but to guide. Faeryland is no less difficult and puzzling than middle earth, but it is middle earth with its issues made clearer for the reader though seldom for the characters except in moments of revelation which are the equivalent for them of the poet's whole vision for us; moments which allow us to see our way, or at least to see that there may *be* a way, if we can only hit upon it. Calidore's wanderings within the maze of Book VI bring him to the protected pastoral place, which is poetry's place because it is a metaphor for what the poet sees and recreates, the golden world, or other nature, that Sidney speaks of. Within the pastoral again is the sacred hill where we see poetry coming into being. This place is Acidale, made numinous by the poet Colin's vision of the Graces as Arlo Hill, in fact the "most unpleasant and most ill" of mountains, becomes the fairest of "this holy-islands hights" (*Mutabilitie* vi.37), the temple at the center of the cosmos, because the poet Spenser sees it so. Vision can reveal significance in the depths of confusion, the sacred in the midst of what is most defiled. So Milton sees the templar Eden in "The haunt of Seales and Orcs, and Sea-mews clang" (*PL* XI.835), and Paradise in the "pathless Desert, dusk with horrid shades" (*PR* 1.296), where our Morning Star arises. It is the visionary Paradise within which alone we can see meaning in our surroundings. Or as Meliboe puts it to Calidore, "each hath his fortune in his brest./It is the mynd that maketh good or ill" (*FQ* VI.ix.29–30). Meliboe's terms make a more modest claim than Michael's, as befits his difference in station; but when we are shown Colin rapt in his own sight of the Graces, dancing to the music he makes for them, we recognize the radiance of the vision which lies behind Meliboe's simple faith and practice.

The trust of the prophetic poet is, then, in vision, and his work is to articulate vision into a fiction that contains its own lesson in interpretation, so that the reader may in reading learn how to read, how to see the fiction in the light of those epiphanies and visions which from time to time irradiate it. If this "vertuous discipline" is well enough managed by poet and reader it may extend to the world in which we move visionless except for the prophetic poem itself, which is to us as is Michael's revelation to Adam of the atonement and of the final joy when "the Earth/ Shall all be Paradise, far happier place/ Then this of *Eden*" (*PL* XII.463–65), or, in Spenser's less great argument, the ecstatic prophecy in which Merlin reveals to Britomart the future of her line up to the reign of the royal virgin.

But at the same time Merlin and Michael, Meliboe and Colin, direct us to another aspect of the prophetic. The prophetic epic runs parallel, on its own level, to Holy Writ, and to the Book of Revelation itself, the culmination of biblical prophecy. And like the biblical prophets, the prophetic poet has at once a supreme faith in the vision, and a certain scepticism about the effect of the vision in the world.[10] The hope, indeed, is that the poem as vision will inspire and as cyropaedia will instruct us how to live in such a way that the inspiration will have practical daily effect. But it is a hope at best, and often the hope is, understandably, faint. It could scarcely be other, when all our history shows how little we have learned even from the prophets and evangelists, themselves not sanguine about the power of men to remember, much less make use of, that which has been authoritatively revealed to them. Men must be moved, said Sidney, to wish to know and do right: *hoc opus, hic labor est.* This moving is the poet's task as it is the prophet's, but even emotion fades all too quickly, and sight grows blurred once more. The examples cited above of revelation within the poems point in this direction as clearly as they show the skill with which Spenser and Milton try to teach us to apply revealed truth to our inner life and our practical action. Vision sees what is, the dance of the Graces but also the mindless destructiveness of brigands and cannibals to whom the vision is invisible, and the foolish forgetfulness of more amiable characters blundering through their lives. Michael reveals to Adam the continuing goodness of God, though in future more hidden since the clouding of the eye of reason at the fall means we can no longer walk with God in the garden and live easily and daily in the clear sight of the truth. But Adam is shown, too, that one of his own sons will so far forget the garden as to kill. Even Michael is moved by the sight of this "bloodie Fact," and he hastens to give such comfort as he may and to fulfill the Father's charge to "send them forth, though sorrowing, yet in peace" (XI.117). The blood is part of what must be seen, and it must be grieved for. Vision is never an easy way. But Adam must fix his eye steadily not only on the "Fact" of violent death, but on the revealed truth that

> the bloodie Fact
> Will be aveng'd, and th' others Faith approv'd
> Loose no reward, though here thou see him die,
> Rowling in dust and gore.

(XI.457–60)

10. The books cited above (Murrin's in some detail) discuss the doubt of the prophet.

Human blindness and wickedness do not destroy the vision of the divine intention. But they do obscure it, and what is not easy for Adam is still harder for his descendants. The one just man, the fit audience though few: what more has the prophet—that practical and realistic man—ever really found reason to expect? The poet's and the prophet's task must be done, as a duty and a desire and a gift, as Spenser sees it to be in *The Shepheardes Calender* and *The Faerie Queene* and Milton in *Lycidas* and *Paradise Lost*. But it is done as often as not with a sense that it will not be much understood, and will not have much effect:

> What could the Muse her self that *Orpheus* bore,
> The Muse her self for her inchanting son
> Whom Universal nature did lament . . .
> Alas! What boots it with uncessant care
> To tend the homely slighted Shepherds trade,
> And strictly meditate the thankless Muse . . .
>
> (*Lycidas*, 58–66)

Merlin's prophecy to Britomart is, *mutatis mutandis*, of similar import and result to Adam's vision of the future. The canto is introduced by an exalted address to the most sacred fire of love, kindled in the realm of eternity, "Emongst th' eternall spheres and lamping sky" (*FQ* III.iii.1), poured into men for the fulfilling of the divine purpose. Thus even the world of human relationships, changing as the sea, lamented by the sea nymph Cymoent as a place of careless, irresponsible cruelty and oracular evasiveness, is, when seen with the eyes that holy light may plant within, a world of indirect divine direction. The poet, commenting on Cymoent's predicament, does not deny the reality of the world's treacherous uncertainties; but he affirms a certainty too, and this depends on "things invisible to mortal sight":

> So ticle be the termes of mortall state
> And full of subtile sophismes, which doe play
> With double sences, and with false debate,
> T'approve the unknowen purpose of eternall fate.
>
> (III.iv.28)

Even prophecy is under direction, and Proteus himself, deliverer of the oracle to Cymoent, is as much an instrument of destiny as is Merlin, whose prophecy occurs immediately before that of the sea-god. Prophets and poets, after all, share the ambiguous universe with all of us, though they do also, by nature nurtured in the disciplines of their art, see on occasion through and beyond it.

Thus Merlin, who had "in magick more insight" than any before or after him, and could command the sun and moon, was of very mixed parentage, born of a nun and a "guilefull spright," and his skill appears, indeed, to come from that very fact. Moreover, all his art cannot save him from the treachery of Nimue, through which he is finally to be "buried under beare,/ Ne ever to his worke returnd againe" (III.iii.11). Spenser emphasizes all this, and describes Merlin as living already deep underground, where he takes counsel with his sprights; his fate seems to be part of his whole life, his origins, and his art itself. But Merlin, for all his fearful heritage and his troubled life and desperate end, has the sight. His vision is as exact and detailed as is that granted to Adam, and he sees it so vividly that he cries to Britomart to look too:

> Behold the man! and tell me, Britomart,
> If ay more goodly creature thou didst see . . .
> (III.iii.32)

And at the end he is by some "other ghastly spectacle dismayd,/ That secretly he saw" (iii.50). He also interprets his vision as clearly and forthrightly as Michael does his, explaining just what is happening and what it means. Essentially, his interpretation is like a biblical prophet's interpretation of Judaic history; victories and defeats, joys and sorrows, are equally part of "hevenly destiny,/ Led with Eternall Providence" (III.iii.24). God shepherds his people by punishment as well as reward, bringing them at last through all their waywardness and blindness to the destined end. Of this process, extending over centuries, Britomart's agonized personal passion is a fated part, and so therefore is Merlin's vision—like the second vision, within his own, that prevented Cadwallader from returning to Britain before the due period of British thralldom was ended.

The vision saves neither Britomart nor Merlin himself from bitter grief at the senseless evils to be committed and the sufferings to come, any more than the vision saves Adam or Michael. Spenser's sense of the prophetic poet's task is as austere as Milton's, and he shares, he tell us, the griefs of his characters.

Britomart, though she now knows her own sufferings have a
purpose, is by no means enabled, as a result, not to feel them. In
the canto following Merlin's revelations we find her bitterly la-
menting her lot on the rocky shore, addressing the

> Huge sea of sorrow and tempestuous griefe,
> Wherein my feeble barke is tossed long,
> Far from the hoped haven of reliefe . . .
>   (III.iv.8)

and the sea becomes as it has become through the ages, and is
again in *Lycidas*, a figure for the felt lack of meaning in the weary,
directionless tossing of our lives. Prophecy, vision, insight, neither
deny experience nor deprive it of its power to hurt. They give us
not necessarily happiness or ease but what they give to Britomart,
Merlin, and Adam, faith and "great courage." The best that God
can give his two fallen creatures, through Michael's revelation and
instruction, is peace in sorrow.

The prophecy of Proteus shows another way in which prophecy
may work to instruct us. Proteus too is a genuine seer, "with
prophecy inspir'd," but he is unable to do more than impart what
he has received "through foresight of his eternal skill" (*FQ* III.
iv.25), for he is not part human, part spirit, like Merlin, but a
creature of nature, and he cannot interpret what his prophecy may
mean in human terms. It is as if the sea itself has spoken,
expressing all its mystery, which is the mystery of the universe and
in which life and death, creation and chaos, are mingled and
merging, each necessary to the other. Cymoent, another sea being,
struggles to interpret the words on behalf of her beloved half-
human son, but in trying to find a clear meaning for her guidance
she finds only an incomplete and so wholly misleading one which
brings about the very result that was so oracularly prophesied.
Spenser uses here the familiar ambiguity of the subtle sophisms
and double senses of the pagan oracle, a prophecy made without
the clarity of sight that knowledge of the true God brings, so that
the prophet is an unknowing instrument where Merlin is a knowing one. The story of Cymoent and her son is one of gradual
understanding. They jump to, or force, conclusions and act wrong-
ly as a result; but by degrees, through suffering, they learn to
move quietly under direction, and not to try to force events. At

last they learn to understand the full meaning of the prophecy, of which its ambiguity was a necessary expression. Cymoent's shocked realization of the complexity of human things, expressed in a paradoxical play of deceptively simple words, is one stage in her and our education:

> I feared love: but they that love doe live,
> But they that dye doe nether love nor hate . . .
>
> Who dyes the utmost dolor doth abye,
> But who that lives is lefte to waile his losse:
> So life is losse, and death felicity:
> Sad life worse then glad death . . .
>
> (III.iv.37–38)

It is part of the strategy of Spenser's instructive prophecy to point out that the poet himself shares the terms of mortal state, and that even he cannot always interpret or express clearly what he is shown. He cannot see how Florimell can escape from Proteus; the "confused rout of persons" in the Masque of Cupid have names he finds "hard to read," and some of their names and natures are not told us because he cannot read them well (III.xii. 25–26). Sometimes his tentative interpretations are ambiguous. He writes as the vision is revealed to him, but this is a deeply inward experience that may well be difficult to translate into terms which will be communicable. Spenser exemplifies this aspect of the prophetic predicament within his fiction. Merlin is shown something by a force outside himself, and he sees it so intensely that he speaks as if Britomart must see it too. Yet it is visible only to him, to the inner eye, for "the mind is the eye of the soul,"[11] and as his ecstatic fit deepens he goes entirely into himself and is silent.

The priest of Isis, in Book V, has a similar experience, though it does not deprive him of speech and he is able to give Britomart an inspired interpretation of her dream, and a practical and helpful one. But even this inspired explanation is clearly only a partial account of the richly numinous impressiveness of the dream. It gestures toward a greater mystery than can be explicated in its

11. Christophoro Giarda, quoted by E. H. Gombrich, "Icones Symbolicae," in *Symbolic Images: Studies in the Art of the Renaissance* (London and New York: Phaidon, 1972), p. 154.

definition of the meaning of Isis's crocodile, which differs from that already given by the poet himself. In the perspective of the whole poem the relation of "forged guile" to "the sterne behests" of Osiris can be seen to be part of the difficult justice administered in our world. But this relationship can only be presented in its full paradox in the visionary dream itself, which is described in terms that beautifully convey both the frightening numinosity and the warm womblike intimacy of such experiences, as Britomart merges in dream into the nature of Isis the mother, the protective clemency. "In the midst of her felicity" the altar fire flames up through the temple, and the crocodile beneath the goddess's feet wakes to unite itself with Isis-Britomart. She wakes no longer in bliss but in "fearefull fright" and "doubtfully dismayd" (V.vii.14–16).

This state of brooding, dreaming vision is one in which Spenser himself moves, practical poet and man of affairs though he was, naturally as to the manner born. In the minor poems we are often in such an atmosphere, with the poet descending into himself in troubled thought and then "seeing" a vision which though given to him yet arises from the depths of the self and externalizes what is deeply personal. This is so in the *Visions of the Worlds Vanitie*, in *Daphnaida, Prothalamion,* and the *Fowre Hymnes;* and the sense of personal yet true dreaming in *Virgils Gnat* or *Muiopotmos* is unmistakable. The dreamlikeness of *The Faerie Queene* has been remarked over the centuries, and a modern reader is perhaps especially impressed by the way in which places and events, if they can be referred to in such solid terms, follow and merge with one another with the narrative inconsequence and the convincing psychical logic of the dream.

The atmosphere of dream is one aspect of the inwardness that characterizes all Spenser's poetry and that even in the epic, which we think of as so objective a form, grows ever deeper. Another aspect is the poet's marked reluctance to speak. It grieves him, as much as it grieves his prophetic characters or Milton's, to look upon what is revealed to them whether they like it or not. He is distressed by Amoret's and Florimell's troubles and often wishes "it never had been writ" (IV.i.1). His uneasy reluctance is visible as *The Faerie Queene* progresses; like the snake in the Cupid tapestries Spenser shines unwillingly.

To call this a topos of reluctance is not to end the matter; one chooses among topoi, and Spenser chooses this one frequently and emphatically. Its use in the first stanza of all, it is true, is hardly surprising except in its excellence. The pastoral poet expectably begins his epic in proud humility, proud because chosen by the sacred Muse, humble because he is "all too meane" in his lowly shepherd's weeds. But the emphasis on the inescapable nature of the difficult task he is "enforst" to do, the compulsion to speak, however reluctant, is repeated throughout. In the Proem to Book III, "my lucklesse lott doth me constrayne/ Hereto perforce" (III. Proem. 3); repeatedly the voyaging poet, traveling the difficult seas of the poem, longs to reach his final port. We are reminded of that inevitable alarm at the prophet's rather fearful responsibility which made Jonah flee from the demands of his God. Moreover, the poet's worst fears are justified by the reception of his poem, as we find in the Proem to Book IV. The sacred Muse's insistence has got him into trouble with Burleigh, for whom his poem is "vaine," who, to use the terms of the Proem to the legend *Of Temperance,* sees it as "th' aboundance of an ydle braine," "painted forgery," not as the true antiquities revealed by the Muse (II. Proem. 1). The prophet may find that his vision is not only difficult and even painful to contemplate and express; it can be difficult and painful to his audience too, and their reaction may be one not only of inattention and incomprehension, but of positive hostility. His answer to such a situation is likely to be that of the Hebrew prophets or of Milton: I will go on seeing and expressing truth because I must, but I will no longer expect you to look at it. "To such therefore I do not sing at all" (IV. Proem. 4), says the poet defiantly after trying to explain how Burleigh has wholly mistaken the nature of generous virtue. His hearers will be the few who can respond to him, and for these alone he will, like his great successor, write.

To some degree this is, of course, the unavoidable problem of the prophet-poet in any age. His vision will be incomprehensible, and therefore uncomfortable, to most of his hearers. He cannot hope to explain to everybody who hears him this deeply secret and inward thing; he can only hope to stimulate some of them to commit themselves to it. The mysteriousness of the Orphic poet is neither affectation nor deliberate obfuscation. It can no more be helped in Spenser, Milton, Blake, or Ovid, than in St. John of the Book of Revelation or Hermes Trismegistus. Spenser and Milton both keep as fine a balance between inner and outer—what I have elsewhere called vision and rhetoric and what one might also call, in another aspect, revelation and its practical application—as a visionary poet may. But the inwardness, the secretness, natural to them both, is marked in their epic poems, as they react, more and more, to their inevitable prophetic disappointment by turning in upon themselves: upon the mind, the pastoral place, the paradise within, where poet and prophet are free not from self-indulgent ease but for the strenuous creation of a visionary truth which is not aimed at the many (the comparatively many; no major Renaissance poet, of the line of Orpheus, David, Virgil, Ovid, would be likely to suppose that his audience could ever be anything but small) but at the few rare spirits willing to undertake the poet's discipline.

This prophetic inwardness has recently been the focus of some brilliant critical attention. For Spenser, Harry Berger, Jr., in a series of articles on Spenserian "retrospection," and Angus Fletcher, in *The Prophetic Moment,* have done finely perceptive work, and my debt to them will be immediately apparent to any student of *The Faerie Queene.* A discussion of Milton's prophetic inheritance can do no better, at this point, than to quote from Professor Fletcher's last chapter, where he speaks of the essential problem of all epic, from Virgil on: "What is the good of empire, if it forces men to overextend themselves?" Or, to enlarge upon this question, what is the relation of the prophetic poet to the demands of heroic achievement? Is not his visionary freedom threatened by the increasing rigidity of encroaching empire—most of all, the freedom of his imagination, gripped by the ambitious yet limited values of heroic?

The imitators of Spenser, while recognizing the danger of a mechanic expansion of poetic cosmologies, could not solve the problem, either because their views were superficial or regressive. The creation of a Purple Island does restrict the compass of a world, and so does the Castle of Indolence, but in both cases we get a return to neomedieval or gothic allegory. By contrast Milton asked what was the inner drive of the expansive Spenserian vision, which he found in that introverted, elegiac, prophetic strain—the atmosphere which steadily asserted itself more strongly as *The Faerie Queene* progressed.[12]

12. *The Prophetic Moment,* p. 301.

The prophetic strain does, certainly, assert itself more strongly as the poem develops, but of course in a way it was an inward poem from the start and in its whole conception as compared with Homer or even the more introspective Virgil, though the difference would have seemed much less to a Renaissance poet who saw the classical epics as instructive allegories, in some sort, of human life.[13] *The Faerie Queene* is set wholly within the mind of man, though there are analogies with political action. But it does, nonetheless, become not only "introverted" but "retrospective" as it proceeds, and critics (the reference is again primarily to Fletcher and Berger) have seen the sixth (and last, or last complete) book as especially so. For one thing, it is preeminently the book about poetry, existing within poetry and so within the mind of the poet. From this point of view one may approach rather differently certain passages cited earlier in this essay, the deliberate construction of a series of "temples" one within another, each set off by contrast with the world without—the pastoral peace, for instance, follows immediately on the most savagely ironic presentation of human destructiveness in the whole poem, the sacrifice of Serena— or Meliboe's insistence that our pastoral, like Paradise, must be, can now only be, within the individual mind. We may now see these passages in relation to the "introverted, elegiac" strain which for Spenser seems to characterize the prophetic vision. The movement from labyrinth through pastoral to poetic creation itself at Mount Acidale not only draws us inward: it leaves us inward, by eliminating in turn the vision at Acidale and the pastoral life, destroyed by the slave-merchant brigands who are such absolute enemies of individual and creative freedom. Calidore returns, for the last two cantos, to a dismal enough Faeryland, a broken-down heroic world like that of his immediate predecessor Artegall, Knight of Justice. He engages first the brigands and then the utterly dreary object of his quest, the Blatant Beast, whose mark is left everywhere: Meliboe and all his people but the exceptionally cloddish and rustic Coridon are dead. The creature is not only omnipresent, it is powerfully evil, and Spenser compares Calidore

13. See Don Cameron Allen, *Mysteriously Meant: The Rediscovery of Pagan Symbolism and Allegorical Interpretation in the Renaissance* (Baltimore: Johns Hopkins Press, 1970).

with Hercules overcoming the Hydra (again, as in Milton, true
heroism is the defeat of inner temptation, here the wish to
belittle, which is what the Blatant Beast is). The contest is squalid
rather than exhilarating (and so all the more heroic), squalor being
the nature of the Beast. It is a creature that uses its voice in the
most nonpoetic, nonheroic, nonvisionary of ways; it makes all
things, good or bad, indiscriminately mean, sordid, meaningless,
worthless. A world wholly given over to the Beast would be a
world in which the poet could not survive.

All of Calidore's quest has been rather subdued, as has Artegall's, and both are partial failures. The Beast is captured, but he
escapes as he always will, "So now he raungeth through the world
againe" (VI.xii.40), more than ever unrestrained, and strong
enough to attack the very center of all that he hates and that is
inexorably opposed to him: poetry, the creative word which is the
human analogy of the divine creation, the word used *to make,* to
express the vision of truth revealed by the sacred Muse, not to
reduce all things to baseness because baseness is all the Beast can
"see."

> Ne spareth he most learned wits to rate,
> Ne spareth he the gentle poets rime

or even this very poem. The book ends:

> Ne may this homely verse, of many meanest
> Hope to escape his venemous despite,
> More then my former writs, all were they cleanest
> From blamefull blot, and free from all that wite,
> With which some wicked tongues did it backebite,
> And bring into a mighty peres displeasure,
> That never so deserved to endite.
> Therefore do you, my rimes, keep better measure
> And seeke to please, that now is counted wisemens threasure.
>
> (VI.xii.40–41)

The "rugged forhead" of Book IV and the other more creeping
embodiments of the Beast have gained in effrontery, and the bitter
irony of the last couplet in effect destroys even such doubtful
hope of prophetic (which is heroic) efficacy as had existed. Rimes
that "seeke to please" are not poetry at all, in the sense that the
poems of the shepherd-poet-prophets Spenser and Milton are.

One should not, of course, read into this passage too much of absolute and final statement, or of biographical statement. Colin Clout has broken his pipe before, in *The Shepheardes Calender,* and his gesture is part of a "true fiction," meaningful there and only there. One must see this second gesture in the same way, and here too it is fictionally meaningful. The book has opened with a delighted contemplation of the inward joy of the visionary poet. It would be hard to quote from the Proem in a way that would demonstrate adequately how delicately it presents the conceiving of the poem as a profound creative joy, the sense of intimate, sensitive revelation "deep within the mynd,/ And not in outward shows, but inward thoughts defynd" (Proem 5). Poetry is "secret comfort" and heavenly pleasures, the finding of strange untrodden ways known only to the Muse and her children. The emphasis in the Proem is less on the thing made than on the inner joy of the making. For how can Burleigh and his like understand the vision? How can that vision survive in the world of the Beast? And how does epic succeed in not partaking of the values of this world?

The whole of Book VI, then (one can see how rightly it is called *Of Courtesy*), is contained by the thought of poetry, by the serious joy of the Proem and the bitter withdrawal at the close. Within these containing passages we are quietly but inexorably compelled to contemplate the predicament of prophetic poetry. It is in some ways the most romantic, the most contrived, of all the books. Events are as sordid and as evil as those in the legend *Of Justice,* and some are carefully paralleled with Artegall's adventures. But their inventor makes them come right, often against all likelihood, and easily, without Artegall's heart-searchings and struggles. Increasingly the rightness is the result of "fortune," fortune so remarkable and so orderly that it can only be guided by the intention of divine providence. One might say that this is a magnificent use within the epic form of the resources of romantic comedy, to intimate as do Shakespeare's last romances that there is a meaning and a benign intelligence behind the foulest of labyrinths; that the labyrinth is in fact Pope's maze. And I think that this would be altogether true. But we may also focus our attention on the fact that it is, and is only, the prophetic or Orphic vision of the poet that sees it so, that has deliberately and brilliantly presented it so. And like Shakespeare in *Pericles* or *The*

Tempest, Spenser does seem to be drawing our attention to this fact in the sixth book to a degree he has not done before. Vision is within the poem as the creation of the poet's mind; perhaps, the last stanza seems to suggest, that is where it should stay. The sixth book leaves the reader with nowhere else to go. Even the poem, as a verbal, external embodiment of the poet's vision, is in varying senses destroyed, by the vanishing of the Graces as Calidore blunders in upon Colin and by the tongues of the Beast at the end.

Yet it need not be that this is a literal farewell to the poem, a literal abandonment of the divine task of the prophetic poet. We do not know Spenser's intention for the *Mutabilitie Cantos*, but it does seem likely that they were to be part of another book, and they are manifestly mature work. All we need consider, given the nature of Spenser's rhetorical fictions, is that he has persuaded us in Book VI to consider what was increasingly borne in upon his own mind, the inevitable problems of visionary poetry when it seeks to communicate its vision to others. And this too is part of the vision, the encyclopaedic teaching, the gentle discipline, the revealing of the true heroism within the individual mind. The quiet, inturned quality, the creative mind brooding over its creation and its "secret comfort," which is common to Spenser and Milton throughout their poetic lives for all the vigor of their heroic battles and heroic speeches, absorbs again at the last those speeches and those battles; and we experience the enormous scope and richness of their creations as, precisely, creations: as something "taught them by the Muse," but taught *them* by the Muse, for only they can see and hear, only they can find the words by which the Muse can communicate.

Thus *The Faerie Queene* is throughout the most intimate of epics. The poet seldom allows us to forget his presence—thoughtful, amused, ironic, sometimes puzzled; and the effect of his comments is not so much that of a poet within the poem as of a poem within the poet. Even in epic he never wholly ceases to be recognizably the maker of the minor poems which rise into vision out of his own self-absorption, his "sullein care" (*Prothalamion*, 5), his musing "on the miserie/ In which men live, and I of many most,/ Most miserable man" (*Daphnaida*, 36–38), his "meditation deepe/ Of things exceeding reach of common reason" (*Visions of the Worlds Vanitie*, 3–4). If we take *The Faerie Queene* as we find it, we may see *Mutabilitie* as a further penetration within, an afterword, complete and perfectly shaped in itself, which reveals to us the substructure of Faeryland as we have experienced it—the substructure, that is, of the prophetic poet's personal vision of the world, with Arlo Hill as temple of temples, center of all centers of meaning, loving and joyous creation enclosed in a haunting sadness. Having turned our attention, in the legend *Of Courtesy*, upon poetry and this poem as the poet's sight of truth, revealed and yet deeply personal, Spenser can move to show us, at the poem's end, the heart of his vision. Though it is here wider and deeper, and the power vastly greater, one is reminded still of the visionary processes of *Prothalamion, Daphnaida, Visions of the Worlds Vanitie*. The vision begins with a cry of personal yet cosmic pain, the unceasing Spenserian grief for the passing of things:

> What man that sees the ever-whirling wheele
> Of Change, the which all mortall things doth sway,
> But that therby doth find, and plainly feele . . .
> > (*Mutabilitie* vi.1)

And Nature, after uttering her mysterious truths to the assembled creatures on Arlo Hill, vanishes as suddenly as the Graces on Mount Acidale, and with a more heart-breaking finality:

> Then was that whole assembly quite dismist,
> And Natur's selfe did vanish, whither no man wist.
> > (*Mutabilitie* vii.59)

The poem—the *Cantos* and the whole, as I think, of *The Faerie Queene*—is drawn to its overwhelming close with the most moving of all Spenser's laments, most moving because of the perfection of its placing; a cry of deeper grief because, in seeing the heart of his vision, he has seen too how little it can do. Nature has gone: the world, once more, is mutability, the ever-whirling wheel. Even prophecy, inner sight given shape in poetry, can do no more than comprehend this fact. We are thrown back on the secret comfort, the paradise within from which the poetry arose, and the hope of the ultimate vision to which all prophecy directs us: "O that great Sabbaoth God graunt me that Sabaoths sight!" (viii.2).

Spenser is doing so much here that one can only snatch at some of the effects that this fine close achieves. The immediate point for which I have quoted it is to suggest that the *Mutabilitie Cantos* carry further that process for which the ending of the sixth book has prepared us, the drawing of the poem finally in upon itself, its presentation of itself as poetry rising from the depths of a mind. The poem which began by calling attention to its poetic and personal being in the Virgilian "Lo! I the man" ends with withdrawal into the mind from which it came. Poetry returns from the world, the place of its making, the mind inspired by that mind's own source: for poetry, as the *Argument* of the *October* eclogue had claimed years before, is "a divine gift and heavenly instinct, not to bee gotten by laboure and learning, but adorned with both, and poured into the witte by a certain ἐνθουσιασμός and celestiall inspiration." The heavy and even sorrowful responsibility of the chosen prophet-poet, heir of St. John as well as of the divine Orpheus, can never have been more finely expressed than in the last cantos of *The Faerie Queene,* where poetry itself, prophecy itself, undertakes, as part of its inspired and disciplined task, to point us to its own limitations as a human creation, and to define its own ultimate worth, moving back into the poet's mind so that it may draw us with it into our own. The whole structured world which has made us see more clearly now directs us to the place within, where alone vision and heroism have value.

It can never have been more finely expressed, but Milton equals it. And I should like to begin this aspect of my topic again with a quotation from Angus Fletcher:

> By turning inward, which indeed had always been his tendency, [Spenser] saved the life of his poem. In this he dimly anticipated the poetical career of Milton, whose *Il Penseroso* associated poetical powers with the mood of melancholy. Milton appears to have believed that the great epic vision could not come from a merely technical imperial expansion over vast territories. This was for him a problem of intense personal significance, since he was by nature and training one of the most learned poets in the English tradition. If syncretism is a major requirement for Spenser, it is far more taxing in the case of Milton. The Miltonic choice has a special importance to later poetic tradition, for he early holds that the only legitimate route toward true poetic vision will be a return to the self, by introspection and introversion, by rejecting the external pleasures of *L'Allegro.* Prophecy thrives on the mystery of *turning inward,* on the sense that the self can achieve Ovidian metamorphoses for whatever can turn inward may also turn outward.[14]

14. *The Prophetic Moment,* pp. 299–300.

This inward movement is visible as early as the *Vacation Exercise* and *Elegia Quinta,* where the most memorable passages are those which describe the creative mind rapt in contemplation of the most ancient past, "secret things that came to pass/ When Beldam Nature in her cradle was" (*At a Vacation Exercise,* 45–46). "Kings and Queens and Heroes old" (47), the persons of traditional epic, take second place to the cosmic revelations of prophecy, secret things not to be known through concern with the outer world alone but through the gaze of the "deep transported mind" (33). The *Elegia* is similar:

> Perque umbras, perque antra feror penetralia vatum,
> Et mihi fana patent interiora Deûm.
>
> *(Elegia Quinta,* 17–18)

Il Penseroso is as brooding as is the indrawn pose and downward gaze of Dürer's Melancholy herself, and *Lycidas* is as self-enclosed, existing within the forced reluctance of the opening lines and the quiet courage of the close—within, that is, the concerns of the inspired, devoted, troubled shepherd-poet. *The Shepheardes Calender* is similarly enclosed as is the legend *Of Courtesy;* Spenser has accustomed us to these reluctances, these distresses, these half-sad, half-spirited decisions to accept the burden and go on. Those who have in the past disapproved of *Lycidas* have often done so precisely because of this inwardness, feeling it improper for an elegy to concern itself with the writer, even the writer-as-poet. Now, we would suppose that such a poem is just where the "introverted, elegiac, prophetic strain"—and the prophetic is plain in *Lycidas*—might be expected to make itself felt. Again *Comus* may be thought of as unfolding like Spenserian allegory wholly within the mind, in the "heavy labyrinth," the "tangl'd Wood" and "perplex't paths" that are those of Faeryland rather than of the Welsh marches.

As for prophetic epic itself, the brooding inwardness of the great Miltonic poems has always been evident, and I wish only to call attention to those aspects of it which make Milton's understanding of and closeness to Spenser so plain despite the differences in epic structure and method. Spenser's serpentine, infolded stanza, and the echoings and repeatings and lookings before and after, which characterize his style, have their equivalent in the sweeping paragraphs in which Milton seems to scoop all the world

and all our experience of it inward to become part of the contemplating and re-creating mind. The perpetually astonishing opening
lines, plunging downward into the vast abyss of creation, provide
the best of all examples, and the further descent that follows is
felt as a descent into the "deep transported mind" as much as it is
into Hell, if indeed one has to differentiate. For Hell as well as
Paradise is within, and Satan's words, though not his meaning, are
true enough. The mind *is* its own place, and embraces all things, as
the experience of the fallen Adam and Eve or of the incarnate Son
of God in *Paradise Regained* so richly demonstrates. The movement is similar in the invocation to Holy Light which opens Book
III and modulates into a parallel with the Orphic hymn and the
Orphic descent. The mysteries of cosmos and of spirit dwell in the
depths of the mind. This theme is developed in the intimately and
movingly personal lament for sight lost. Here Milton makes supreme use of the age-old tradition of the blind seer, whose dark
world opens inward upon the shining of celestial light, irradiating
"the mind through all her powers" (*PL* III.52) to draw all things
within. *Paradise Lost* is indeed "Res cunctas," the story of "all
things,"[15] but it is the story of all things as they exist in the mind
of the prophetic poet. Milton's lists of epic names are famous, yet
it is a truism to say that *what* echoes through the lines, *what*

> resounds
> In Fable or *Romance* of *Uthers* Son
> Begirt with *British* and *Armoric* Knights;
> And all who since, Baptiz'd or Infidel
> Jousted in *Aspramont* or *Montalban*
> (*PL* 1.579–83)

is not heoric expansion but contemplative melancholy; not Charle-
magne's establishment of a great Christian empire but the poet's
sad response to the end of it all "When Charlemain with all his
Peerage fell" (1.586) as all have fallen and will fall save the Son of
God. All outer human events exist within this brooding elegiac
vision.

Such passages bring us back to the much-discussed "anti-heroic"
nature of Milton's heroic poem, in which the false heroism of

---

15. Frye, *The Return of Eden,* p. 4, quoting the prefatory poem by Samuel Barrow
in the second edition of *Paradise Lost.*

Satan defines the true in both the Messiah and Adam, and of the even more inward *Paradise Regained* with its starkly opposed figures in a visionary and symbolic landscape.[16] Here the Spenserian tradition is especially evident, for, though Milton's use of the heroic to establish the far greater and more valuable heroism of endurance and inner struggle is more coherently and insistently developed, such use of the heroic is equally sustained in Spenser. The grief of the Red Crosse Knight when he recognizes the inescapable guiltiness of all his earthly battles, and at the same time the dearness of that familiar world and of the heroisms that were the best he knew, is as touching as Malory's:

> "But deeds of armes must I at last be faine
> And ladies love to leave, so dearely bought?"
>
> (*FQ* I.x.62)

The legend *Of Holinesse* is full of the sadness (the word "sad" is repeated with unusual frequency) of the life of heroic endeavor. Even Red Crosse, whose armor is the allegorical armor of the Christian, can yet mistake the nature of what he is about, and can fight Sansjoy in Lucifera's palace, fleeing from it only when he sees in its dungeons "the dreadful spectacle of that sad House of Pryde" where the heroic virtue of paganism is flung aside and forgotten: "Wide were strowne/ The antique ruins of the Romanes fall . . ." (I.v.49)—great Romulus, Sulla, Scipio, Hannibal, high Caesar, and great Pompey.

The poem yields such examples in book after book, and in the sixth book the deficiency of the heroic is an implicit part of a more complete and inclusive movement within. But the book in which the criticism of the old heroic values is most systematically presented is that *Of Temperance,* which has so clearly made its contribution to the setting and development of *Paradise Regained.* By the very nature of the virtue he tries to live by, the virtue

---

16. It is of particular interest to the concerns of this paper that J. B. Broadbent ("The Private Mythology of *Paradise Regained,*" in *Calm of Mind: Tercentenary Essays on* Paradise Regained *and* Samson Agonistes *in Honor of John S. Diekhoff,* ed. J. A. Wittreich [Cleveland and London: Press of Case Western Reserve Univ., 1971], pp. 77–92) remarks in a section of his paper entitled "Real or Allegoric I Discern Not, IV, 390" (pp. 77–80), "The structural weakness is overlaid with a general air of dreaminess," and proceeds to discuss the poem in terms of dream and of theories of psychoanalysis.

essential to all others, Guyon's heroism has to be exercised, and interpreted to us, as a deliberate denial of heroism as one expects to meet it in epic or romance. Though warlike and chivalrous by nature, he subdues himself to the low-keyed, unexciting pursuit of self-control. He does not kill, but only wards off, his opponents; he tramps about his business on foot though in full armor; he is jeered at and regarded as a prudish bore. To bear all of this, of course, is what his heroism consists in. To ride down upon all these irritations with spear brandished would be much easier and more satisfying, and would win him more respect and interest from his fellow characters and even, unfortunately, from some of his readers. But Guyon does not only endure and resist. Through self-control he also learns, and his urbane and ironic intelligence is one of his most attractive characteristics.

The "adventure," if any of the events in Guyon's understated story can be called so, on which Milton makes his fine piece of critical comment[17] is the descent from a "desert wilderness" into the dwelling of Mammon, the cave of the self where the desire to sweep aside our careful daily discipline and mount again to ride roughshod in the exercise of power lies buried in Guyon and in us all. It must be faced, refused (seen and known and abstained from), and made part of a real power within. Guyon looks carefully at all he sees—"fild his inner thought" (*FQ* II.vii.24)—and his replies to Mammon's offers show an increasing self-knowledge and an increasing clarity of recognition about the issues involved. Time after time he looks into himself and corrects, with a precise and elegant irony, Mammon's misuse of such terms as riches, lord, slave, bliss, and grace (for Mammon too, "God of the world and worldlings" [vii.8], has his grace to bestow, and the choice is essentially between God and that which is not God). Guyon, then, overcomes by the denial of lordship: of riches, honor, dignity, the rule of the world. The denial itself constitutes another kind of lordship over the world, a truer lordship, achieved by establishing power over the mind, where all the real battles are fought. The importance of his victory is seen in the garden in the depths of

17. Commenting on the Cave of Mammon episode in *Areopagitica* (see *CM*, IV, 311), Milton makes a factual mistake (the Palmer is not present in the cave) but no mistake about the bearing of the incident as a whole.

Mammon's realm, where we are exposed to all that failure would ultimately mean. The Garden of Proserpina is a place of profound sadness where dwell Tantalus and—as Milton must have seen with satisfied understanding—Pilate, who also had to choose between God and Mammon. It is a garden of Eden with all the life gone from it, silent, filled with dark and poisonous plants, with an empty silver seat in an arbor where the goddess of the dead, who was once the young goddess of the flowering spring, is wont to sit near a tree of golden apples.

That the temptations of *Paradise Regained* were written out of a full appreciation of Mammon's cave and its meaning is very evident. The denial of heroic superhuman achievement and of power, the quiet struggle within, is the essence of Christ's experience in the wilderness as it is of Guyon's, and indeed it is equally evident that Spenser had the temptations of the biblical Christ in mind. Thus Milton's meditating Son of God has "Into himself descended" (*PR* II.111), and before his inner thought move the temptations by which, like Guyon, he comes to know himself, and wholly to command himself and all things, through the exact definitions he is compelled to make. Like Guyon, having conquered, he is ministered to by angels, but the close, like other Miltonic endings, is as unheroically quiet as if nothing had happened—nor has it, to the outer eye. Christ merely

> unobserv'd
> Home to his Mothers house private return'd.
> (*PR* IV.638–39)

It would be out of place to make more detailed comparisons here, but the more closely they are made, the more each set of temptations illuminates and shows the profundity of the other—and shows too the depth at which the Spenserian works in Milton.

One would like also to examine the ways in which the Garden of Proserpina and the "loss of Eden" echo and re-echo each other. Spenser's tree of golden apples is, he tells us, the source of all the desired and trouble-making apples of the myths—those of Hesperus (this Milton remembered), and that of Discord, which gave rise to the fall of Troy and the wanderings of Odysseus and Aeneas, and to the first of our sorrowing epics. The Garden holds the same sad irony of loss, endless loss brought about through the attempt

at immoderate and more-than-human gain, that we feel in Milton's
haunting puns:

> the Fruit
> Of that Forbidden Tree, whose mortal tast
> Brought Death into the World, and all our woe,
> With loss of *Eden* . . .
>
> (*PL* I.1–4)

> Serpent, we might have spar'd our coming hither,
> Fruitless to mee, though Fruit be here to excess . . .
>
> (IX.647–48)

The same sense of loss is there again in the intricate weavings of
the figure of Eve among her flowers, "fairest unsupported Flour"
(IX.432), with "Pomona when she fled/ *Vertumnus*" and Ceres
"Yet Virgin of *Proserpina* from *Jove*" (IX.394–96), and most of
all in the chanting sorrow of:

> Not that faire field
> Of *Enna*, where *Proserpin* gathering flours
> Her self a fairer Floure by gloomie *Dis*
> Was gatherd, which cost *Ceres* all that pain . . .
>
> (IV.268–71)

So, for both of the great Renaissance heroic poets, heroic
effort, outer event, history, is part of their material, as it must be
in epic and in prophecy. But their history is—if one may for a
moment separate these two elements—the history of prophecy
rather than of epic. It is history contained within the inward-
looking prophetic vision and seen in eternal relation to Heaven and
Hell, God's garden and Proserpina's. This is the kind of superiority
that Sidney attributes to poetry as compared to the work of the
historian proper, and for the poets of prophecy history will be
urgently important as the scene to which their vision has such
compelling relevance. Historical event past, present, or future—the
trial of Mary of Scots or the outrage of the Sons of Belial,
Fontarabbia or Hevenfield where good King Oswald died—is transformed in prophecy. Spenser insists that his "historicall fiction" is
exactly that, paradoxical though the term may seem, and in the
Proem to Book II he devotes five stanzas to the truth of the things
he describes. But in the same Proem the emphasis is equally on the

existence of the "antiquities," the "famous antique history," within "just memory," mother of the Muse. Faeryland is England, but England prophetically understood.

The point is made again within Book II, which summarizes the contents of two fictious history books: *Briton Moniments,* which is like something written by "Cambden, the nourice of antiquitie" (the phrase is from *The Ruines of Time*), and *Antiquitee of Faery Lond.* The first is, in terms of the materials it draws on, an account of that amalgam of fact and legend that made up for Spenser's time the history of Britain from the arrival of Brutus. But the facts are filtered through a mind which sees history as a record of human sin and weakness. The second book is a history of Faeryland, so nearly eventless that it can be recounted in seven stanzas to the *Moniments'* more than sixty. Faeryland's peaceable succession of good and public-spirited kings, over seven hundred of them hardly distinguishable one from another, has ensured its quiet. Ideal history stands as implicit comment on the greed and cruelty of the actual. And both books are kept and read in the House of Alma, the temperate soul dwelling in the orderly house of its body. They are kept, of course, in the head, in the hindmost of the three chambers in which sit the three sages who can, respectively, "things to come foresee," "of thinges present best advize," and "things past . . . keepe in memoree" (*FQ* II.ix.49). Eumnestes is "of infinite remembraunce," and he spends his time turning over his scrolls and books. It is here, in the furthest chamber of the mind, that history is rightly known and the past can be creatively related to present and future time, so becoming part of our "knowledge of a mans selfe, in the Ethike and Politique consideration."[18] History becomes, in prophetic vision, a version of biblical revelation or of the Ovidian mythology of the creation of things and their enduring though shifting life ("eterne in mutabilitie" is Spenser's memorable phrase).

For both these poets, Spenser and Milton, have the intense energy of the visionary maker, seen perhaps most gloriously in

18. See the excellent discussion by Harry Berger, Jr. ("Two Spenserian Retrospects," *Texas Studies in Literature and Language*, 10 [1968], 5–25) of the "enacting of the mythopoetic process" in Spenser's pageant of rivers at the marriage of Thames and Medway, where British historical geography rises out of and returns into the changing movement of the waters.

their celebrations of the joy and power, the "enormous bliss," of created and creating life:

> So fertile be the flouds in generation . . .
>
> (*FQ* IV.xii.1)

> Infinite shapes of creatures there are bred . . .
>
> (*FQ* III.vi.35)

> All be he subject to mortalitie,
> Yet in eterne in mutabilitie,
> And by succession made perpetuall . . .
>
> (*FQ* III.vi.47)

> The Earth obey'd, and strait
> Op'ning her fertil Woomb teem'd at a Birth
> Innumerous living Creatures, perfet formes . . .
>
> (*PL* VII.453–55)

> Flours worthy of Paradise which not nice Art
> In Beds and curious Knots, but Nature boon
> Powrd forth profuse on Hill and Dale and Plaine.
>
> (*PL* IV.241–43)

Yet what we go on to remember always is the gathering of this rich fertility, of the whole created world, into the steady, sorrowing contemplation which is the mark of these two poets of the prophetic moment, the ingathering of the poem into an elegiac vision of the fate of men caught in changing time, and only glimpsing "the pillours of eternity."

> Great enimy to it, and to all the rest,
> That in the Gardin of Adonis springs,
> Is wicked Tyme . . .

> Yet pitty often did the gods relent,
> To see so faire thinges mard and spoiled quight:
> And their great mother Venus did lament
> The losse of her deare brood, her deare delight . . .
>
> (*FQ* III.vi.39–40)

And even—especially—in Eden, the nostalgic Miltonic ironies echo:

> Others whose fruit burnisht with Golden Rinde
> Hung amiable, *Hesperian* Fables true,

> If true, here only . . .
> Flours of all hue, and without Thorn the Rose.
>
> (*PL* IV.249–56)

For in this garden

> the Fiend
> Saw undelighted all delight, all kind
> Of living Creatures new to sight and strange:
> Two of far nobler shape erect and tall,
> Godlike erect.
>
> (*PL* IV.285–89)

The Garden of Proserpina is that which replaces Eden, expressing and resulting from the Satanic undelight. The undermining is almost coeval with the "enormous bliss"; divine and human creation, goodness, joy are all poisoned by the tooth of the Beast. "What could the Muse her self that *Orpheus* bore"? There is no place for prophet or poet or instructed reader but in the inner pastoral, the paradise within, which is for each of them, as it is for Calidore, a point of reference, and a strengthening for prophetic action.

Sidney and Milton: The Poet as Maker

S. K. HENINGER, JR.

Milton's overt references to Philip Sidney are few. There are four entries in the Commonplace Book which indicate a close knowledge of the *Arcadia*. A scattering of verbal similarities echo in the poetry, most insistently in the description of Eden in *Paradise Lost*. And of course there is the celebrated incident of Pamela's prayer, which had been clumsily adapted for use in the *Eikon Basilike* and which Milton scored with considerable profit and pleasure in *Eikonoklastes*. But that is all we can point to and say confidently, "Milton took this from his reading of Sidney." There is no direct evidence that Milton was familiar with, or even aware of, Sidney's *Defence of Poesy*.

It might seem unwarranted, therefore, if not downright perverse, to suggest that this treatise underlies the poetic theory adopted by Milton in his best (and best-known) poetry. Yet the poetics of Sidney's manifesto had prevailed in England by the end of the sixteenth century. It had been confirmed by critics and exemplified by an increasing number of poets. Though academicians tend to call this movement the school of Spenser, the theoretician was Sidney. Or at least, his *Defence of Poesy* is the extant document which propounds the theory.

We should note, of course, that Sidney arrived at his view in those halcyon years of the Areopagus, when he and Spenser and Gabriel Harvey were in close and frequent converse on the subject of poetry. These are the years that culminated in *The Shepheardes Calender* and the *Arcadia*. It is interesting to speculate on the literary relationship between Sidney and Spenser—and especially on the relationship between Sidney's *Defence of Poesy* and the treatise entitled *The English Poet* which, according to E. K. in the argument for *October*, Spenser had ready for the press in 1579. But Spenser's *English Poet* was never published. What we have is Sidney's treatise. And it was to Sidney's treatise that later critics— William Webbe, George Puttenham, Sir John Harington, Ben Jonson—addressed themselves. In any case, whether we speak of the school of Sidney or the school of Spenser makes little difference. Colin Clout would willingly share our praise with his beloved Astrophel.

In the *Defence of Poesy* Sidney touches upon a large number of topics—indeed, upon most of what concerns us as critics. His apology is a sweeping survey of the *ars poetica:* its ontology, its epistemology, and its teleology. But running through the entire argument is a concept of the poet as a creator analogous to the divine creator of our universe. Quite early in the treatise Sidney defines the poet as a "maker," deriving the very name from the Greek word ποιεῖν, "to make."[1] Moreover, Sidney soon indicates that these "makers" are the "right Poets" (C2), in contradistinction to the poet-prophets, who do no more than repeat the eternal truths of religion, and also to the didactic poets, who use only the data of sense experience as the subject matter for their knowledge. For Sidney the best poet is a "maker"—an artifex working in the likeness of God to create a nature comparable to the physical world that lies about us. This poetics was brilliantly demonstrated by Spenser in *The Shepheardes Calender,* and for that reason he was hailed as "the new poet."

Together these two giants of late Elizabethan literature established a poetics that has conditioned the practice of English poetry down to our own century. Generations of poets have striven to embody its tenets, or have shaped themselves in opposition to it. Certainly, this was the dominant tradition in England at the turn of the seventeenth century, the tradition to which Milton allied himself in his formative years, and the one to which he paid heed throughout his career.

Quite apart from poetic theory, of course, Sidney and Milton shared a great deal. Both had great reverence for learning and both were learned men, especially as humanistic education had defined learning in terms of the *litterae humaniores.* Both were zealous in

1. (London: William Ponsonby, 1595), B4.

the Protestant cause, equally partisan in politics on behalf of Puritanism, though entering the movement at different phases of its development. Both saw literature as a legitimate and effective means of furthering this cause, thereby attributing to poetry a novel teleology. While poetry had long been used for moral instruction, this instruction had served primarily the ends of religion. Sidney and Milton, however, saw literature as serving the ends of politics—politics in the literal sense, the habits and customs of the πόλις. Not since Plato had any writer credited poets with a greater influence upon the commonwealth.

Sidney and Milton shared also a favorite French author, one who compiled their beliefs and hopes in a magnum opus. In 1578 Guillaume Salluste du Bartas, a Protestant, had published his versified commentary on the six days of creation, *La sepmaine.* And immediately it became a success in England. It took its place on the shelf of books between the Bible and the current almanack, and filled a need in family affairs similar to that filled by *Paradise Lost* in later generations. Its influence, literary as well as theological, is incalculable. Gabriel Harvey reports that Spenser knew the fourth day of *La sepmaine* by heart,[2] and Sidney translated the whole of it into English.[3] There is no doubt that Milton had this text ready to hand throughout his mature years, probably in the sympathetic translation into English by Joshua Sylvester.

In Sylvester's Du Bartas, as *La sepmaine* was affectionately known in England, the reader could ponder the wide-ranging mysteries of creation. He could contemplate God's intention, His methods, His results. The text is characterized by a Protestant passion for the truth—*the* truth, at once universal and concrete. It is also characterized by a Protestant devotion to the word—*the* word, at once comprehensive and knowable, λόγος though it may be. The hexameron is laid out in its diversity for human perusal, and yet Du Bartas's single-minded purpose is never obscured: to magnify the Lord, who in His benevolence has created the heavens

---

2. Harvey, *Marginalia,* ed. G. C. Moore Smith (Stratford-upon-Avon, 1913), p. 161. If Harvey is any bellwether, the bardolatry of Du Bartas in England was excessive: already in 1579 "divine" Du Bartas was wiser even than Euripides, who was "poetarum sapientissimus" (ibid., p. 115); and about the same time, if not slightly earlier, he was "Homerus divinus" in French (ibid., p. 168).

3. Sidney's translation was not published and has not been found by later scholars. It is incontrovertibly attested, however, by contemporary references; see *The Poems of Sir Philip Sidney,* ed. William A. Ringler, Jr. (Oxford: Clarendon Press, 1962), p. 339.

(and man) to declare His glory, and to parvify man, who lost the original paradise through a proclivity to sin. Though man was created in the image of deity, a passage in Genesis dear to the hearts of humanists, he had proved unworthy of his divine prototype, a point reiterated by the Protestants.

The success of *La sepmaine* soon produced a sequel, a longer (and unfinished) second week of hexameral discourses printed in 1584 as *La seconde sepmaine*. This volume deals with man's early history after the fall. Included is a book entitled "Les colomnes," in which Du Bartas paraphrases the arcane knowledge that the heirs of Seth supposedly had inscribed on a pair of pillars, thereby preserving the antediluvian wisdom of the ancients through Noah's flood and transmitting it to future generations. The subject matter of this book is mathematics—specifically, the quadrivial disciplines (arithmetic, geometry, astronomy, and music) as they had been formulated in the Pythagorean school and recorded by Boethius.

The section on astronomy appropriately contains a full description of the zodiac. There as a summary comment Sidney[4] and Milton could have read the following passage, which touches upon the age-old question of whether God created out of pre-existent matter or out of nothing or out of Himself:

> Before th'All-working Word alone
> Made Nothing be Alls wombe and *Embryon*,
> Th'eternall Plot, th'*Idea* fore-conceaved,
> The wondrous Forme of all that Forme received,
> Did in the Work-mans spirit devinely lye,
> And, yer it was, the World was wondrously.[5]

Du Bartas's answer to the problem is ingenious. He syncretizes in a typically Renaissance fashion. He uses poetry to conflate and equivocate in a way that must have won Sidney's whole-hearted approval.

In this passage Du Bartas begins within a Christian framework, drawing upon the familiar tradition based upon St. John that Christ as λόγος was God's effective agent in the creation. "In the

---

4. Although *La seconde sepmaine* was not printed until 1584, Sidney may well have known it earlier in manuscript. Certainly anyone who had translated *La sepmaine*, as Sidney had done, would have eagerly sought its equally famous sequel.

5. *Devine Weekes and Workes*, tr. Sylvester (London, 1605), p. 483.

beginning was the Word, and the Word was with God, and the Word was God." Milton cultivates the tradition in its fullest bloom in Book VII of *Paradise Lost,* when God gives Christ the commission to create the world:

> And thou my Word, begotten Son, by thee
> This I perform, speak thou, and be it don.[6]
>
> (VII.163–64)

In this tradition there is an essential ambiguity in the terminology. The term λόγος is a physical utterance, a word to be heard, the sense-perceptible result of Christ's action; but also it is a plan or design, the Latin *ratio,* the insubstantial idea in the mind of God. Christ's act of creation—the miracle of it—lies precisely in the translation of the λόγος from the conceptual realm into a world of three dimensions. The ambiguity of the term is a semantic aid to understanding the coordinates wherein this miracle transpired. In any case, by citing the tradition of Christ as the implementor of God's λόγος, Du Bartas begins on ground well known to Renaissance Christians.

But then Du Bartas shifts his ground and chooses a different set of referents for his discourse. He uses the term "All" for the universe, and punningly counterposes it against "Nothing," the *nihil* out of which the Schoolmen said that God had created. Furthermore, he uses the term "Idea," and he glosses it in the next line with a synonym, "Forme." And soon we find that the creator was a "Work-man." Without more prompting, we should realize that Du Bartas is operating within a Platonic framework, and specifically within the framework of cosmological postulates laid out in the *Timaeus.* This dialogue was, with the *Symposium* and the *Republic,* the best known of Plato's works in the Renaissance, and the only one that had been known continuously through the centuries since their composition. It had enjoyed unbroken popularity, and had early entered the mainstream of Christian thought through approving paraphrases by most of the Church Fathers. It was, in fact, but slightly less Christian than St. John's gospel of the λόγος.

Nevertheless, we can distinguish between creation by the Word

---

6. Cf. also "So spake th'Almightie, and to what he spake/ His Word, the filial Godhead, gave effect" (*PL* VII.174–75). See also *PL* VII.208, 217.

and creation by a divine Workman. And while we recognize that both traditions had been assimilated into Christian thought (and that both traditions are enormously important for any theory of poetry, the art form using words as its medium), we can profitably separate the Timaean cosmogony and consider it as an autonomous tradition.

The Timaean cosmogony is simple and straightforward, yet surprisingly complete. It presupposes a benevolent and rational deity that proceeds to a creation which is good and beautiful. Starting with an archetypal idea, equivalent to the insubstantial λόγος in St. John's gospel, the creating deity gives physical extension to this design by projecting its form into a receptive void. He continues to create by a mathematical process—that is, according to proportion and harmony—until his idea is fully realized. The result is the three-dimensional time-space continuum that we recognize as our universe. The divine idea is thereby rendered palpable to mortal senses. And it is perfect, in the literal meaning of the Latin verb *perficere,* since the deity has carried out his plan to completion. It is therefore described as τό πάν, "the all." In this cosmogony the world may be thought of in its conceptual state as the permanent idea in the mind of the deity, or in its physical state as the mutable phenomena of natural events. There are two realities to which we must respond. And time may be defined according to two distinct coordinates, one for each of these realities. Within the unchanging, all-inclusive stasis of the divine mind, time is eternity; within the variable circumstances of the sublunary world, it is a procession of moments, hours, days, months, years.

We can see now how closely Du Bartas echoes the Timaean cosmogony. Our universe is τό πάν, and the creating deity is identified as "th'All-working Word." He is a unique potency who begins with an archetypal plan described by two epithets, "th'eternall Plot" and "th'*Idea* fore-conceaved," and in the next line by yet a third epithet, "the wondrous Forme of all." This "idea" or "form"[7] lies in the mind of the divine "Work-man," continuously and eternally residing there as a concept without substance. But being generous and omnipotent, the deity has projected his arche-

7. Gr. ἰδέα = "form."

typal idea into a time-space continuum, described as the "Nothing" which became the "wombe and *Embryon*" of this "All." Thereby our universe as a physical entity came into existence. And time as a measured sequence of events began. Nevertheless, even before this moment when the timeless became timely, our universe had being—"yer it was, the World was wondrously." Our universe had being as a noncorporeal concept in the mind of the creator. The ultimate reality of our universe, therefore, resides with that archetypal idea in the changeless and inclusive mind of God. But the mutable objects and transient phenomena perceived by our senses are reflections of thoughts in God's mind, and consequently represent a correspondent though subordinate order of being. They are a lower level of existence with a secondary reality, once removed from truth itself.

Milton follows this cosmogony in his own account of creation in Book VII of *Paradise Lost*. He sophisticates it by dichotomizing the creating deity: God the Father conceives the idea, while God the Son translates it into physical fact. And there is considerable Christian coloration by means of angelology and liturgical vocabulary. But the essentials of Du Bartas's theory are clearly evident. Christ is identified as "th'Omnific Word" (VII.217), a latinate version of Du Bartas's epithet, "th'All-working Word," and the inchoate nothingness that He harmonizes into order is "the vast immeasurable Abyss" (VII.211).

Very quickly the Judeo-Christian tradition of Genesis takes over in Milton's narration and a paraphrase of the Mosaic hexameron ensues. But not before we are treated to the majestic image of the deity as archgeometer, delineating the perfect circle of the finite universe:

> He [Christ] took the golden Compasses, prepar'd
> In Gods Eternal store, to circumscribe
> This Universe, and all created things.
>
> (VII.225–27)

Then the perfection of τό πᾶν takes shape before our mind's eye as Genesis recounts. But this tradition for a mathematical creator derives from the *Timaeus*, where the universal harmony of our world is attributed to the careful ratios which the deity prescribed in composition of the world-soul (34C–37C). Although the *auctor*

mathematicus of the *Timaeus* can readily conflate with the Hebrew Jehovah, who created according to number, weight, and
measure (Book of Wisdom xi. 21), the image of God as geometer,
as Plutarch well knew,[8] reflects the Platonic commitment to a
mathematically designed universe. And the rational design which
we detect in nature is the physical manifestation of the form
which pre-existed as idea in the mind of God.

It is tempting to argue that Sidney also was familiar with this
passage from Du Bartas,[9] though not essential, since he could have
known the Timaean cosmogony from a variety of sources, including the original text itself. In any case, one focal passage in *The
Defence of Poesy* depends upon the cosmological assumptions set
forth in the *Timaeus*. In this section Sidney delivers his most
fulsome praise of the poet. According to the Greeks, says Sidney,
the name "poet" is "the most excellent," and "it commeth of this
word $\pi o \iota \epsilon \hat{\iota} \nu$ which is to make" (B4). Therefore, Sidney observes,
"We Englishmen have met with the Greekes in calling him a
Maker." Behind this epithet of "maker" lies the epithet applied to
the creating deity when he first appears in the *Timaeus*: $\dot{o} \pi o \iota \eta$-
$\tau \acute{\eta} \varsigma \ldots \tau o \hat{\upsilon} \pi a \nu \tau \acute{o} \varsigma$, "the maker of this all" (28C). From this point,
Sidney assumes an analogy between the mortal poet and the
heavenly maker; and just as the heavenly maker produces the
universe, so the mortal poet produces a poem. Since the corresponding elements in a metaphor are interchangeable, the uni-

8. In his collection of table-talk, "Of Symposiaques" (VIII.2), Plutarch includes an
entry: "How *Plato* is to be understood, when he saith: that God continually is exercised
in Geometry" (in *The Morals*, tr. Philemon Holland [London, 1603], pp. 767–68). Here
is the locus classicus for this Renaissance canard.

9. Sidney, of course, could not have seen the Sylvester translation, since it was not
prepared until the 1590s. Therefore it behooves me to provide the text in French as
Sidney likely knew it:

> Tout ainsi
> Que plustost que le Rien par une voix feconde
> Fut fait et la matrice et l'embryon du monde,
> L'exemplaire eternel, l'avant-conceu portrait,
> Et l'amirable seau de tout ce qui s'est fait,
> Logeoit divinement dans l'esprit du grand Maistre,
> Et l'univers avoit essence avant son estre.

(*The Works of Guillaume De Salluste Sieur Du Bartas*, ed. Urban T. Holmes, Jr., et al., 3
vols. [Chapel Hill: Univ. of North Carolina Press, 1935–40], III, 186.)

verse is God's poem, or a poem is the poet's universe. To speak more broadly, nature is God's art (i.e., artifact), and the poem is the poet's nature.

Sidney continues this analogy in minute and literal detail. Since the poet works in the likeness of God, in his poem he creates "an other nature" (B4^v), which is related to our physical world as one projection of an idea is related to another projection of the same idea. The poet's universe and material nature are cognates. Both the physical world and the poet's imagined world derive ultimately from the same archetypal idea, and therefore retain the same basic form. But the material world is subject to the accidents of change: to deficiencies of this or that, and to the mutability brought by passing time. The poem, of course, lies beyond the unstable sphere of the four elements. It resides in a permanent world of art, approximating Plato's changelss world of being comprised of eternal ideas. Therefore, Sidney asserts, "Nature never set foorth the earth in so rich Tapistry as diverse Poets have done . . .: her world is brasen, the Poets only deliver a golden" (C1). The poet, using the nonmaterial medium of words, avoids the flaws of the physical creation and approximates the perfection of God's poem.

Sidney goes so far in this analogy between poet and heavenly maker as to extoll the validity of the poem over that of ephemeral nature. Wherein lies truth, he asks *sotto voce*. In our kaleidoscopic impressions of material objects? Or in the artifacts of poets? Sidney boldly formulates the difference between nature and art, and daringly suggests that the creation of the mortal poet more nearly approaches perfection than does the material world produced by God's agent, Nature:

Neither let it be deemed too sawcy a comparison, to ballance the highest point of mans wit, with the efficacie of nature: but rather give right honor to the heavenly maker of that maker, who having made man to his owne likenes, set him beyond and over all the workes of that second nature, which in nothing he sheweth so much as in Poetry; when with the force of a divine breath, he bringeth things foorth surpassing her doings.

(C1–C1^v)

Here we have the age-old motif of who is superior in the arts, man or deity? Sidney the humanist would have recalled that this issue had been decided when Arachne challenged Athena to a contest, an occasion amply interpreted by Spenser in *Muiopotmos;* and

Sidney the Christian self-consciously saw his assertion of primacy for the poet as an act of pride. Therefore he suggests that we praise not the poet, "but rather give right honor to the heavenly maker of that maker." For after all, the deity is the prototype for the poet: " . . . the heavenly maker of that maker, who having made man to his owne likenes, set him beyond and over all the workes of that second nature." So man by divine fiat is lord of God's creation. And nowhere more than in his poetic ability does man show his superiority over the other creatures and his proximity to deity: "which in nothing he sheweth so much as in Poetry." Uttering the poem, in fact, takes on something of the godlike impetus of the λόγος. Just as God animated Adam, so the poet blows his inspiriting afflatus into his creature. And then, "with the force of a divine breath, he bringeth things foorth surpassing her [Nature's] doings."

This passage in *The Defence of Poesy* is so compact that it requires careful explication. Sidney's premises must be exposed as a foundation for his meaning. But his intention and his dependence upon Timaean cosmology are evident. A poetics emerges in which the poet is a "maker," in the sense that the Timaean godhead is a maker, equivalent to the Greek word ποιητής, from ποιεῖν. His "poem," likewise from ποιεῖν, is that which he makes, his artifact[10] —a synonym with "fiction," which comes from *fictus* (the past participle of the Latin verb *fingere*) and means that which has been made. And just as deity begins with an idea, to which He gives extension in terms of time and space, thereby creating our physical universe, so the poet begins with an idea, to which he gives extension in terms of human events, thereby creating a narrative. The poet creates a universe out of people (characters) who perform episodes (actions) in a time-space continuum (setting). But the ultimate reality of the poem remains its original idea, the conceit in the mind of the poet that informs its several components but nonetheless continues apart as an unchanging entity on some level of existence beyond the events of the narrative. The characters and actions and settings are but the palpable manifestation of the original idea, what make it com-

---

10. In *Eikonoklastes* Milton refers to Sidney's *Arcadia* as a "Poem" (*CM*, V. 86), though certainly he knew that the work was written in prose, not verse. Clearly Milton is using the word "poem" in this special sense of something made.

municable. But they are at best ancillary to the idea, a correspondent though subordinate level of being. They are not a substitute
for the idea. In no wise do they replace it as the ultimate meaning
of the poem.

Sidney is unequivocal on this point. He states more dog-
matically than is his wont: "Everie understanding knoweth the
skill of ech Artificer standeth in that *Idea,* or fore conceit of the
worke, and not in the worke it selfe" (C1). Clearly we are in a
Platonic cosmology where reality lies among the essential ideas in
an unchanging world of being. And the act of creation consists in
projecting the "*Idea,* or fore conceit"—"th'eternall Plot, th'*Idea*
fore-conceaved" of Du Bartas—into the coordinates of time and
space. Thereby the idea is transported across the discontinuity
between insubstantial and material, and the divine is rendered
mortal. The limitless is mirrored in the finite, and the eternal is
shadowed in a cavalcade of successive events. But the essence of
the poem still resides in its original idea, or fore-conceit.

In his account of creation, Raphael gives Adam a lesson in
epistemology which we should heed. The angel instructs our
parent about that moment when the λόγος was rendered physical,
and comments on the difficulty of explaining the event to men:

> Immediate are the Acts of God, more swift
> Then time or motion, but to human ears
> Cannot without process of speech be told,
> So told as earthly notion can receave.
>
> (*PL* VII.176–79)

The "Acts of God" are "immediate," both instantaneous and
uninterruptedly continuous. They transcend the coordinates of
time and space which determine the world perceptible to our
senses. For human understanding, therefore, they must be construed in a medium which our limited faculties can apprehend.
This is the function of words: to bridge the conceptual and the
physical realms. And this is the role of the poet, the vatic maker.
In his fiction, using the medium of words, the poet renders
knowable to our "earthly notion" that which "without process of
speech" would remain ineffable. The maker, then, does not have
license to create indiscriminately or even whimsically—as Sidney
puts it, his "delivering foorth ... is not wholly imaginative, as we
are wont to say by them that build Castles in the aire" (*Defence,*

C1). He must stick to God's truth. His raison d'être, in fact, is to re-create in our terms "the Acts of God."

Such a poetics predetermines the way in which a poem must be read. Necessarily the reader begins with the data of the narrative, with the episodes that pass in sequence before his mind's eye. This, however, is but the starting-point for a reading. The discursive experience of such data is superficial and not an end in itself. Rather, the reader must work through the surface of the narrative in his search for the underlying idea; he must seek the concept that informs all the parts and gives them coherence. With slight tampering, we can extract this advice from a later passage in *The Defence of Poesy*, in which Sidney says: "Use the narration . . . as an imaginative groundplat of a profitable invention" (G1^v)—where "invention," from the discipline of rhetoric, is the equivalent of "fore-conceit." This "invention" is the essence of the poem.

We might note in passing that this method for reading a "poem" by a maker is quite different from the method of interpreting an allegory. In an allegory, one thing stands for another, and a series of things stands for a series of other things. There is a one-to-one equation between each abstraction and its counter in the narrative, and reading an allegory consists in a relatively straightforward transfer from the physical to the abstract, or vice versa. The reader extrapolates from the counters and their relationships on the one hand, to the abstractions and their relationships on the other. To speak mathematically, the reader constructs two parallel series of ciphers which are more or less interchangeable. But reading a "poem" is more like the mathematical operation of doing a sum. The meaning is cumulative, pieced together bit by bit, until the entire design is perceptible.

Furthermore, since the idea is the ultimate reality of a "poem," its form becomes a salient feature. The poem must be seen as a totality—composed of disparate parts presented in temporal sequence, but nonetheless interrelated to form a single whole. This is what Andrew Marvell, in the second line of his commendatory poem "On Paradise Lost," calls the "vast Design." Idea and form and totality and design are synonymous in this poetics.

Consequently, the first reading of a poem—the discursive procedure of beginning with the opening line and continuing to the finish—is hardly reading at all. That initial experience of the poem is innocent of its totality, and therefore of its idea. In fine, the proper reading of a poem can take place only after the discursive experience of the first reading is completed and the total pattern of the poem is in mind. Then each part can be seen in proper relation to the whole. The meaning of each episode can be determined, in fact, only when it is related to the whole, only when it is seen as a constituent part of the totality. In such a poem the meaning of the episodes does not derive from sequential relationships as we progress from one incident to the next through the temporal sequence of the narrative—that is the way we read a novel—but rather from the part-to-whole relationships as we go from one quasi-discrete episode to the next quasi-discrete episode. Usually the episodes are discontinuous with their neighbors, showing disregard for a recognizably normal passage of time. It is for this reason that epic poets begin *in medias res;* thereby they announce that in their poetic universe measured time has been abandoned. There is no distinction between beginning and end, and middle is cotemporaneous with both. Time is reduced to an ever-present now—the totality of the sequential parts, the idea of the poem.

It is Sidney's treatise on poetry that most succinctly codifies this poetics of making, though likely *The English Poet,* the lost treatise of Spenser, would have expressed similar views of the poetic craft. Certainly, the poems of Spenser exemplify this poetics in a concrete and convincing way. They demonstrate the most effective techniques of "fiction," and therefore have earned for Spenser the highest accolades from his fellow-poets. He is, to deal in a phrase already coined, "the poet's poet."

The Shepheardes Calender, incidentally dedicated to Sidney, is a prime example of a maker's poem. The design of the work, as the title pointedly announces, is a commonplace, the annual unit of time comprising twelve disparate parts. The subtitle insistently calls attention to this design: "twelve Aeglogues proportionable to the twelve monethes."[11] Each eclogue, identified with a month, is rigidly distinguished from its neighbors, almost isolated unto itself. Yet the twelve eclogues build cumulatively to a complete calendar.

11. Citations for Spenser refer to *The Works: A Variorum Edition,* ed. Edwin A. Greenlaw et al., 10 vols (Baltimore: Johns Hopkins Press, 1932–57).

The discrete parts taken together achieve an unmistakable totality, the annual unit of time. And this annual unit of time, the year, is the integer of eternity, because, repeated endlessly as the heavens turn in their interminable courses, it generates eternity.

In the design of the poem, then, a limited portion of time, the month, is related to limitless time, eternity. Furthermore, a well-known motif in medieval art correlated each month with an appropriate human occupation, so that March is the month to prune, April the month to woo, May the month to plant, and so forth. The twelve occupations represented by the twelve months exhaust the possibilities of human experience—that is why Colin Clout must bid adieu at the end of *The Shepheardes Calender*. But conversely, by exhausting the possibilities, the twelve months in their totality achieve an inclusive completeness. The year becomes an icon for *all* human experience, and Spenser's design becomes a means of relating each particular human activity to an ideal concept of the full life.

The same statement is made visually by a diagram used to illustrate the section on "Time and Its Parts" in a French translation of Bartholomaeus Anglicus' *De proprietatibus rerum* printed at Lyons in 1485 (see fig. 1). This diagram enjoyed wide distribution in England because a close adaptation of it was included in the numerous editions of that compilation of kitchen astrology imported from France and published throughout the sixteenth century as *The Kalender of Sheepehards*. The diagram is composed of three concentric circles, each distinct but all interrelated by correspondences. The outermost circle contains the twelve signs of the zodiac (proceeding in the direction of counterclockwise). The middle circle contains the corresponding human occupations appropriate to each month. The inner circle reduces these twelve-part cosmoi to the simplest possible form: a pair of contraries. A woman gathering flowers in a meadow beneath leafy trees represents summer, while a man warming himself before a fire in a barren field beneath leafless trees represents winter. The two halves of this circle are exact counterparts, and of course together they comprise a perfect circle. Each of these three perfect circles, be it noted, provides an ideogram for time.

Another perfect circle is completed each year by the seasons as they roll round in orderly sequence. If we make a slight adjust-

1. *From* Bartholomaeus Anglicus, *De proprietatibus rerum* (Lyons, 1485), r5. *By permission of the Huntington Library, San Marino, California.*

ment and think in terms of seasons rather than months, as E. K. does in the argument for *December*, we can see that our period of youth is a spring, our manhood a summer, our middle-age an autumn, and our dotage a winter. This icon, as Ovid knew, is as old as Pythagoras.[12] Every man goes through this temporal sequence, of course, but the equally important point is that each season contributes directly and independently to the whole. Spring is essential, just like summer and autumn and winter. To use the terms of E. K., the folly of youth, the love at manhood, the harvest in maturity, the chill of old age—each performs a

12. Cf. *Metamorphoses*, XV.214–36.

prescribed function. Each season is necessary to complete the pattern. The effect of *The Shepheardes Calender,* therefore, is an orderly progress through the variety of human experience in measured time, but the final result is a perfect paradigm, a static image of all human experience *sub specie aeternitatis.* This is the point of Spenser's envoy: "Loe I have made a Calendar for every yeare,/ That steele in strength, and time in durance shall out-weare."

In addition to its relevance to contemporary affairs (which is extensive), *The Shepheardes Calender,* then, has a cosmic dimension. It is Spenser's icon or image by which to render knowable the relationship between our present moment (the Aristotelian νῦν) and eternity, and to make us realize that the variety of experience, both good and bad, is necessary to complete the pattern predestined as a paradigm for the human condition. Each man must suffer the vicissitudes of time, symbolized by the changing seasons, but the optimist sees that by perfecting the pattern he participates in eternity. That is the design of Spenser's poem, the idea that informs its twelve parts and makes them whole.

Returning now to the quotation from "The Columns" quoted on p. 60 above, we shall see that Du Bartas attributes to God a similar intention when He displays the zodiac in the heavens. Just before this passage Du Bartas has described each of the twelve signs in turn, from Aries through Pisces. Next comes the passage quoted, which Sylvester glosses in the margin with a pertinent comment: "A deeper & more curious reason of the same [i.e., the zodiac]." And then in the same verse paragraph, the text continues:

> Th'Eternall *Trine-One*, spreading even the Tent
> Of th'All-enlightning glorious Firmament,
> Fill'd it with Figures; and in various Marks
> Their pourtray'd Tables of his future Works.

According to Du Bartas, the zodiac makes palpable the vast design of God, just as Spenser's calendar does. The zodiac is God's poetic calendar, in the same sense that His universe is a poem. He has filled it with signs ("Figures" and "Marks") to render knowable to man His eternal intention ("his future Works"). In the next verse paragraph Du Bartas reiterates the point, to emphasize the inclusiveness and timelessness of God's calendar in the skies:

> There's nothing precious in Sea, Earth, or Aire,
> But hath in Heav'n some like resemblance faire,
> .   .   .   .
> And sacred patternes, which to serve all Ages,
> Th'Almighty printed on Heav'ns ample stages.

Spenser, creating in the likeness of such a deity, emulates His subject-matter and His method in *The Shepheardes Calender*. By gazing thereon, as by gazing upon the zodiac, man can ascertain divine truth.

In *The Shepheardes Calender* the icon for time is a twelve-phase cosmos composed of the months. In the argument for *December*, E. K. represents time as a four-phase cosmos composed of the seasons. In these instances, the year, the annual unit of time, is used as the integer of eternity. However, other portions of time can also be used as the basic unit from which to extrapolate eternity by infinite repetition. By far the most frequent of the alternatives is the *diurnal* unit of time, the twenty-four hours from sunrise to sunrise. The entities of day and night are seen as two equal counterparts which together make up the daily term. And this diurnal period can be extrapolated into eternity just like the annual unit of time.

The idea that day and night in their endless repetition signify eternity is an ancient one, widely promulgated in the literature of alchemy and hieroglyphics. It is ubiquitous in the Renaissance, appearing in places so diverse as the first emblem in Horapollo's *De sacris Aegyptiorum notis,* the lament of Shakespeare's Cleopatra over Antony (*Antony and Cleopatra* V.ii.79–81), and the title page for the first edition of the King James version of the Bible. No one, however, expresses the thought more concisely than Milton:

> . . . light and darkness in perpetual round
> Lodge and dislodge by turns, which makes through Heav'n
> Grateful vicissitude, like Day and Night.
>
> *(PL* VI.6–8)

The greater light and the lesser light, set in the heavens to mark the passage of time, follow one another "in perpetual round."

We can bring the idea into precise focus, and relate it to our discussion of ideograms for time, by means of an illustration from a text which the Renaissance chose to rescue from the Middle

2. *From* Albertus Magnus, *Opus philosophiae naturalis* (Brescia, 1493), a1 [title page].
By permission of the Huntington Library, San Marino, California.

Ages, an edition of Albertus Magnus' *Opus philosophiae naturalis* printed at Brescia in 1493 (see fig. 2). This woodcut appears on the first page of the volume in lieu of a title page, and holds a similar position in several later editions of the work. There are no other illustrations in the text—this is a summary statement of its contents. In the center of the diagram we see microcosmic man, composed of four humours which correspond to the four elements. He is circumscribed by a circle divided into two halves indicating daylight and darkness, and marked with the sun and moon. There are also twenty-four dots to represent the hours of the diurnal unit of time. At the top, the godhead peers over his creation; and the ten digits, the scales, and the compasses aver that he creates according to number, weight, and measure. The rule and square at the botton aver that he is the archgeometer.

In Albertus's text there are chapters on time and eternity and on the human soul, but nothing specifically in explanation of this woodcut. A cogent gloss is provided, however, by a chapter in that old favorite, *The Kalender of Sheepehards:*

Hereafter foloweth the iiii. elementes, and the foure complexions of man and howe and in what time they raigne in man. Cap. xxix.

Ayre, Fyre, Earth, and Water. The xxiiii. houres of the day & night ruleth Sanguine, Cholerike, Melancolike, & Flumatike. Six houres after midnight bloode hath the maistry, & in the vi. houres afore noone coller raigneth, and vi. houres after noone raigneth melancoly, and vi. houres afore midnight raigneth flumatike.[13]

There is no doubt that the lore epitomized in figure 2 continued as the most self-evident of popular truths. It reappears, for example, though in a highly sophisticated metamorphosis, in Robert Fludd's compendium of human knowledge, *Utriusque cosmi . . . historia* (see fig. 3).

It should come as no surprise if our discussion at this point turns to Milton's first unqualified success as a poet, the companion poems *L'Allegro* and *Il Penseroso*. It has long been recognized that *L'Allegro* begins at dawn and ends at dusk, and chronicles the events of daytime; correspondingly, *Il Penseroso* records the passage of a night and ends at the break of the next day. This design

13. (London, c. 1550), 13^V.

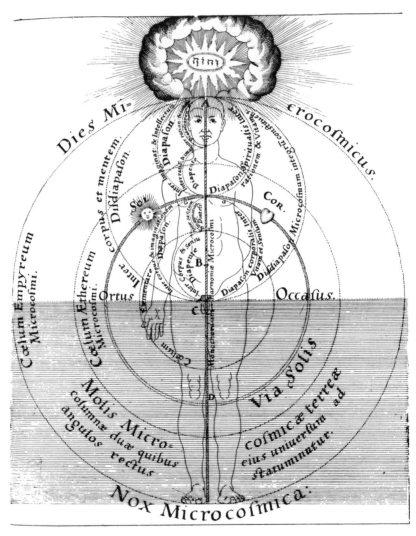

3. *From* Robert Fludd, *Utriusque cosmi majoris scilicet et minoris metaphysica, physica atque technica historia* (4 vols.; Oppenheim, 1617–19), III, 275. *By permission of the Huntington Library, San Marino, California.*

is obtrusively obvious. It is equally clear that the contrast between the joyful man and his pensive counterpart stems from a difference in temperament, from their respective "complexions," to use a technical term. "Temperament," however, is also a technical term and applies to the mixing (or tempering) of the humours in the body. Furthermore, from these two differing temperaments derive two contrasting attitudes toward life, two lifestyles—what we may call, to summon antique terms, the *vita contemplativa* and the *vita activa.* These are the clichés of Renaissance psychology.

What may not be so obvious, however, is the interrelationship, even interdependence, of these two poems. They belong to a distinct genre of literature, companion poems, a class that literary historians have not yet fully defined and documented. The proto- type of companion poems in Elizabethan literature is the beguiling colloquy known as "The Passionate Shepherd" and "The Nymph's Reply," attributed to Marlowe and Raleigh, respectively, though on dubious evidence. In those matched pieces we have two world views in point-to-point contrast. The Shepherd begins his seductive proposition with the well-known lines: "Come live with mee, and be my love,/ And we will all the pleasures prove"; and the Nymph closes her tart rebuttal with a mocking echo:

> But could youth last, and love still breede,
> Had joyes no date, nor age no neede,
> Then these delights my minde might move,
> To live with thee, and be thy love.

Milton recalls these lines at the ends of both his poems. The joyful man concludes, "These delights, if thou canst give,/ Mirth with thee, I mean to live"; and the thoughtful man, in almost the same words though addressed to the opposing goddess, concludes, "These pleasures *Melancholy* give,/ And I with thee will choose to live."[14] Each of Milton's poems comes to the same (though opposite) conclusion.

Other examples of companion poems are common in the Tudor period, if not legion. A most interesting instance is the song that rounds off *Love's Labour's Lost,* a duet between a cuckoo repre- senting spring and an owl representing winter. The cuckoo sings about a green world of young love and idealized beauty, "When daisies pied and violets blue . . . ," while the owl sings about cruel weather and human debility, "When icicles hang by the wall . . . . " Shakespeare, of course, was adapting for his purpose the literary *débat,* which in turn derived from the academic debate—the sort of thing that Milton undertook so laboriously in his first prolusion, "Utrum Dies an Nox praestantior sit?" In the

14. Cf. also *L'Allegro,* 37–40.

Middle Ages the genre had taken viable form in the many balanced
dialogues between body and soul that rationalized the difficulties
of living in this world while contemplating the next. Donne's
Anniversaries are a late mutation of this contention, and should be
read as companion poems. Perhaps more to our purpose are the
disputants in *The Owl and the Nightingale* from the early thir-
teenth century. They sit very near Shakespeare's song, and each
could find a happy perch in *L'Allegro* or *Il Penseroso*.

The cosmological context for companion poems no doubt harks
back to Greek thought. It should be traced to the dichotomy
between the world of being and the world of becoming in Platonic
cosmology, or to the antithesis between two contraries which
Aristotle in the *Physica* (I.vi) postulated as a necessary condition
for orderly change in nature. In either case there is a duality, but a
duality composed of two exact counterparts. To cite an ideogram
from another culture, we could point to the symbol of yin and
yang that the Chinese have used for centuries to indicate the
dynamic equilibrium between light and darkness. The point is that
each half defines the other. Each exists only by virtue of the
other, just as in chiaroscuro the highlights are defined by the
patches of shadow. In consequence, there is a close identification
of one with the other. One is a mirror-image of the other. One, by
inverse relationship, *is* the other. Each is both itself and the other.

Furthermore, the two counterparts fit together in mutual dependence to form the perfect whole. And this whole is greater
than merely the sum of the two constituent parts. Two simple
opposites can make a sum of two parts, and no more. But two
exact equals, by being identical—by each being both itself and the
other—produce internal bonds that apply homogeneously, and not
just at the seams. Between such counterparts there are continual
inner resonances, so that the whole is greater than the arithmetic
sum of its parts. To use a phrase of Gerard Manley Hopkins, "It
gathers to a greatness." And this greatness, to continue with
Hopkins, is "God's grandeur."

These thoughts are largely alien to us, who are conditioned by a
scientific culture to analyze into parts rather than cumulate to the
limit of infinity. But they were commonplace in the Renaissance,
the unexamined premises of the period. They underlie much of Du
Bartas's cosmology in *La sepmaine*. For example, in a passage that

Sylvester glosses, "Why God ordained the Night and Day alternately to succeed each other," Du Bartas explains the symbiosis
between two halves of a perfect contrast:

> . . . because all pleasures waxe unpleasant,
> If without pawse we still possesse them present:
> And none can right discerne the sweets of Peace,
> That have not felt Warres irksome bitternes
> And Swannes seeme whiter if swart Crowes be by
> (For contraries each other best descrie)
> Th'Alls-Architect, alternately decreed
> That Night the Day, the Day should Night succeed.[15]

Pierre de la Primaudaye in *The French Academie* speaks even more
broadly, though no less cogently, to the same point. In the other
Protestant encyclopedia to come from France, this one in prose,
La Primaudaye deals first with "the providence of God in the
harmonie of the seasons of the yeere," to quote the marginal gloss;
and then he turns to "the succession of day and night." With his
accustomed eloquence, as R. Dolman rendered it into English, La
Primaudaye then expatiates on this theme:

By how much the more we consider of these things, by so much the more
shall we finde occasion to woonder at the works and providence of God. For
whereas the propertie of one contrarie is to destroy another: he hath so well
tempered and reconciled them, that he causeth the one to be preserved by the
other: yea that one cannot subsist without the aide of his companion. Which
taketh place not onely in these things, which we have here alreadie mentioned, but likewise in all creatures, which are in the universall world. For it is
all composed of contrarie natures. And yet God their father maketh them to
fit so well togither, that he reduceth all discord into concord, and all enmitie
into amitie: as the example is notable in mans bodie being compounded of
elements and qualities cleane contrarie one to another; and yet conjoined by
such a unitie, that the composition and preservation is most firme and
assured, so long time as it pleaseth God to maintaine his worke.[16]

This passage elucidates Milton's ultimate concerns in *L'Allegro* and
Il Penseroso. It documents his essential subject-matter.

In fact, were it not an affront to our literary sensibility, I would

---

15. *Devine Weekes*, tr. Sylvester (1605), p. 19.
16. *The Third Volume of the French Academie*, tr. R. Dolman (London, 1601), pp. 160–61.

say that this quotation from La Primaudaye is an accurate prose paraphrase of Milton's thematic statement. We must see these two companion poems as balanced components of a larger whole. And that larger whole is an image of microcosmic man in a temporal setting of the diurnal unit of time. And this ideogram in turn must be synchronized with God's providence—with the idea in the mind of the divine creator that exists throughout, as well as before, creation.

In such a context, *L'Allegro* and *Il Penseroso* are more than youthful *jeux d'esprit*. They are more than poetic profusions, pretty images, and pleasant sounds. They are even more than admirable examples of the poetic craft. As Milton says of *The Faerie Queene*, "More is meant then meets the ear" (*Il Penseroso*, 120). These companion poems are a serious and profound description of the grandest of all designs. They are a young poet's earnest attempt to express his understanding of God's intention in the universe, especially as it relates to man. They are an *étude* for *Lycidas*.

My purpose, however, is not to provide a reading of *L'Allegro* and *Il Penseroso*, and so I will offer no *explication de texte;* nor is my aim to praise Milton for his aspiration or achievement. But rather I wish to apply to the poetry those traditions and conventions that instruct us about companion poems. *L'Allegro* and *Il Penseroso* taken together, as they must be, produce a single whole, a cosmos—but a cosmos with internal articulation, a variant of the twelve-phase cosmos of *The Shepheardes Calender*. Furthermore, they derive from the same poetics as *The Shepheardes Calender* and share many similarities with that first work by Spenser, similarities of technique as well as subject-matter. Most pertinent to my argument, much of the meaning is conveyed through the form. An *"Idea*, or fore conceit," organizes the parts into a unified whole, which is the poet's ultimate statement. In these poems Milton, like Spenser, is a maker, as Sidney defined this "most excellent" name for a poet.

Of course, Spenser was a maker throughout his career, not just in *The Shepheardes Calender*. His usual method was to begin with an idea, which he then projected in terms of time and space. In *The Teares of the Muses* his design consists, with crude obviousness, in the familiar motif depicted in the symphony of Muses.

Each of the nine sisters plays a different instrument and makes her unique contribution to the whole, but all participate in the universal harmony under the tutelage of Apollo. In the *Epithalamion* Spenser deploys the stereotyped diurnal unit of time, the procession of twenty-four stanzas from one sunrise to the next. By recounting the events of his wedding day and night, he projects an image of microcosmic man who by joining with his female counterpart rises to cosmic love—the temporal pattern that Milton uses in *L'Allegro* and *Il Penseroso*, though without the female component. In *Fowre Hymnes* Spenser structures his poem in accord with the Pythagorean tetrad, a sophisticated form with subtle internal bonds of the same sort as those between the two halves of a contrariety. There is, expressly, the antithesis between two earthly hymns and two heavenly hymns; but also the ascent in a scale of values from Cupid through Venus and Christ to God the Father, who sits in supremacy with a female companion, Sapience, by His side. Finally, in *The Faerie Queene* Spenser again begins with a fore-conceit, as he tells us in the letter to Raleigh. He begins with the concept of glory embodied in Gloriana, mirrored in her male counterpart Arthur, and exemplified twelvefold in each of the knights that were to predominate in the twelve books of that dark conceit. But certainly the twelve-part structure informs the poem with something of the same meaning that the calendar infuses into *The Shepheardes Calender,* especially when we remember that the Fairy Queen holds an annual feast, when all the knights gather in her honor. With few exceptions, then, the poems of Spenser exhibit carefully articulated structures with cosmic analogues. *Mother Hubberds Tale* and *Colin Clouts Come Home Againe* are notable exceptions, but they are first and foremost occasional works. The *Epithalamion* is also an occasional work, but Spenser gives it cosmic dimension by structuring it in accord with the diurnal unit of time, giving it a vast design.

Because Milton had been conditioned by the poetics of making, he would have been more sensitive than we to the structures in Spenser's poems. He would have looked for the overall design, and would have considered each episode in relation to it. He would not have rested with a discursive reading. To point up the difference between his likely response and ours, we may say that we have been conditioned by the aesthetics of the novel. We are most likely to read a literary work as a series of words to which we respond in temporal sequence, joining *a* to *b* to *c* until we reach *x* and *y* and *z*, at which point we lay the book aside. We seek a literary experience that has the spontaneity and verisimilitude of a finite portion of passing time. And we assume that the work has no existence apart from these phenomena. The first commandment of the modern critic is "Read the text," as though that collocation of words was concrete, absolute, real. Whether we deal with the words as objective entities or whether we deal with our subjective responses to them, when we read in this fashion we employ a critical method based upon the phenomenalistic assumptions of modern science. We ignore the large component of meaning which genre, metrical form, and recondite allusion infuse into the poem. We ignore tradition. We ignore authorial intention. Worst of all, we begin to read (i.e., infer meaning) before we perceive the comprehensive design of the work. And that, in the poetics of making, is to count the trees, perhaps, but not to distinguish hardwood from underbrush, and never to see the forest in the beauteous fullness of its entirety.

Readers have long sensed that *L'Allegro* and *Il Penseroso* together comprise a "poem" of this special sort, the microcosm of a maker. A poet must express his design in ways that are readily perceptible; secretiveness, or even coyness, is self-defeating. It is most unlikely that he would resort to hidden patterns embedded, for example, in arcane numerologies. God works in mysterious ways, but that license does not extend to the mortal maker. Not surprisingly, therefore, readers have long perceived the pattern of these paired pieces and have responded to it. What I have done is merely to provide an intellectual framework which makes explicit a set of beliefs that would have been activated spontaneously for a Renaissance reader. I have reconstructed a cosmological context that had been prevalent until Milton's day, but that was sloughed off during the next century, so that modern readers no longer think in these terms. I hope to have raised the level of our consciousness in reading *L'Allegro* and *Il Penseroso,* and thereby to have imputed high seriousness to them. But my reading is hardly revolutionary.

I do have some proposals to make about two of Milton's earlier poems, however, that are unhandseled. I should like to suggest that *The Nativity* and *The Passion* are a similar pair of poems, intended by the young poet as companions. Both *The Nativity* and *The Passion*, scholars agree, date from a few months in the winter of 1629–30, and they are linked together by the opening lines of the second piece. There Milton is careful to bring the one to bear on the other:

> Ere-while of Musick, and Ethereal mirth,
> Wherewith the state of Ayr and Earth did ring,
> And joyous news of heav'nly Infants birth,
> My muse with Angels did divide to sing.
>
> (*Passion*, 1–4)

Through his persona Milton goes on to philosophize glibly about the fleetingness of joy. And rather pointedly he tells us that *The Nativity* belongs to a different time of the year, to the winter solstice, the nadir of the sun in its annual journey through the zodiac:

> But headlong joy is ever on the wing,
> In Wintry solstice like the shortn'd light
> Soon swallow'd up in dark and long out-living night.
>
> (*Passion*, 5–7)

But now at the vernal equinox, at the time of Christ's passion, a contrary note must be sounded:

> For now to sorrow must I tune my song,
> And set my Harp to notes of saddest wo,
> Which on our dearest Lord did sease e're long.
>
> (*Passion*, 8–10)

The Passion is manifestly, insistently, in the same time continuum with *The Nativity*, which began with a similar placement in the annual cycle: "This is the Month, and this the happy morn. . . ."

My argument, quite simply, is that *The Nativity* and *The Passion* began as companion poems. Like *L'Allegro* and *Il Penseroso*, which set forth the contrariety between joy and melancholy in terms of the diurnal unit of time, these two pieces were intended to set forth the same contrariety, but in terms of the equally valid seasonal cycle. And again, *The Shepheardes Calender* is the touchstone. *The Nativity* and *The Passion* reduce the ideogram for time to its simplest form, to the seasonal extremes of winter and spring, like the song at the end of *Love's Labour's Lost*. And the human figure in this temporal setting, the microcosmic man who stands for each of us, is not Colin Clout and not the abstracted persona of *L'Allegro* and *Il Penseroso,* but rather Christ. According to orthodox theology, He is the universal everyman who not only died for our sins, but also provides an exemplum for each of us to emulate. We can best conceive the complexity of this model, its subtleties and its ambiguities, when it is presented as a two-phase cosmos of joy and sorrow, spring and winter, light and darkness.

It is a commonplace of biblical exegesis that the sorrow of the passion is inherent in the joy of Christmas, and likewise that the despair of Calvary is a necessary prelude to the exultation of Easter morning, which in turn as rebirth is analogous to the Nativity. Christmas and Easter together produce a closely woven pattern of comparisons and contrasts. Firmly within this tradition, the opening stanza of *The Nativity* harshly asserts the meaning of the Crucifixion: Christ is "our great Redemption" (4) and He pays "our deadly forfeit" (6). Comparably, the opening stanza of *The Passion* wanly recalls the "joyous news of heav'nly Infants birth." These two pieces were intended to mirror this pattern of parallels and oppositions, a design for the total meaning of Christ with a system of inner resonances to account for alternating joy and sorrow in human affairs. For that reason, the joyfulness of Christmas comes paradoxically at the winter solstice—at that time of year when daylight is shortest. The greatest joy is attended by the least light. But this paradox is appropriate in a contrariety, since each half is both itself and the other. Or to put it differently, as the joy decreases in the cycle, reaching its low point at the passion, the light (and the hope it symbolizes) increases, culminating in the blaze of divine majesty that bursts from the opened tomb.[17]

This paradox is most successfully presented in a poetic contrariety. For the same reason, the owl in Shakespeare's lyric "nightly

17. The opening of St. John's Gospel, quoted earlier in part, is again pertinent here: "In the beginning was the Word, and the Word was with God, and the Word was God. The same was in the beginning with God. All things were made by him, and without him was not any thing made that was made. In him was life, and the life was the light of man. And the light shineth in darknesse, and the darknesse comprehended it not." In the King James version this passage bears a marginal gloss: "The Divinitie, Humanitie, and Office of Jesus Christ."

sings . . . a merrie note." In contradiction to the simple view, there
is joy in darkness, and incipient melancholy in the morning light.
The wholeness of the pattern, and the interrelationship (even
interchangeableness) of its parts—that is what the poet tries to
project.

So *The Nativity* and *The Passion* should be seen as companion
poems, a preliminary exercise in the poetic art of making. They
are a dry (and incomplete) run for *L'Allegro* and *Il Penseroso*,
which are a secular interpretation of the same cyclic pattern of
time and each man's changing experience in time. The earlier
pieces use Christ as the "most perfect *Heroe*" of the work (*Passion*, 13); the later pair use as hero a speaking-voice abstracted
from the poet himself. Reflecting Milton's greater maturity, the
later poems are at once more personal and more confident.

Milton did not finish *The Passion*, and perhaps it is idle to
speculate why. In the 1645 edition of his *Poems*, he inserted a
brief note that explains very little: "This Subject the Author
finding to be above the yeers he had, when he wrote it, and
nothing satisfi'd with what was begun, left it unfinisht." For
reasons unspecified, Milton was discontented with his effort. Perhaps he felt inadequate to his grand design, the sort of inadequacy
he professes at the beginning of *Lycidas*. When we read the poem,
we sense an increasing difficulty (and growing embarrassment) as
the joy of Christmas transmutes to the sorrow of the Crucifixion,
and as the divine Christ stoops his regal head beneath a mortal
yoke until he suffers the stroke of death (stanza iii). The embarrassment grows to an obstacle as the young poet turns from the
plight of Christ to his own perusal of that plight, and the speaking
voice comes more and more to be the subject of the poem until
the persona replaces Christ as its focus. By the time of writing
Lycidas, Milton could modulate his own sense of uncertainty and
suffering, and could control the transubstantiation of these emotions into cosmic significance. But not in 1630. At any rate he
broke off, with his design incomplete.

We have, then, only a fragment of *The Passion*. But clearly
Milton planned this fragment as an induction to a fiction that
would be the hymn proper, just as *The Nativity* has two parts, an
induction and a hymn. The fragment of *The Passion* is composed
in the same stanza form as the induction to *The Nativity*: a

seven-line stanza of iambic pentameters with a concluding alexandrine, rhyming *a b a b b c c*, which Milton uses nowhere else. Furthermore, the rhetorical structure of the fragmentary *Passion* is identical with that of the induction in *The Nativity*. The first two stanzas of *The Passion* indicate the time of year and designate the season as sorrowful in terms of Christ's life, like the first stanza of *The Nativity* (though of course in this opposite piece the season is happy). The next two stanzas of *The Passion* relate how God the Son took on the woes of mortality, like the second stanza of *The Nativity*. The fifth stanza of *The Passion* is a plea to the goddess Night for inspiration, like the third stanza of *The Nativity* addressed to the "Heav'nly Muse." And the last three stanzas of *The Passion* are an invitation to view some celestial vision beginning with the exhortation "See," like the last stanza of *The Nativity*, which in exact parallel begins with the same exhortation, "See." The celestial vision would be the subject of the hymn in *The Passion*, as it is in *The Nativity*. But Milton presumably did not produce this fiction.

Some critics might note that the number of stanzas in the induction to *The Passion* is eight, exactly double the number of stanzas in the induction to *The Nativity*—just as the number of stanzas in the "December" eclogue of *The Shepheardes Calender* is exactly double the number of stanzas in the "January" eclogue. In consequence, the second poem is proportional to the first in the ratio of 2:1. This, of course, is the proportion of the octave in music, and therefore the continuum between the two poems represents a diapason, an all-inclusive unit, an integer of infinity. I shall argue neither for the significance of this fact, nor against it. I merely point to the circumstance. Perhaps it is additional evidence that *The Passion* and *The Nativity* are related.

In any case, Milton did not provide a hymn for *The Passion*. We have the prelude, but not the fiction itself. We do have the other half of the vast design, however—*The Nativity*, containing both prelude and fiction, both an induction and a hymn. And when we read *The Nativity*, we should place it in the context of Milton's total design, which includes *The Passion* as a companion piece. Then, I think, we shall see that a work already recognized as good is even better, because it resonates within a larger dimension. The stasis of the scene in the manger that concludes *The Nativity* is indeed a fit ending for that phase of the cycle, but the same bright-harnessed angels who sit in service there will accompany the risen Christ to heaven after His passion. The inclusive vision of the Nativity conjoined to the Passion will "work us a perpetual peace" (*Nativity*, 7).

The high point of Milton's career as a maker is *Paradise Lost,* comparable to *The Faerie Queene* in Spenser's career. Milton begins his magnum opus with a statement of the fore-conceit, "Mans First Disobedience," just as Spenser proclaims in his letter to Raleigh, "In that Faery Queene I meane glory in my generall intention." And just as Spenser announces a "generall end"—"to fashion a gentleman or noble person in vertuous and gentle discipline"—so Milton is explicit about the teleology of his poem—to "assert Eternal Providence,/ And justifie the wayes of God to men." So concludes the first verse paragraph of *Paradise Lost.* The poem that Milton saw as his great work is like the masterpiece of Spenser in this fundamental way: both poets begin with a fore-conceit that they then extend into a narrative, thereby creating a universe of time and space filled with beings in the human mold.

The poetics of making accounts for Milton's heavy dependence upon the techniques of drama in *Paradise Lost:* the frequent dialogue, the strong characterizations, the distinct sense of setting. Of course, Milton uses dramatic scenes for a variety of reasons and to a variety of ends. But basically, he chose to present his fiction in a quasi-dramatic mode because drama is the most objective of genres, allowing the poet to externalize and examine—much as God externalized and examined His creation. Then the poet, like God, can say, "It is good." Moreover, drama is the most objective of genres in the sense that it allows the reader to experience a datum, to hear and see an event. Drama is the most experiential of genres, the most nearly verisimilar, the best mode for giving the impression of passing time in the realm of physical nature. But all this action transpires, we must remember, within the stasis of eternal providence.

Milton is consciously working also within another literary tradition, the epic. There is repeated evidence that he thought of himself as the blind epic poet dressed in his garland and singing robes, immortalizing the glories of his race. But it would be wrong to dissociate the epic tradition from the poetics of making.

Rather, the epic is the greatest example of the poem, as critic after critic in the Renaissance theorized, and as poet after poet demonstrated in practice. Sidney is typical in his praise of "the *Heroicall,* which is not onelie a kinde, but the best and most accomplished kindes of *Poetrie*" (*Defence*, F2). Epic was the peak that poets struggled toward; the earlier poems in their careers were, in large part, preliminary exercises in the art of making, preparatory to essaying the heights of the heroical poem. The epic at the end was the summit of achievement, a vantage point just beneath heaven from which the poet surveyed our landscape. It was a comprehensive world-view, the universal poem that included all human knowledge.

So the epic poet is a maker, embodying his world-view in a fiction. The epic theme—the hero who triumphs, or at least survives, despite catastrophic vicissitudes—is best projected in a narrative poem with a fore-conceit. Virgil, the undisputed master of the epic, began the *Aeneid* by announcing such a fore-conceit in the first line: *Arma virumque cano.* Before him Homer had begun his poems in similar fashion. The *Iliad* opens with a blunt demand that the muse sing of Achilles' wrath: Μῆνιν ἄειδε Θεά, Πηληϊά-δνω Ἀχιλῆος. The first line of the *Odyssey* likewise contains a plea for inspiration so that the clever hero may be publicized: Ἄνδρα μοι ᾽έννεπε, μοῦσα, πολύτροπον. Milton obediently falls into line behind this procession of ancient practitioners in the epic genre: "Of Mans First Disobedience . . . Sing, Heav'nly Muse." These poets are makers. After announcing a fore-conceit, they proceed by extending their vast design in terms of characters and actions and settings. They create a universe of time and space with the hero at its center.

In *Paradise Lost,* we can see that Milton's fore-conceiit, "Mans First Disobedience," is the ultimate being of the poem, the basis of its ontology. And its teleology is openly declared: to "assert Eternal Providence,/ And justifie the wayes of God to men." An epistemology is also implied by Milton's adherence to the poetics of making. We can know the essence of the poem, its idea, through the discursive experience of its fictive narrative. This quasi sense-experience in durational sequence—the procession of episodes before our mind's eye—can be abstracted to its conceptual underpinnings. To use Sidney's terms, the narration must be used as a groundplat for its profitable invention. The result is a fiction that occurs in measured time, but also a correlative idea or form that is timeless.

This is exactly the experience of reading *Paradise Lost* that Andrew Marvell records in his commendatory poem printed before the second edition of the work. Marvell reports that his first response upon perusing the argument was doubt:

> When I beheld the Poet blind, yet bold,
> In slender Book his vast Design unfold,
> *Messiah* Crown'd, Gods Reconcil'd Decree,
> Rebelling Angels, the Forbidden Tree,
> Heav'n, Hell, Earth, Chaos, All; the Argument
> Held me a while misdoubting his Intent.
>
> (1–6)

Marvell was less than satisfied by the sequence of narrated episodes. Yet as he read, he grew more approving. Marvell liked Milton's "Project" (12), but still doubted its success. He feared that the poem might obscure what should be evident, or that by fictionalizing the events of creation, Milton would overdramatize them and present the hexameron as though it were a silly play (21–22). But Milton rises to an exhaustive greatness: "Thou hast not miss'd one thought that could be fit" (27). His work is "infinite" (17), "so that no room is here for Writers left,/ But to detect their Ignorance or Theft" (29–30). The poem produces the static permanence of the best art: "Things divine thou treatst of in such state/ As them preserves, and thee, inviolate" (33–34). Marvell responds to the contrariety of the paradoxes: "At once delight and horrour on us seise" (35); and he wonders at the inclusiveness as well as the majesty of the poem: "Whence furnish such a vast expence of mind?" (42). Most tellingly, Marvell closes with a couplet that recognizes *Paradise Lost* as a fictional universe created according to the poetics of making:

> Thy Verse created like thy Theme sublime,
> In Number, Weight, and Measure, needs not Rhime.
>
> (53–54)

In his final salute to Milton, Marvell approves his omission of rhyme while applauding his mastery of metrics. The poet, as Sidney had argued, is not identified by the jingle of rhyming words. Rather, "the skill of ech Artificer standeth in that *Idea,* or fore conceit of the worke." The skill of the maker resides in the formulation of a "Theme sublime," to which he gives palpable form "in Number, Weight, and Measure," thereby imitating the creative act of King Solomon's Jehovah.

As Marvell read *Paradise Lost,* the fiction of the poem is durational; its fore-conceit, sublimely permanent. There are, in fact, two distinct coordinates of time which persist throughout *Paradise Lost,* perhaps best described as a pair of opposites: the temporal and the atemporal—or, if that terminology seems solipsistic, the earthly and the eternal. One inheres in the finite realm of the four elements, the other in the mind of God.

A clear illustration of this sort of ambiguity is provided by Hans Holbein the Younger in his depiction of Eve's creation (see fig. 4).[18] The woodcut focuses on God, who is extracting Eve from Adam's side. In the sky above we see the sun and the moon, originally placed in the heavens to mark the passing of time—and so they do here in this physical setting. As night follows day and succeeding day follows night, the perfection of paradise becomes vulnerable to decay. This was the understanding of Robert Frost: "So Eden sank to grief,/ So dawn goes down to day,/ Nothing gold can stay." The creation of Eve is a forecast of Adam's fall, the subject of the next woodcut in Holbein's series of illustrations for the Old Testament. Figure 4 is also the first item in Holbein's famous *Icones mortis* (Basle, 1554), a fit introduction for a series of woodcuts portraying the Dance of Death in its manifold manifestations.

But shining conjointly, as their stylization and symmetrical arrangement in figure 4 suggest, the sun and moon also symbolize eternity (see p. 73, above). They are the compound of day-and-night, the whole that is composed of two counterparts but is larger than their sum. As we have said, they represent the daily term, the diurnal integer that extrapolates to eternity. So by their conjunction, they place this scene within the context of perpetuity. The creation of Eve then becomes an atemporal principle, an integral

18. The Huntington copy from which figure 4 is taken at one time belonged to Gabriel Harvey. The title page bears both his initials and his signature, as well as the date "1580" in his handwriting. It also bears his marginalium: "Sallust du Bartas, the only brave poet in this sacred vein."

4. *From* Hans Holbein the Younger, *The Images of the Old Testament* (Lyons, 1549),
A4. *By permission of the Huntington Library, San Marino, California.*

part of God's everlasting intention, as well as a temporal act, a
climax in the hexameral process. The event can be considered
within the domain of passing time, but also within the domain of
God's λόγος. Time is both differentiated into measureable portions
and undifferentiated.

In similar fashion, any incident in *Paradise Lost* can be related
to either of these two coordinates for time. Therefore each incident in the narrative will have two meanings, dependent upon
whether the incident is interpreted as a phenomenon occurring in
mutable nature or a phenomenon residing in the mind of God.
These two meanings are distinct, though interrelated. And their
relationship is that of contrariety.

An example will clarify the point—actually, the example which
is prototypical of all the other actions in the poem. The fall of
Adam—man's first disobedience, which is the fore-conceit of *Paradise Lost*—was (according to the Bible) a historical incident that
took place in measured time. It required a period of time for its
enactment. It was an eventuality capping a period that began on
the sixth day of Genesis when God created Adam. But also the fall
of Adam may be generalized to represent the fall of man, or even
further abstracted to some concept of our innate proclivity to·sin.

In other words, it may be a one-shot occurrence, or it may be a pattern that is in constant operation. As Spenser puts it after Red Crosse succumbs to Duessa and suffers the mortification of Orgoglio's dungeon, "Ay me, how many perils doe enfold/ The righteous man, to make him daily fall?" (*FQ* I.viii.1). Red Crosse as a historical personage has fallen once, but as "the righteous man" he daily falls. Just so, the tense of Adam's fall is both pluperfect and progressive.

Furthermore, when considered as an incident in the transient world of mutable events, Adam's fall is evil. It is a fall from pristine goodness, a decline. It is an action leading to man's nadir. But paradoxically, this extreme implies its contrary. And when considered within the other coordinate of time in the poem, when seen in the context of eternity, this isolated episode becomes part of a larger pattern. The nadir begins an ascent to the zenith. The fall, which is evil *sui generis,* becomes an integral contributor to a whole which is good. Thereby the fall becomes fortunate, the opposite of its meaning when considered as an isolated incident in human history. The fall both is and is not evil, and it is and is not good. Evil and good are mutually dependent, each inherent in the other, just like darkness and light, or melancholy and joy. This is the vast design of *Paradise Lost.* Its foreconceit has this form; the idea of man's disobedience imposes the pattern of the fortunate fall on his experience.

This analysis in terms of the paradox of time can be applied also to the title of the poem. The title includes two successive states: paradise, the state of innocence, followed by the fallen state of sin. There is, moreover, a temporal progression from the first to the second, expressed by the arrangement of noun and adjective in that inverted sequence. Indeed, this unusual arrangement of noun and adjective invites an extrapolation to complete the expected order: "Paradise Lost Paradise." Then "Paradise" can be played against "Lost Paradise." The result is an action, a flux. However, this flux nonetheless ends in a finality. The temporal progression concludes in a final state that subsumes both, a complex reconciliation of opposites that is ultimately stable. The first five lines of the poem condense this action to the familiar pattern of the fortunate fall: man's disobedience brings death, but divine love restores us to the *sedes beata.* Through eternal providence this pattern, like the fortunate fall and like the cycle of the seasons, has become the permanent condition of man. "Paradise" and "Lost Paradise" are the two halves of the paradoxical contrariety that we saw operate in the companion poems, "The Nativity" and "The Passion." They are Christmas and Easter in cyclic alternation. The distance between them and the period of time from one state to the other provide dimension for the universe of *Paradise Lost.*

Both these coordinates—the temporal and the atemporal—coexist in *Paradise Lost,* then, and bear upon its every incident. When this fact is realized, many questions that have exercised scholars and critics resolve themselves, because each question admits of two diametrically opposed answers, depending on which coordinate is called upon as the referent. When any question is answered, be it noted, the answer implies its opposite.

For example, is Christ coeternal with God, or younger than God? If Christ is the son of God, then He must be junior to God. Indeed, He was born at a moment in time. But certainly as a member of the Holy Trinity the son is coeternal with the father. Only by application of both coordinates of time can we resolve this conundrum and expose the shifting sands of semantics on which it is based. Christ is the son of God when we regard His life as a series of mortal events in our time-space continuum. When considered in terms of the created world of four elements, Christ is subsequent to God as son to father. But of course Christ is also the immortal coregnant seated beside God in heaven. When considered in terms of eternity, which is indivisible and homogeneous, Christ is coexistent with God. Even when considered as son to father, Christ is a duplicate of God, embodying the same attributes and virtues. When Christ goes forth to implement God's edict for creation, He is indeed His father's son:

> Girt with Omnipotence, with Radiance crown'd
> Of Majestie Divine, Sapience and Love
> Immense, and all his Father in him shon.

> (*PL* VII.194–96)

So, like the two halves of a contrariety, Christ and God are separate, yet exact counterparts. And Christ is both Himself and the other, so that we can see Him in isolation as an incomplete and therefore restless part, or integrated as a nonextractable form for the whole. In temporal terms, Christ both is and is not junior to God. He is both mortal and immortal, timely and timeless.

The same pattern of paradox saves the appearances when we ask if God predetermined the fall of Adam or if He merely had knowledge of the event in advance. When the fall is considered to culminate a series of actions in temporal sequence, it is predestined. God is active. However, when the fall is considered to be part of an eternal plan, it is a matter of foreknowledge, because the plan continuously operates and all its component parts are cotemporaneous. God is patient. Foreknowledge and predestination, though at first glance mutually exclusive, are in fact mutually dependent, and even identical when placed in the relationship imposed by Milton's fore-conceit. The contrariety rests in the two coordinates of time within which we can make our judgments. But the poem bridges the discontinuity between the ever-changing world of phenomena and the static world of essence, largely through synchronizing the double coordinates of time.

One final point which has pervasive significance for reading *Paradise Lost* as the fiction of a poetic maker: just as God made the universe and is immanent in every portion of His creation, so the poet is immanent throughout the universe of his poem. Spenser in *The Shepheardes Calender*, for example, ranges the entire work. He has an express persona, Colin Clout; but the other shepherds, even the most sardonic and most dissolute, also represent moods of his psyche, facets of his being. The twelve eclogues taken in their entirety are a comprehensive projection of Spenser himself in 1579. Thereby the poet becomes an everyman to populate his microcosm, or the hero of his own epic poem.

In such a way, I think we must read *Paradise Lost*, as a personal as well as universal statement. Milton is immanent in every component of the poem, and conversely the poem in its entirety is a comprehensive projection of the poet. Milton is Adam, of course, the prototype of man who is dichotomized between evil and good—whose native evil is made good by divine grace. Milton wishfully identifies with Christ, the agent of divine grace, who creates the world with golden compasses just as Milton circumscribes a personal Eden for the paradox of a fortunate fall. And Milton further identifies with both God and Satan—the essential good who always is and His opposite who transposes the referents so that evil becomes his good (IV.110). Milton is also Eve and Raphael and even Michael—but there is no need to labor the point. Just as God provides the continuum wherein the multifarious items of the universe subsist, so also the poet encompasses the multeity of his poem. And just as God rested on the seventh day, so the poet achieves a sabbath, a happy stasis, having brought psychic order out of chaos. Each disparate element is appropriately placed; each contrary is balanced by its opposite. "Day and Night,/ Seed time and Harvest, Heat and hoary Frost/ Shall hold thir course" (XI.898–900). Eternal providence, after long and arduous effort, has been affirmed.

"A Poet Amongst Poets":
Milton and
the Tradition of Prophecy

JOSEPH ANTHONY WITTREICH, JR.

In dealing with individual poets the critic . . . is dealing with tradition, for they live in it. And it is in them that tradition lives.

—F. R. Leavis

You struck out into new paths, I walked in old ones.

—Tasso to Milton

"*His was the cultural inheritance of Sidney and Spenser*"[1] —the words are spoken of Milton, but they imply what for a long time

Research for this essay was completed during my tenure as a fellow of the Folger Shakespeare Library, and the essay was written while I held grants from the National Endowment for the Humanities and from the University of Wisconsin's Institute for Research in the Humanities. The title of my essay, I should say, observes the spirit, if not the letter, of De Quincey's remark that Milton "is not an author amongst authors, not a poet amongst poets, but a power amongst powers." De Quincey explains his assertion by saying that "there is this great distinction amongst books: some . . . are . . . no more than a book—not indispensable. . . . But with regard to Milton . . . the case is far otherwise" (*On Milton*, in *The Romantics on Milton: Formal Essays and Critical Asides*, ed. Joseph Anthony Wittreich, Jr. [Cleveland: Press of Case Western Reserve Univ., 1970], p. 478). De Quincey's intention, then, is not to deny that Milton is "a poet amongst poets" but to find a rhetoric that will distinguish Milton from other poets by way of asserting Milton's special status among the English poets. In that same spirit, I have written the following essay whose epigraphs derive from Leavis's *Revaluation: Tradition and Development in English Poetry* (London: Chatto and Windus, 1949), p. 3, and the anonymous *Il Tasso, a Dialogue* (London: R. Baldwin, 1762), pp. 4–5.

1. A. S. P. Woodhouse, *The Heavenly Muse: A Preface to Milton*, ed. Hugh MacCallum (Toronto: Univ. of Toronto Press, 1972), p. 16 (my italics). Though Woodhouse

has been evident, that the tradition of poetry encompassing Donne, Dryden, and Pope (the so-called "line of wit") is manifestly different from the visionary tradition including Sidney, Spenser, and Milton. Before New Criticism, the discrimination was made by Thomas De Quincey when he differentiated between the literature of knowledge and the literature of power; and before De Quincey, it was drawn, even more emphatically, by William Blake, who lamented that "the Works . . . of Pope & Dryden are looked upon as the Same Art with those of Milton." "Their art," Blake could be expected to say, "is to lose form, his art is to find form, and to keep it. His arts are opposite to theirs in all things."[2] With a different set of biases, De Quincey and Blake simply anticipate the truth that New Criticism has focused for the modern age: both aesthetic considerations and ideological ones separate Donne's metaphysics from Milton's apocalyptics—an obvious enough perception but one which turns a fact of literary history into one of its ironies. The very terms later used to disparage the metaphysicals, "metaphysical ideas and scholastic quiddities," had already been deployed against the visionary line of poets. Deploring

positions Milton within this English tradition, he prefers to study him within the context of "the European classical tradition" (p. 32) and thus underplays the poet's "theoretical conviction that the Bible will yield forms and models at least comparable with the classics" (p. 180). My own essay, then, explores a context for Milton's poetry that Woodhouse himself ignores and thus, more than to Woodhouse, owes its debt for inspiration to the work of Kathleen Williams, and Angus Fletcher especially. Like my essay, Harold Bloom's new book, *A Map of Misreading* (New York: Oxford Univ. Press, 1975), is concerned with "literary origins"; however, my understanding of Milton's literary origins—of the attitude Milton assumes toward his precursors, especially Spenser—is different from Bloom's.

2. See both *Public Address* and *A Descriptive Catalogue* in *The Poetry and Prose of William Blake*, ed. David V. Erdman, rev. ed. (Garden City, N.Y.: Doubleday, 1970), pp. 564, 529. And Blake remarks further: "I do not condemn Pope or Dryden because they did not understand Imagination but because they did not understand Verse" (p. 564). By quoting Blake, I do not intend to imply that Milton's influence on neoclassical poets is negligible. However, I do mean to endorse Leslie Brisman's conclusion that Milton's influence on Dryden and Pope is "of a different kind" than his influence on the Romantics or, for that matter, than the influence of Chaucer, Sidney, and Spenser on him (see *Milton's Poetry of Choice and Its Romantic Heirs* [Ithaca, N.Y.: Cornell Univ. Press, 1973], pp. 7–8). Even further, I would argue that standing behind "the line of wit" and "the line of vision" are two different aesthetic systems and that implicit in each is a different poetics of influence.

Elsewhere in this essay I quote from Blake's poetry, always from the Erdman edition cited above, and in these instances I have given a reference parenthetically within the text of my essay (supplying plate and where appropriate line number); for Blake's prose, I give a short footnote citation and provide pagination.

this tradition (in terms similar to those used in our own century to ridicule Milton's poetry), John Harvey speaks of the *"hellish* Rhetorique" that carries a load of "Metaphysicall *Idees"* and "philosophicall quiddities."[3] Once noted, however, this irony which would blur distinctions can be pushed aside as Milton's place in the history of English poetry, in relation to both his precursors and his successors, is reassessed. Such a reassessment, as De Quincey has acknowledged, is of special importance when we have grown accustomed to seeing a great poet through the clouds of years that have gathered around him, when it becomes difficult to separate the poet from the orthodox view of him established by those who have quoted, copied, and echoed him.

John Milton (to which *he* added the word *Englishman*) possesses obvious ties with the European classical tradition, but his most fundamental connections are with the tradition of English poetry in whose history he represents a decisive turning point, achieving a unity of aesthetics and ideology—both different from those informing the poetry of Donne and his school, both deriving from the Bible, which for Milton (as for Blake) was the great code of art, and both impinging upon (though not always in equal measure) the great poetry of England: Chaucer's and Langland's; Sidney's, Spenser's, and Shakespeare's; and after Milton, the poetry of the Romantics and some moderns. The line of wit is one tradition of English poetry that exists alongside, sometimes even flowing into, another tradition, the line of vision, whose great exemplar is Milton and whose holding spool is the Bible—its prophecies and especially the Book of Revelation.

It may be that the apocalyptic tradition, of which Virgil is an imitator, "contains nothing like the form of the Christian Apocalypse";[4] and it may be, too, that secular prophecy, both of the Middle Ages and of the Renaissance, never really developed a form of its own, investing itself instead with a variety of received forms. But to extrapolate from these phenomena the conclusion that "no

3. *A Discoursive Probleme Concerning Prophesies* (London: John Jackson, 1588), pp. 88, 92. Harvey describes prophecy as one of England's "pretended traditions" and singles out "Merlin" and "Pierce Plowman," "Coridons" and "Colin clowtes," as "supposed prophet[s]" (pp. 2, 80).

4. Austin Farrer, *A Rebirth of Images: The Making of St. John's Apocalypse* (1949; rpt., Boston: Beacon Press, 1963), p. 305.

particular literary form ever came to be recognized as the only proper vaticinal expression," that "the only quality prophecies had in common was obscurity,"[5] is to ignore how St. John's Apocalypse had come to be regarded. Moreover, to postulate that John undertook to make "a new form of literature" and then to argue that "he had no success"[6] is to ignore how the Apocalypse affected the development of poetics and, subsequently, the whole course that English poetry would take during the Renaissance and later.

The Bible—as Blake observes in *Jerusalem*, "builded with immortal labour,/ . . . canopied with emblems & written verse./ Spiritual Verse, order'd & measur'd"—culminates in "Revelations everlasting" (48:5–11). "Much more excellent then all the other prophecies"; "the conclusion & sum of the holy scriptures in and about those things that concerne prophecy"; "a Prophecy full of Majestie," wherein "all things are . . . delivered more distinctly and explicitly, then ever before"; a work of "singular workmanship" to which nothing in the Old Testament, not even the psalms of David, is comparable; the work not just of another prophet but of "the Prince of Prophets"[7]—encomiums like these derived from the belief that the Book of Revelation yielded the aesthetic and ideological bases for visionary art. Thus, those who would write prophecy, and those who would read it, can do no better than be "subtile exercised Interpreter[s] of the *Revelation* of St. *John*"; and that exercise comes from a style, both "cutting and searching," wherein "Every word is . . . marshalled," every sentence given "its apt cadance," and every syllable "so stuft . . . with substance" that matter and manner, sound and sense, always agree.[8]

5. Rupert Taylor, *The Political Prophecy in England* (New York: Columbia Univ. Press, 1911), p. 109.

6. Farrer, *A Rebirth of Images*, p. 313.

7. I quote from John Bale's *The Image of Both Churches* (1548; rpt. London: Printed by Thomas East [1570?]), sig. Aiii^V; James Brocard's *The Reveled Revelation of Saint John after Divers Learned Authors* (London: Thomas Barth, 1582), sig. B2^V; Thomas Brightman's *The Revelation of S. John* (Leyden: Printed by John Class, 1616), p. 7; Joseph Mede's *The Key of the Revelation*, tr. Richard More, 2d ed. (London: Printed for Phil. Stephens, 1650), p. 92; and Arthur Dent's *The Ruine of Rome, or an Exposition upon the Whole Revelation* (London: Printed for Simon Waterson, 1633), p. 24.

8. See Anon., *Catastrophe Mundi: or, Merlin Reviv'd* (London: n. p., 1683), p. 99; Henry More, *An Exposition of the Seven Epistles to the Seven Churches* (London:

Poets like Milton about whom it can be said (as Coleridge did
say) that to alter a word, or even the position of a word, is to
destroy the artifact, or like Blake who says of his own poetry that
"every word and every letter is studied and put in its fit place: the
terrific numbers are reserved for the terrific parts—the mild &
gentle, for the mild & gentle parts, and the prosaic, for inferior
parts: all are necessary to each other" (*Jerusalem,* plate 3)—such
poets found in the Book of Revelation a model for their art. And
for those poets who discovered in the Apocalypse what the Cambridge Platonist, Henry More, had seen, it was an appropriate
model indeed. "There was never any Book penned with that
artifice as this of the *Apocalypse,*" says More; it is "as if every
word were weighed in a balance before it was set down."[9] Moreover, those poets who shared with More this view of the Book of
Revelation recognized that it extended to them not only a model
of intrapoetic relationships but a whole system of aesthetics; and,
besides, the Apocalypse constituted for these poets a newly recognized literary form, possessing, like any other genre, its own
thematic concerns and rhetorical strategies, along with a distinctive structure and ideological fix. In Milton's art, from *Lycidas* to
the epics and *Samson Agonistes,* prophetic structures articulate
prophetic themes and underpin the ideology of prophecy; furthermore, both themes and ideology are advanced through rhetorical
strategies characteristic of prophetic art. By virtue of his uniting
all aspects of the genre in his own writings, Milton restored the art
of prophecy to its original perfection and thus should be regarded
as the father of a poetic tradition resurrected by the English
Romantics and used by later poets, British and American, both in
the nineteenth century and now.

The strategies of John's Apocalypse are an indispensable guide
to understanding its genre: they unlock the meaning of the fusion
of epic and prophecy that, initiated by Spenser, is completed by
Milton. That Spenser and Milton should both write themselves
into prophetic tradition may be explained in terms of the way in
which their culture viewed both itself and the arts. England was,

---

Printed by James Flesher, 1669), unpaginated Preface; and John Trapp, *Gods Love-
Tokens, and the Afflicted Mans Lessons* (London: Richard Badger, 1637), sig. a^v.

9. *An Explanation of the Grand Mystery of Godliness* (London: Printed for W.
Morden, 1660), p. 179.

for both poets, the new center of the Christian world, possessing the same disjunctive relationship with Rome as Christ possesses with Antichrist. Here in England, as one visionary put it, Christ would "begin to reigne" again—"England shall have first the revelation of truth";[10] and that revelation, both Spenser and Milton believed, was to be invested in England's poets who would transmit it through poems, epical in their dimensions, all imbued with a prophetic center.

Differences exist between epic and prophecy, yet certain features are also shared by them. Like epic, prophecy is a composite form, subsuming a variety of literary forms and, with them, the various structures and styles, the different value systems and rhetorical strategies, to which those forms are allied. In union, as they are in Milton's poetry, epic and prophecy constitute the ultimate transcendental form; they represent total form by containing within themselves all other forms and by achieving perfect harmony through a combination of styles. The achieved form of Milton's epic-prophecies thus finds its analogue in the perfect form of God's creation—a creation, as Milton describes it in *Paradise Lost*, that is teeming with "perfet formes" and mapped out in "various stile" (VII.445; V.146).

Like the epic poet, the prophet assumes an analogy between himself and the Creator and thus commits himself, as Milton does in *Animadversions*, to making "a creation like to Gods" (*CM* III, i, 164). Prophecy, then, is wrought out of various combinations, all of them evident in John's Book of Revelation. The accepted model for prophecy, it encompassed the extremes of style, the one plain and simple (in the opening chapters), the other difficult and enigmatic (in the later ones); and, according to one commentator, John's Revelation was "a posy of all flowers, a vision composed out of all visions; as Solomon's Song was a song of songs."[11] A fusion of all the literary forms, the Revelation prophecy was thought to unite Aeschylean tragedy and Homeric epic, lyrics and comedy, history, philosophy, and oratory, and thereby developed, as Hugh Broughton explains, the capacity to "give the realistic emphasis of dramatic presentation to its ideas, while [being] free

10. Quoted from a Newberry Library Broadside, *A Vision, Which One Mr. Brayne . . . Had in September, 1647* (London: Printed for John Playford, 1649).

11. Thomas Goodwin, *An Exposition of the Revelation* (1639), in *The Works of Thomas Goodwin*, 12 vols. (London: James Nisbet, 1861–66), V, 33.

at any point to abandon drama for discourse or lyric meditation."[12] But more than just a synthesis of literary forms, the
Book of Revelation came to be understood as a multimedia
performance. Joseph Mede, for instance, "was of the opinion that
those visions concerning the Seals were not written by Characters
in letters, but being painted by certain shapes, lay hid under some
covers of the Seals; which being opened, each of them in its order,
appeared not to be read, but to be upheld and viewed." For Mede,
therefore, the Book of Revelation is the prototype of picture-
prophecy, conceived in such a way that the pictorial and the
verbal can be "joined together"; and he concludes, then, that
"according to this apprehension, those words of John, *Come and
see*, seem not unfitly to agree."[13] Subsequent to Mede, prophecy
was commonly understood to contain "visionary scenes"—it was a
form of "picture-writing";[14] and thus poets who would designate
themselves as prophets were obliged to include such scenes either
figuratively (as Spenser and Milton do by letting verbal description
be determined by iconographic traditions) or quite literally (as
Blake does by creating poems that are firmly ensconced in this
tradition of the picture-prophecy). So doing, Spenser and Milton
raise their poems to the status of word-pictures, while Blake,
observing prophetic tradition to the letter, establishes a truly
collaborative relationship between word and picture. His poems
are, in the strictest sense, pictorial prophecies.

When it is understood that all literary forms possess their own
world-view, offer a distinctive perspective on the human predicament, and when it is remembered that every art form represents a
different mode of perception, then the prophet's objective becomes clearer: he assaults the mind by opening the doors of
perception and enlarges its perimeters by imposing upon it not one
but many perspectives. What Joan Webber describes as "characteristic" of epic poetry is the motive force behind prophecy: "To
probe and extend the limits of human consciousness."[15] Epic

12. *A Revelation of the Holy Apocalyps* (London: n. p., 1610), p. 70.

13. *The Key of the Revelation*, unpaginated translator's note.

14. See both the anonymous *A Key to the Mystery of the Revelation* (London: W. Goldsmith, 1785), p. 96, and James Bicheno, *The Signs of the Times* (West Springfield, Mass.: Printed by Richard Davison, 1796), p. 10 (Bicheno's commentary was written in England between 1793 and 1795).

15. I quote from Webber's monograph, still in manuscript, "The Literary Epic from Homer to Milton."

poets and prophets alike are theorists of vision, both concerned with the expansion of consciousness, but within that likeness there is a difference. If epic articulates a new stage of consciousness, prophecy is more ambitious still, attempting to bring man to the highest peak of consciousness that is possible, its objective being not to equip man to live in an advancing state of civilization but to enable man to enter the heavenly Jerusalem. Epic may record a culture's shift from one state of consciousness to another as the old culture is invaded by a new one; but prophecy would alter the very eye by which the new culture has conceived of itself. This it accomplishes, first, by altering the eyes of the populace on the assumption that the eye altering alters all, that by bringing individual men to the pinnacle of vision, the ultimate state of consciousness will be realized. Prophecy thus locks arms with epic— but only so that it may advance beyond it. Like epic, prophecy operates according to principles of discontinuity and continuity; but again similarity focuses distinction. The epic poet enters into a contentious relationship with his precursors and into a harmonious one with his culture; he transcends their achievement by enshrining the value systems of his own time, which themselves transcend the less adequate systems celebrated by his predecessors. On the other hand, the prophet asserts discontinuity between himself and his culture, whose collective mind he is assaulting, and continuity between himself and his precursors, whose visions he releases and then expands.[16] Neither conservers nor confirmers of the prevail-

16. See, for an opposing view, Harold Bloom, *The Anxiety of Influence: A Theory of Poetry* (New York: Oxford Univ. Press, 1973), where he argues that "the Covering Cherub . . . is a demon of continuity; his baleful charm imprisons the present in the past, and reduces a world of differences into a grayness of uniformity." A few lines later Bloom says, "Discontinuity is freedom. *Prophets* and advanced analysts alike *proclaim discontinuity*" (p. 39; my italics). Since Bloom is talking about the way prophets (and poets) relate to one another and not the way in which they relate to their culture, one must conclude that he fails to appreciate discriminations, translating revolutionary ideology into mental perversity. The anxieties explored by Bloom are attributable less to poets than to critics; indeed what is offered there is "a theory" of criticism, not of poetry, and that theory explains many of the aberrations in Bloom's adventurously perverse book: the very language of the book looks back to Leavis (the "ruminative" line, for example); and its conclusions coincide with those of Leavis, at least insofar as they involve Milton. Within the book itself, there is ample evidence "of distortion, . . . [of] wilful revisionism," especially when it comes to laying out the evidence intended to substantiate Bloom's theory of poetic influence, a theory he extrapolates from the Blake-Milton relationship. This relationship does, in fact, yield up a theory of poetic

ing orthodoxies, prophets are the agents through which new, more perfect and enduring ones are created; prophets thus band together, sharing a common purpose founded upon the same ideological suppositions.

Like any other genre, prophecy, for all its variables, contains a set of thematic constants: it attributes a providential pattern to creation, which subsequent history has deformed; the prophet's objective, then, is to re-form history—an objective dependent upon the renovation of individual men, upon transforming the natural man into the spiritual man. Since apocalypse occurs only after mankind is readied for it, the prophet submits others to the processes of purgation and purification. Committed to brightening the mind, to exalting all its faculties, the prophet employs a series of strategies designed to force open the doors of perception, teaching men to see not with but through the eye. One of these devices, generic mixture, has already been alluded to; it is designed to extend the limits of human consciousness, to bring before the eye what it has not been able to see before. Another of the prophet's devices is obscurity, a veil that can be penetrated only by the spiritual eye; and still another is that "multifarious Allusivenesse"[17] which turns prophecy into a literature of contexts. Those allusions, an antidote for obscurity, erect the contexts that gradually enlarge and perfect man's understanding; and they have the effect, finally, of continually pushing the reader beyond the confines of any one prophecy—back into the earlier prophecy out of which the new one is fetched, and out into the world where it is eventually to be fulfilled. Both the obscurity of prophecy and its allusiveness are calculated to generate an antagonistic relationship between the prophet and his audience. Since his responsibility is to shake men loose from the orthodoxies to which they subscribe,

influence that resembles my own, not Bloom's; and the major evidence supporting it (and by Bloom this evidence is not "distorted" but suppressed) is to be found in Blake's portrayals of Milton and in his illustrations for Milton's poetry, together with alterations in attitude toward Milton evident when one turns from the statement about the poet made in *The Marriage of Heaven and Hell* to the one offered in *Milton*. Such alterations of attitude may also be deduced from differences, especially iconographic ones, that separate the four surviving copies of the poem to which Milton gives his name. For a full discussion, see my study, *Angel of Apocalypse: Blake's Idea of Milton* (Madison: Univ. of Wisconsin Press, 1975).

17. I borrow the phrase from Henry More, *An Exposition of the Seven Epistles*, p. 143.

the prophet subjects his audience to what, now called "reader harassment," was designated in the seventeenth century as "the trial of the Reader."[18] This strategy of prophecy, in particular, finds its extension in the structure of prophecy.

Prophecy is dramatically structured, progressing from shadowy types to truth and substituting for the conflict among characters in a play a conflict among its various perspectives—perspectives deriving from the different forms it incorporates and held in dynamic tension by their various styles. Like the ordinary dramatist, the prophet employs choric devices both to lead an audience toward, and to jostle it into adopting, new perspectives. These various devices led to the Book of Revelation's being called a tragedy, or a comedy, or a tragi-comedy; and these designations fostered still others: John's prophecy, with its "celestial" drama, was eventually described as an "Apocalyptick Theatre"[19] —one

18. See Stanley E. Fish, *Surprised by Sin: The Reader in* Paradise Lost (London and Melbourne: Macmillan; and New York: St. Martin's Press, 1967), and also *Self-Consuming Artifacts: The Experience of Seventeenth-Century Literature* (Berkeley and Los Angeles: Univ. of California Press, 1973). In these two books, Fish has inferred from Milton's poetry and prose many of the elements that make up the aesthetic that I am describing in this essay: Milton's is not an "anti-aesthetic" but a biblical aesthetic, however—one that is ratified by the commentators cited throughout this essay and made familiar in Milton's time by them. To identify Fish with New Criticism, as Brian Vickers does, displays a remarkable insensitivity to historical contexts (there is a difference between the self-consuming artifacts of Fish and the self-presuming ones of New Criticism). What Vickers can accept only as "a peculiar phase in twentieth-century aesthetics," "wholly inappropriate to seventeenth-century writers," should be accepted by us as a vital part of an aesthetic that, however "trendy" it may seem, had in Milton's time the venerable tradition of the Bible standing behind it. Though such a tradition may not have had equal sway over all writers at all times, it obviously would have had great sway over a Christian poet like Milton who would be, by temperament and commitment, compelled by it in a way that he would not be compelled by Aristotle. Prophecy and its traditions provided Milton and his age with exactly what Vickers denies him *and it,* a "problematical concept of the process of writing and reading." For Vickers' views, see his review of Fish in *Renaissance Quarterly,* 27 (1974), 117–22. Fish's idea of "reader harassment" (advanced in both his books) corresponds exactly with the seventeenth-century notion of "the trial of the Reader" (see Samuel Hartlib et al., *The Revelation Reveled by Two Apocalyptical Treatises* [London: Printed by William Du-Gard, 1651], p. 135).

19. See the unpaginated translator's note in Joseph Mede, *The Key of the Revelation,* and also Mede's own comment on p. 30 (the phrase appears as the subtitle for this section of the commentary). Presumably, it is Mede who appears in *Lycidas* under the pastoral guise of "old *Damaetas* [who] lov'd to hear our song" (36). When it is understood that Mede is one of the seventeenth century's great theorists of vision and *Lycidas* one of the century's great examples of visionary art, the line from *Lycidas*

that, taking the whole world for its stage, depicted the struggle of all men as they travel toward a Jerusalem that must be discovered within before it can be established without.

With few exceptions, the Book of Revelation was regarded as "a certayne and distincte order," all of whose parts are "knit together" so as to be "coherent and correspondent."[20] Depending upon the enumerator, the structure of John's visionary drama was described as threefold, or sevenfold, or both. That is, the Book of Revelation contained three prophecies—those of the epistles, the seals, and the book—each of them intermixing vision with narration in a seven-part drama, each of these parts being a labyrinth leading men closer to Jerusalem. These structures organized the prophecy's visionary drama; yet another structure, sixfold and rhetorical, was thought to organize its argument.[21] But whoever the enumerator, Revelation's structure was described as nonlinear, patterned according to a system of synchronisms: events, instead of succeeding one another, were made to mirror one another; insofar as plot lines were discernible, they crossed rather than followed one another sequentially. Complicated but not disorderly, the Revelation structure came to be conceptualized as a series of

---

acquires real point. In a recent study of *Lycidas*, moreover (one that I read after my own essay was completed), David Shelley Berkeley reminds us of what is too often forgotten, that Milton's poem was written for, and thus should be read from the perspective of, "Milton's learned contemporaries"; that reminder is accompanied by the proposal that Mede be thought of as an "ideal" reader (see *Inwrought with Figures Dim: A Reading of Milton's* Lycidas [The Hague and Paris: Mouton, 1974], p. [7]).

20. See Brocard, *The Reveled Revelation of Saint John*, sig. B2; Henry Bullinger, *A Hundred Sermons upon the Apocalypse of Jesu Christ* (London: John Daye, 1573), p. 16^V; and Henry Burton, *The Seven Vials or a Briefe and Plaine Exposition upon the 15: and 16: Chapters of the Revelation* (London: William Jones, 1628), p. 11.

21. William Fulke assumes a threefold structure for the Apocalypse; and Henry Bullinger, though he examines the book's rhetorical organization, acknowledges a sevenfold, visionary structure of which David Pareus provides the fullest anatomy (see, respectively, *Prælections upon the Sacred and Holy Revelation of S. John*, tr. George Gyffard [London: Thomas Purfoote, 1573], *A Hundred Sermons upon the Apocalypse of Jesu Christ* [London: John Daye, 1573], and *A Commentary upon the Divine Revelation of the Apostle and Evangelist John*, tr. Elias Arnold [Amsterdam: C. P., 1644]). During the seventeenth century, both Joseph Mede, in *The Key of the Revelation*, and Henry More, in *Apocalypsis Apocalypseos; or the Revelation of St. John the Divine Unveiled* (London: Printed for J. Martyn and W. Kettilby, 1680), reconcile the threefold and sevenfold analyses, each commentator arguing that the Apocalypse contains three prophecies, each of them divided into seven parts (see figs. 5 and 6).

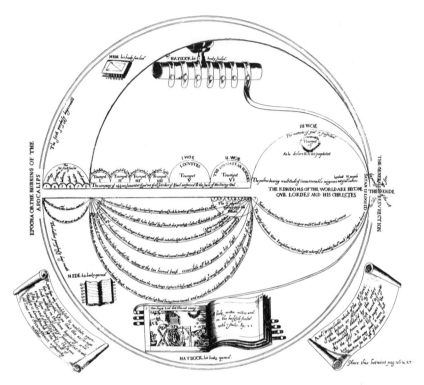

5. *From* Joseph Mede, *The Key of the Revelation*, 2d ed., tr. Richard More (London, 1650), between pp. 26 and 27. *By permission of the Folger Shakespeare Library, Washington, D.C.*

overlapping arcs and concentric circles (see figs. 5 and 6); and perception of it, beneath a chaotic surface, marked the reader as a *seer,* who, after being educated by Jesus through John, was ready to enter the divine vision.

Not only the structure of John's Apocalypse, but also its vision turned downward and inward, forcing the prophet's audience to travel through mental spaces in whose boundaries they encountered Christ and thereupon discovered a perfect pattern of heroism to which they could aspire. As the hero of the Apocalypse (the Mighty Angel, John calls him), Christ is at the center, his warfare being a type of all Christian warfare and his program embodying the revolutionary ideology at the heart of this prophecy. Other angels fall from the divine vision, embracing instead human tradi-

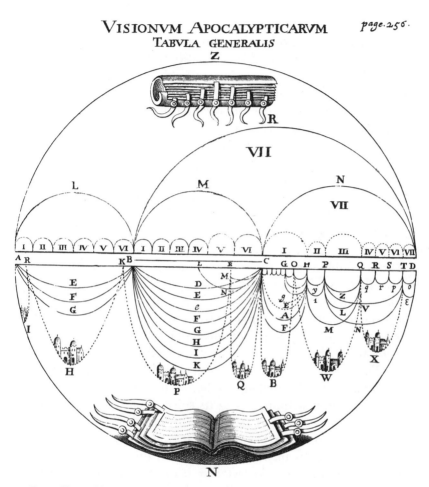

6. *From* Henry More, *Apocalypsis Apocalypseos; or the Revelation of St. John the Divine Unveiled* (London, 1680), p. 256. *By permission of the Folger Shakespeare Library, Washington, D.C.*

tions, the orthodoxies of society; but as the Mighty Angel, representing the principle of subversion fundamental to all prophecy, Christ undermines the institutions of society, political and religious, by way of restoring the Everlasting Gospel.

Anyone familiar with how the Book of Revelation was read by Renaissance commentators will recognize in these elements of prophecy the component parts of a biblical aesthetic to which poets and prose writers, both during the Renaissance and since, have given their allegiance. One may also detect not just similarity but congruence between this aesthetic and the so-called "anti-aesthetic" of the "self-consuming artifact" for which Stanley Fish has provided a descriptive paradigm. That paradigm should now be accepted for what it is—the representation not of a genre but of certain elements that during the Renaissance helped to compose a genre, elements that, instead of having been recently discovered in the past, were, during the Renaissance, recovered from the Bible. What Fish's phrase, the "self-consuming artifact," points to is an aspect of prophecy that, in the Bible, is pointed to by the metaphor of "eating the book." The book, given to John of Patmos by Christ, implies the patient-physician relationship; and beyond that, the act of eating the book implies the consumption of it in a double sense: the reader's inferior self is consumed in a process that allows the spiritual man to rise up and triumph over the natural man; and the prophecy itself, administered in doses (it is negotiated panel by panel and seal by seal), is itself consumed as its reader finds the rungs of his ladder burning away, until, reaching the highest rung, he achieves the pinnacle of vision. Such art, as Fish explains, is "concerned less with the making of better poems than with the making of better persons."[22] Or, to turn from Fish's idiom without losing its spirit, such art battles against the mental obstacles that keep men entombed; it is engaged in a process of liberation that rolls stones away from the mind, thus allowing light to stream forth. Prophecy is therefore literature as process, not literature as knowledge; it exists not for the truths it embodies but for those to which it provides access, and thus, once it has brought man to the final stage of consciousness, it ceases to be functional and then can be discarded. Prophecy, in short, mediates between man and God, between fallen reason and the visionary imagination, and, liberating the mind, enables it to become the mediator between earthly and heavenly things, between time and eternity. This is the end prophecy is made to serve in Milton's poetry, where its various elements are harnessed to a chariot of creativity that draws forth from the poet not just *Lycidas*, but the epics and *Samson Agonistes* as well.

22. See *Self-Consuming Artifacts*, esp. pp. 3–4, 42–43.

Lycidas: An Apocalyptic Theater

Thomas Vogler has said (one wishes with tongue in cheek) that Milton did not consider "the poet's private life or the emotions, conflicts, and turmoils of youth appropriate material for truly serious poetry."[23] What, then, of *Lycidas?* And as we ask that question, we may wonder, too, what impelled Vogler to exemplify through Milton a poet divorcing his own experience from the serious poetry he writes. The answer to this last question is simple enough: the critic, wishing to set Milton apart from his Romantic heirs, devises the terms for a distinction that works to Milton's disadvantage. Divorcing poetry from experience, Milton, we are told, produces lyric poems that are literary exercises, in contrast to the Romantics, who, making their own experiences the subject of their poetry, compose "prelude poems." Such poems, it is argued, give epic import to the lyric impulse; they "retain the intensity and subjectivity of the lyric while achieving the scope and universal reference of epic," and, marked by expectancy, they are less concerned with recording a vision than with the processes by which vision is achieved.[24] In consequence, "prelude poems" survey the remnants of the fallen and fragmented world by way of reaching for a perspective from which a larger, more adequate vision of life can be achieved. Such poems, it is allowed, may not accomplish a renovated society, but they do hold out the prospect for one: their function is to expand man's consciousness; and by showing an individual, usually the poet himself, awakening into a new life, they assert their larger purpose, which is to bring the reader to a similar apotheosis.

If these are the features of the supposedly new genre of the prelude poem, then *Lycidas* is just that. But these same features, many of them identified by Stanley Fish with his self-consuming artifact, are the hallmarks of prophecy; and I suspect that our comprehension of *Lycidas* is the greater if, instead of allowing it to be appropriated to a new genre, we recognize in the poem the same generic elements that caused Blake to designate *Milton,* and

23. *Preludes to Vision: The Epic Adventure in Blake, Wordsworth, Keats, and Hart Crane* (Berkeley and Los Angeles: Univ. of California Press, 1971), p. 14.
24. Ibid., p. 15.

Wordsworth to designate *The Prelude,* as prophecies. These Romantic poems find their closest analogues in *Lycidas* and Milton's epics, which, like the poems they inspired, are prophecies about the formation of the prophetic character.

Lycidas and *Paradise Lost* share with one another a common purpose, the justification of God's ways, the assertion of eternal providence, which for Milton, as for Blake, is "opposed to & distinct from divine vengeance."[25] Like their model, that "admirable *Looking-Glass of Providence*" called the Apocalypse,[26] Milton's poems are inspired by men's questionings, and they would allay such questionings in the manner of John of Patmos— by testifying to providence and ensuring that there will be ministers of it. If such testimony is "the First great Fruit and Use" of the Apocalypse,[27] that is also its yield in Milton's poetry, where providence is asserted not by invoking a god of justice and wrath but by countering such depictions with a god of love and mercy. The vengeful god of Christian orthodoxy was for Milton, as he was for Henry More, an "imagination" of the false prophets, which they would erect within "the Temple of every mans Minde" and which it is the duty of every true prophet to destroy.[28] This Milton undertakes to do, not by advancing the notion that God is the archdestroyer, but by promulgating the idea that he is the master-creator whose presence gives order, however intricate and involved, to the world and to its finest facsimile, the poem.

With calculation, Milton brings both *Paradise Lost* and *Lycidas* into accord with the scriptural book that, enmassing "so many cleare arguments of . . . providence," puts aside all the questioning of it in earlier prophecy—the book that was alleged to supersede all earlier prophecy by explaining God's justice, which earlier prophecy allowed but admitted it could not comprehend.[29] Moreover, by casting himself into the role of witnessing to providence, Milton arrogates to himself the power attributed to God's witnesses in scripture—power over water. If Christ's pastoral function

25. *A Vision of the Last Judgment,* in Erdman, *Poetry and Prose,* p. 549.
26. More, *Apocalypsis Apocalypseos,* p. 356.
27. More, *An Explanation of the Grand Mystery of Godliness,* p. 202.
28. Ibid., p. 206.
29. Thomas Brightman, *The Revelation of S. John* (Leyden: Printed by John Class, 1616), sig. A5$^\text{V}$.

involves his rescuing the church when she is drowning, Milton's prophetic role engages him in rescuing men from a similar fate. Christ presides over the second resurrection, receiving Lycidas into the heavenly kingdom; and correspondingly, the prophet, in this case Milton, presides over the first resurrection, raising up his audience of readers into a new spiritual life. Sharing these themes with the Book of Revelation, *Lycidas* also replicates its design, being an amalgamation of forms and of the styles appropriate to them, those forms impinging on the poem an array of perspectives that its various styles hold in dynamic tension.

Lycidas has been called a poem about poetry: it is more precisely a prophecy about transforming all the Lord's people into prophets, and as a prophecy it exhibits the major characteristics of its genre. In its striving for transcendental form and in its interlacing of "joyful things . . . with sorrowfull,"[30] Milton's poem in conception matches the Book of Revelation. This poem is not, of course, Milton's first attempt to combine a variety of forms by way of achieving multiperspectivism, for the *Nativity Ode* and *Comus,* in different ways, reflect Milton's cosmological striving. In the Nativity poem, Milton joins ode to hymn, and both to the traditions of dream-vision and nativity poetry; in *Comus,* Milton is more ambitious still, encompassing multiple literary forms within a multimedia performance.[31] *Lycidas* continues this experimen-

30. Bullinger, *A Hundred Sermons upon the Apocalypse of Jesu Christ,* p. 129.

31. For a full discussion, see Angus Fletcher, *The Transcendental Masque: An Essay on Milton's* Comus (Ithaca: Cornell Univ. Press, 1972), esp. pp. 116–94. Milton, of course, is not the only poet to seek transcendence of the world as it exists by transcending the forms that have held the world in a state of suspended animation. The great poets of England, who belong to the visionary line, are all masters of *genera mista* and their great poems examples of it—*The Canterbury Tales* and *Piers Plowman,* the Renaissance epics and Romantic ones, exemplify the tradition. Chaucer and Spenser criticism have for a long time recognized this fact, Milton criticism is beginning to; for Langland's debt to the tradition, see Morton Bloomfield, Piers Plowman *as a Fourteenth-Century Apocalypse* (New Brunswick: Rutgers Univ. Press, 1962); and for Wordsworth's and Shelley's, see Herbert S. Lindenberger, *On Wordsworth's* Prelude (Princeton: Princeton Univ. Press, 1963), and Stuart Curran, *Shelley's Annus Mirabilis: The Maturing of an Epic Vision* (San Marino: Huntington Library, 1975). Fletcher provides the best theoretical discussion and application to Milton; but see also, for theoretical discussion, Rosalie L. Colie, *The Resources of Kind: Genre-Theory in the Renaissance,* ed. Barbara K. Lewalski (Berkeley and Los Angeles: Univ. of California Press, 1973), and esp. pp. 120–22 for an application of the theory to Milton; and see, too, E. H. Gombrich, *Norm and Form: Studies in the Renaissance,* 2d ed. (New York and London: Phaidon, 1971), esp. pp. 3,

tation with composite forms, bringing it to a mighty culmination and thus serving as a prelude to *Paradise Lost* and *Paradise Regained*. This poem, as its usual generic label implies, fuses pastoral with elegy, and both with canzone and madrigal; yet these various lyric modes also embrace satire (the invective against the clergy), along with movements both tragic and comedic (the death and resurrection of Lycidas), in a poem whose cosmic dimensions are epical.

Lycidas may not contain all the extravagance of epic tradition, but its poet was aware of the one "gross fact" to which Thomas Rosenmeyer has called our attention: "pastoral lyric was at first composed in the same verse form as epic, and remained faithful to the pattern for over 1700 years."[32] In keeping with this fact, Milton employs certain devices that lodge his poem in epic tradition—the invocation of the muses, along with explicit reference to Calliope (the muse of epic poetry) and direct citation of the lines through which Virgil, in his fourth eclogue, elevates pastoral to a higher mode; and, for all its prosodic irregularities (which are more "regular/ Then most, when most irregular they seem"), *Lycidas* comes to its period in an *ottava rima* stanza, the verse form that during the Renaissance was acknowledged to be the proper one for epic poetry. These devices participate in the process whereby the epic kind is translated into a metaphor—not by reducing it so much as by compressing it into phrases, devices, and emblems "implying far more than they seem to hold."[33] The meaning of this inclusionist operation, a reflex of Milton's cosmological striving, should not be ignored, nor should the fact that pastoral and elegy, canzone and madrigal, tragic movements and comedic ones, satire and epic are all harnessed to the prophetic mode: the process of remaking the forms, of setting them in new combinations and defining for them new relationships, involves an attendant reshaping of the ideas those forms characteristically embodied. Milton's ultimate objective is "to reform man, to re-form

73. Gombrich, talking, of course, about the visual arts, says that the Renaissance produced "a new institutional framework for art," its artists, striving for perfect form, adopting a concept of "total form." Such a concept is adopted by Milton who, following Revelation's commentators, proceeds to identify it irrevocably with prophecy.

32. *The Green Cabinet: Theocritus and the European Pastoral Lyric* (Berkeley and Los Angeles: Univ. of California Press, 1969), p. 14.

33. Colie, *The Resources of Kind*, p. 11.

philosophy"[34] —to re-form the world of which, in *Lycidas*, the church is an emblem. As these forms take a place in Milton's apocalyptic theater, so too do the structures typical of them. In the process, *Lycidas*, like *Paradise Lost*, becomes a poem not of one but of many structures, bearing a striking resemblance to its Revelation model.

Like that model, *Lycidas* is a poem of contexts; and the settings in which the poem at different times appeared provide the quickest guide to the contexts that will open its vision. Initially, *Lycidas* appeared in *Justa Edovardo King Naufrago* as the last of thirteen poems written in English (they form a discrete section in the volume, set off with their own title-page). All these poems seem to be part of a collaborative effort, to participate in "a flexible comprehensive design," with *Lycidas* having unique status in the volume: like the other poems, it participates in an echoing process; but coming last in the volume it organizes not only its own themes "but those of the book as a whole."[35] It accomplishes this task not by simply weaving themes from this poem and that into the fabric of its own vision but, instead, by assuming an ironic, often contentious, relationship with other poems in the volume. They typically decline to "examine Gods decree" or to "question providence," arguing, as does Henry King, that "Discreet Religion binds us to admire/ The wayes of providence, and not enquire"; they celebrate the church and its clergy; and, though all these poems are rhymed, they nonetheless express the impossibility of mourning in rhyme: no one, says John Cleveland, can weep "in tune"— no true mourner can confine his sentiments to "the Muses Rosarie," grief knowing "no laws" but running its course "like the waves." Milton's *Lycidas* dares to do what these other poems recoil from: it questions providence, it inveighs against the clergy, it spurns the device of rhyming, at least of systematic rhyming. In this act of defiance, Milton turns from one tradition of poeticizing to another, and with that turn he positions his poem within a tradition of pastoral—of Christian pastoral—that is brought to a culmination in Christ's parables and to an apotheosis in John's Revelation. The contexts of Christian pastoral and Revelation

34. Ibid., p. 113.
35. Michael Lloyd, "Justa Edouardo King," *Notes and Queries*, N.S. 5 (1958), 432–34.

prophecy are firmly established by the setting assigned to *Lycidas* in the 1645 *Poems of Mr. John Milton.* Positioned between *Arcades* and *Comus,* the one poem an allegory about the Christianizing of pastoral, the other a pastoral masque with visionary dimensions, *Lycidas,* through its epigraph, together with the thick tissue of allusion within its verse, invokes the books of Genesis and of Revelation, both the works of prophets and both prophecies rich with pastoral elements.

By referring to the first and last books of the Bible, Milton stretches the past tense of his poem back to Creation and its future tense forward to Apocalypse. His strategies are those of John: through the pastoral image, he recalls the Edenic world about to be infested with Sin and Death at the beginning of the Bible; and through the genre of prophecy in which that allusion is made, he explores, as does John in the Apocalypse, how man may be released from his fallen condition. The structure of the one experience (Genesis) is negated by the structure of the other experience (Revelation). This John makes clear by inverting in his own prophecy the structure of Moses'; and Milton in his prophecy follows suit by pitting against the structure of pastoral the form of prophecy.

Pastoral, like any other genre, has a set of conventions that provides a poet with a formulaic structure. In *Lycidas,* each verse paragraph turns upon a pastoral convention; and the three panels comprising the poem's overriding thematic structure, each practically equal in length and parallel in pattern, give accents to three of these conventions—the lament of nature, the procession of mourners, and the apotheosis of the lamented. This threefold structure, discovered and anatomized by Arthur E. Barker,[36] is accompanied by a prologue and an epilogue. That this tripartite design resembles the Revelation model, we shall see momentarily; that Milton imagines his poem as a prophecy, and means for us to designate it as such, is made evident by the first and the last lines of his poem.

Lycidas is often read, and too often dismissed, as a poem so "loaded with allusions" that it "can be fully enjoyed only by the

36. "The Pattern of Milton's Nativity Ode," *University of Toronto Quarterly,* 10 (1941), 171–72.

classical scholar who is in the tradition of the Greek pastoralists";[37] yet classical scholars have, finally, done very little to open the meaning of Milton's poem to us. They have tabulated verbal echoes without penetrating Milton's vision, and they have established as the poem's primary context the very tradition of art that *Lycidas* would subvert. The first and last lines of the poem both illustrate and confirm my point. The supposed autobiographical references, as well as pastoral allusions, in these lines have been noted, while one fundamental truth about them has been ignored—a truth suggested by the poem's title that mythologizes Edward King into Lycidas:

Inherent in sympathetic emotion is a tendency to become divorced from the occasion or the subject by which it was called forth. What starts out . . . as a feeling of sadness in sympathy for a bereaved person, may become a condition of sadness as such, no longer associated with the particular person. It may also surpass in intensity the feeling of the person for whom one has sympathy.[38]

As the autobiographical and pastoral references in the first and last lines have garnered more and more attention, the prophetic allusions in them have become so subdued that now they go virtually unnoticed.[39]

"*Yet once more*, O ye Laurels, and *once more*" (my italics) anticipates another occasion in Milton's poetry, much later, when the phrase reappears. The setting for the phrase (again I have added italics) is Sonnet XXIII (" . . . as *yet once more* I trust to have/ Full sight of her in Heaven without restraint")—a setting that underscores the visionary associations of the phrase. Here and in *Lycidas, yet once more* recalls St. Paul's admonition to the Hebrews, not only his advice that if they are to achieve the

37. Henry A. Beers, *Milton's Tercentenary* (New Haven: Yale Univ. Press, 1910), p. 10.

38. Abraham Heschel, *The Prophets: An Introduction* (New York, Evanston, and London: Harper and Row, 1969), p. 126.

39. Notable exceptions are Edward Tayler's unpublished *Lycidas* essay (Columbia University) and James Taaffe's "*Lycidas*—Line 192," *Milton Quarterly*, 6 (1972), 36–38. The allusion to Hebrews 12:26–27 in *Lycidas's* first line was first noted by David Shelley Berkeley, "A Possible Biblical Echo in *Lycidas*, l. 1," *Notes and Queries*, N.S. 8 (1961), 178. See also *Inwrought with Figures Dim*, p. 33, where once again noting the allusion Berkeley again fails to draw out its full implications.

heavenly city they must not turn away from the prophets who speak on earth or from heaven, but also his words:

Yet once more I shake not the earth only, but also heaven.

And this word, Yet once more, signifieth the removing of those things that are shaken, or of things that are made, that those things which cannot be shaken may remain. (Hebrews 12:26–27; my italics)

In Milton's line, there may be the suggestion that, having already written many elegies, the poet is about to write another; but in the line there is also this clear echo of Hebrews—of a passage from it that biblical commentators repeatedly join to the great promise in the Book of Revelation, that a time will come when man can wipe the tears forever from his eyes, that at that time a new Jerusalem will rise in place of the old one. As Henry More explains, this is the time for wiping away the tears, and it is signified by the fact that no one is "oppressed with grief" any more, nor does anyone any more "express his grief by his tears."[40] Now the witnesses of Christ, liberated from injustice and cruelty, from the abuses of institutionalized religion, rise up, like Milton's uncouth swain, doffing their sackcloth and donning the garments of the resurrection, to testify to God's providence. The Epistle to the Hebrews thus anticipates, through "Prophetic Language" and in "Metaphors of the highest Excellencies," man's triumph over the beast,[41] a triumph won through the mental warfare that the true prophets like Milton waged against the false prophets, who are represented in Milton's poem by the corrupt clergy. It is no accident that Milton prophesies in an elegy, for true prophets, wearers of sackcloth, appear as mourners; nor is it an inconsequential detail that the poet, in the epilogue, assumes the prophet's mantle, for the man (who and what he is) is known by his apparel. Milton's point is simple enough: prophets, he recognizes with Thomas Goodwin, are "set out by their *condition*, which is in sackcloth and mourning"; and they are called upon to prophesy, to "feed the church," in those periods when she is in the wilderness.[42]

40. *Apocalypsis Apocalypseos*, pp. 214, 216.
41. Abraham Woodhead, *The Apocalyps Paraphrased* (n.p.: n.p., [1682]), p. 32, and Samuel Hartlib et al., *The Revelation Reveled by Two Apocalyptical Treatises*, pp. 75–76.
42. *An Exposition of the Revelation* (1639), in *The Works of Thomas Goodwin*, 12 vols. (London: James Nisbet, 1861–66), V. 142.

First lines sometimes have hidden in them a poem's resolution—
they prophesy its conclusion. But *Lycidas,* we have been told,
"almost alone among Milton's important poems, does not suggest
at the beginning how it will end": "Of the poem's conclusion we
are given no hint," says Isabel MacCaffrey, largely because "no
literary context" is developed by these initial lines.[43] Such an
argument ignores, first of all, "the sacred well,/ That from beneath
the seat of *Jove* doth spring" (15–16)—a thinly veiled allusion to
the sea of glass before the throne of God, which is a notorious
emblem for "the *Spiritual Kingdom* of Christ, . . . of Regeneration,"[44] so movingly envisioned both in the penultimate chapter
of John's Apocalypse and in the penultimate verse paragraph of
Milton's apocalyptic poem. Even more pointedly, there is the
implied metaphor of the first five lines—Milton's poem is a garland—a metaphor that, in the language of prophecy, identifies
Milton as a Christian poet and that builds, or should build,
expectations for the consolation which comes at the close of his
elegy. But most important of all is the very first line of *Lycidas*—
an allusion to an allusion that, once penetrated, points to the
poem's ultimate resolution, "And wipe the tears for ever from his
eyes" (181). Commentators interpreted this verse, which Milton
lifts from the Book of Revelation (7:17, 21:4; cf. Isaiah 25:8), to
mean that, though this life is "*a vale of teares,*" God "will make it,
that we shall weepe no more, by taking away all cause of teares,
turning our teares into joy according to the promise: They which
sow in teares, shall reape in joy."[45] Milton's consolation implies,
even further, that "It is much better to weepe here in afflictions
for a little time, and to rejoyce for evermore in the world to
come . . . then to have delight . . . for a season, and after to
mourne for ever."[46]

Lycidas, then, begins with the shedding of tears that, before it
ends, are wiped away: "Weep no more, woeful Shepherds weep no
more" (165). The promise that "thou shalt weep no more," the

43. "*Lycidas:* Poet in a Landscape," in *The Lyric and Dramatic Milton,* ed. Joseph H.
Summers (New York: Columbia Univ. Press, 1965), pp. 65–67.

44. More, *Apocalypsis Apocalypseos,* p. 43.

45. Pareus, *A Commentary upon the Divine Revelation of the Apostle and Evangelist
John,* p. 553.

46. George Giffard, *Sermons upon the Whole Booke of the Revelation* (London:
Printed by Richard Field and Felix Kingston, 1599), p. 155.

wiping away of tears, succeeds "the water of affliction" and
signifies that man now sees as his teacher does: now "the eyes of
the blind . . . see out of obscurity, and out of darkness"; "in the
wilderness . . . waters break out, and streams in the desert" (Isaiah
30:19–21; 29:18; 35:5–6). Wiping away the tears—an activity
customarily associated with Christ's pastoral function—drives
home the message of Milton's poem:

> . . . he [Christ] is the shepherd over the whole flocke, which shall be even to
> the worlds end. And seeing we be now in exceeding great dangers in these
> evill dayes (as the last times are perilous) assure your selves he hath a special
> care over us.[47]

In *Lycidas*, the priest who has turned the garments of Christ's
word filthy is made to surrender his duties, as shepherd and
ploughman, as minister and prophet, to the poet, who, becoming a
prophet, acquires great power over water. Ariosto once said that
"a poet hath one step unto a prophet";[48] in *Lycidas* the poet and
the prophet become indistinguishable—they are now one.

Christ's pastoral function, then, is appropriated by Milton, who,
in the act of writing his poem, raises up the reader just as Christ
raises up Edward King. Thus, the nominal subject of *Lycidas* is
King's second resurrection—a raising up into life and eternal glory;
but the poem's real subject is the reader's first resurrection, which
occurs in this life, through the agency of the poem, and involves
moving out of the desolate prison habitated by the natural man
into the mental spaces traveled by the prophet. As in all prophecy,
the real subject of *Lycidas* is its readers; the real locus of the
poem, the reader's mind, represented within the poem by the
uncouth swain. *Lycidas* is about his (our) metamorphosis into
glory, which ensures the still greater one realized by King.

Christ, both in *Lycidas* and in the Book of Revelation, is man's
savior: as commentators so often noted, he made man when he
was nothing and saved man when he was lost; he restored him to
life when he was dead and raised him up to heaven.[49] Literally

47. Ibid.

48. Ariosto's remark is quoted by Rudolf Gottfried in his Introduction to *Orlando
Furioso*, tr. John Harington (Bloomington: Indiana Univ. Press, 1963), p. 10; see also
Augustine Marlorate, *A Catholike Exposition upon the Revelation of Sainct John*
(London: Printed by H. Binneman, 1574), p. 152[V].

49. Bartholomew Traheron, *An Exposition on the Fourth Chapter of S. Johns
Revelation* (London: Printed for Edward Aggas, 1577), sig. Di[V].

this is true for Lycidas, and metaphorically it is true for his mourners. *Lycidas* (and this point needs to be made because it is so often ignored) is a poem written for the living, not for the dead, though it is, of course, lodged in the paradox that it is we, the living, who are dead and King, the dead man, who is truly alive. Just as Christ rescues King from the ocean's floor, so through his prophets he rescues the rest of us from our death sleep, restoring us to a new life and raising up a paradise in the mental wilderness we have until that moment been inhabiting. *Lycidas*, therefore, like the Book of Revelation, is about two resurrections, the first in which the living rise from error and the second in which the dead rise up into eternal glory. Ostensibly a celebration of the latter, *Lycidas* is actually an invitation to and exploration of the former—a poem that figures forth through the second resurrection (the moment when men take possession of eternal life) the first resurrection (the moment when they take possession of divine truth and thus enter into what Blake calls the Divine Vision).

A poem that is a prophecy, *Lycidas* emerges as a poem that is also about how to read prophecy. Commentators on the Apocalypse remark insistently that "Nothing is more common . . . in Propheticall visions . . . than to represent . . . figurative matters by . . . outward and external action."[50] Thus, in the Book of Revelation, what appears to be a record of outward history is regularly understood as the spiritual history of everyman. Analogously, in *Lycidas* what seems to be about an event involving the metamorphosis of Edward King is actually about an event, perpetually recurring, wherein "moving graves" are transformed into mantle-bearing visionaries. The promise of the Book of Revelation is thus translated into the master-theme of *Lycidas*: those who overcome their death sleep will reign in glory both in this world and in the world to come. The theme here is the theme there. The method there is the method here. In the Apocalypse, "things visible" reveal things "invisible"—"outward" events delineate the experience of the "inward man."[51] *Lycidas* thus observes what was, throughout the Renaissance, regarded as the fundamental law of prophecy—that it not be made to refer "onely to . . . particular

50. John Napier, *A Plaine Discovery of the Whole Revelation of Saint John* (Edinburgh: Printed by Robert Walde-grave, 1593), p. 231.
51. Samuel Hartlib et al., *The Revelation Reveled by Two Apocalyptical Treatises*, pp. 18–19.

occasions, and circumstances of times, of places, and of persons, in, by, and to whom [it was] uttered"; rather, prophecy universalizes such occasions and persons so that it may be "*universally understood.*"[52] Always in prophecy (and thus in *Lycidas*), there is "cortex" and "pith," which are made to "cohere one with another singularly well"[53] —the cortex, or natural death and resurrection of King, covers the real subject of Milton's poem, its pith, which is the spiritual death and resurrection of the poet and his readers, both of whom are figured in the uncouth swain. But, besides these connections, there are still others to be observed between *Lycidas* and the Book of Revelation.

Certain phrases (this is true of pastoral and epic and also of prophecy) achieve the status of generic commonplaces and thereupon can be used as a kind of shorthand for invoking generic traditions and with them certain expectations. *Yet once more* is such a phrase, as is suggested by its centrality to two prophecies, both of them later than *Lycidas* and one of them concluding that the heaven of man's making is shaken, not the heaven of God's making, which is "the Kingdom of Heaven . . . within."[54] It is the paradise within, the calm of mind, that *Lycidas* restores to the grieving poet; and this restoration comes only after the message of the Apocalypse is ingested. Within John's prophecy, to which the twelfth chapter of Hebrews is persistently related, the phrase nurtures expectations to be realized through mental revolution: building a new heaven and a new earth is predicated on renovating the world, which begins, as Pareus observes, with "the preaching of the Apostles" and continues as "spiritual renovation" that, culminating in the purification of the church, is accomplished only by first turning all the Lord's people into prophets.[55]

Milton is not the only mourner of 1637 to meditate upon the Book of Revelation or to invoke Hebrews 12 as consolation for

52. Ibid., pp. 22.

53. Henry More, *A Plain and Continued Exposition of the Several Prophecies or Divine Visions of the Prophet Daniel* (London: Printed for Walter Kettilby, 1681), p. 285.

54. See the prophecies by John Glover and Anna Maria King in *A Collection of Prophetical Warnings of the Eternal Spirit* (London: Printed by B. Bragg, 1708), pp. 78–79, 104 (the quotation above is on p. 104). See also Hartlib et al., *The Revelation Reveled by Two Apocalyptical Treatises*, pp. 75–76.

55. *A Commentary upon the Divine Revelation of the Apostle and Evangelist John*, p. 549.

the bereaved. In a commentary on Revelation, occasioned by the death of Lady Susanna Cranfield, John Trapp invokes Hebrews 12:9 by way of identifying the deceased with the young plant transplanted into paradise.[56] Milton uses the same equation in the ninth verse paragraph of *Lycidas* where his poem turns out of lamentation into rejoicing. Like the amaranthus, which was transplanted from Eden to protect it from the corruption attendant upon the fall, Edward King, rescued in his innocence, is drawn by death into a new life, into the bosom of God, where he is protected from the fallen world, one of whose manifestations is a corrupt church. Whether the meditator be Trapp or Milton, or one of their readers, what is meditated upon is the Book of Revelation; and what each meditator discovers is that the world, even with its sorrows, is rife with evidence of God's providence.

A work about the death and resurrection of the church, about its drowning at sea and then being raised up from it, such as John's Apocalypse was thought to be, could easily be appropriated for a poem about the death and resurrection of one of its members, especially when the metaphors employed by biblical commentators were strikingly literalized by Edward King's death. The church in times of trouble was like a ship upon a stormy sea: according to one commentator, "God hath set his powerfull word on the sea and floods, and set barres and dores unto them. . . . Christs word makes *Peter* walke safely on the waters" and ensures that all men who live in Christ "are safe in high floods."[57] Or as still another commentator puts it: "Peters shippe may with billowes and waves of tempestuous storms be overwhelmed, but can never be drowned."[58] God's mission is to save not just the church but its members when they are lost, to rescue them when they are drowning. This he did not just for Peter but for others:

Moses was cast on the waters, God provides him a basket. . . . *Jonas* was cast into the sea: God provides a whale. . . *Noah* was tossed on a world of floods: but God became pilot. . . .[59]

56. See *Gods Love-Tokens, and the Afflicted Mans Lessons* (London: Richard Badger, 1637), sig. A2.

57. Thomas Taylor, *Christs Victorie over the Dragon: or Satans Downfall* (London: Printed for R. Dawlman, 1633), p. 813.

58. Bullinger, *A Hundred Sermons upon the Apocalypse of Jesu Christ*, sig. Aii.

59. Taylor, *Christs Victorie over the Dragon*, p. 811.

In each instance, the situation tests God's providence; and in each situation, in God's response to it, is found evidence of his providence. The circumstances of *Lycidas* strike a clear analogy with these scriptural episodes, an analogy apparently violated by God's failure to rescue the drowning poet.

Here, then, is the dilemma of Milton's poem. Like Orpheus, King met his fate at sea; but unlike St. Peter, he was not rescued from it. Nevertheless, the same scriptural book that focuses Milton's dilemma also provides him with a resolution for it. That resolution is achieved by Milton's extrapolation of spiritual truth from literalistic narrative. God, Milton retorts, as did Henry Bullinger, renews men to life when they are dead; He raises them up to heaven. Through *Lycidas*, Milton asks how the dead, swallowed up by the sea, are to be judged; and he answers this question by asserting that the sea, obeying its maker, compelled by "Gods almightyness," yields up the dead. The metaphor of drowning at sea, yoked by Revelation commentators to the ideas of death and resurrection, is an insistent way of saying that those who go into the sea are the hardest to retrieve: they are buried the deepest; yet they also, through the agency of Christ, rise the highest.[60] Lycidas, we are told, "sunk low, but mounted high/ Through the dear might of him that walk'd the waves" (172–73).

John's Apocalypse showed both to commentators like Trapp and Bullinger and to Milton and his readers, that afflictions and sorrows are evidence not of God's wrath but of his mercy: out of them comes the perception that "the crowne of life . . . [is] wrought out unto us by the afflictions of this life," and with it the realization that this crown is the only one that matters, for connoting eternal life and happiness it "fadeth not away."[61] Given the coincidence that exists among these three meditations— two of them commentaries on the Book of Revelation, the last a poem modeled after it—it is noteworthy that both commentaries point to the Bible as "the standard of all humane writings," elevating its aesthetic, especially as it manifests itself in the Book of Revelation, over all other aesthetic systems, observing at the

60. Bullinger, *A Hundred Sermons upon the Apocalypse of Jesu Christ*, pp. 284^V–285.

61. See Trapp, *Gods Love-Tokens*, p. 64, and Pareus, *A Commentary upon the Divine Revelation of the Apostle and Evangelist John*, p. 41.

same time that this aesthetic involves a way of "seeing," of "forc[ing] open our eyes."[62]

Opening our eyes—that is finally the objective of all prophecy and the obligation of all prophets. That *Lycidas* is about the making of the prophet, the natural man's becoming the spiritual man, is confirmed by the final lines of the poem. In them, the uncouth swain, donning his mantle, stands transfigured by the experience he has undergone just as we, Milton's readers, should be transfigured by it. The primary allusion here is to the relationship of prophets: just as Elijah passes on his mantle to Elisha, Lycidas bestows his mantle on the uncourth swain and Milton passes his on to us; and as Marjorie Reeves observes, Elijah is the "prototype in the Old Testament of the new spiritual man."[63] If the first line, apparently an easy reference to pastoral convention, had hidden in it a reference to prophecy, a key for unlocking the poem's meaning, so these last lines, seemingly wrapped in pastoral cliché, have encapsulized in them a reference to the very process that *Lycidas* involves. The natural man's becoming the spiritual man is a matter of opening his doors of perception, and that process is represented in small by the way in which a pastoral allusion is overwhelmed by a prophetic one and in large by the way in which the mechanical structure derived from the pastoral tradition is subdued by the living form of prophecy.

The structure of *Lycidas* possesses all the earmarks of Revelation prophecy, and the poem itself employs all its strategies and many of its themes. There is the lonely hillside occupied by the uncouth swain in the sorrowful absence of Lycidas, a setting in which the poet experiences and from which he transmits his theophany. There are, besides, the seasonal markers of prophecy: August, the month of mortality and of King's death, a time of devastation and devouring, of affliction and woe, is set against November, the month in which *Lycidas* is composed and during which the feast of two King Edwards is celebrated, a month signifying the dawning of peace and presaging the coming of

---

62. See esp. Trapp, *Gods Love-Tokens*, sigs. [a], A12.

63. *The Influence of Prophecy in the Later Middle Ages: A Study of Joachimism* (Oxford: Clarendon Press, 1973), p. 154, and also Taaffe, *"Lycidas*—Line 192," p. 36. Valuable, too, is the note by James F. Forrest, "The Significance of Milton's 'Blue Mantle'," *Milton Quarterly*, 8 (1974), 41–48.

Christ. There is the cryptic art of prophecy evident in both the poem's rhyme scheme and its numerical symbolism, together with the cosmic dimensions achieved by looking backward to Creation and forward to Apocalypse. The story of the church's perversion, focused by the poem's epigraph and represented in Revelation commentary under the metaphor of drowning at sea, is tied to the theme of providence that steadily emerges from the poem's questionings. There is, most conspicuously, the tripartite structure and within it a repeated pattern of what Austin Farrer would call "mental music,"[64] this pattern mirroring thought processes as they shift in the movement from panel to panel of Milton's poem.

This structure finds a very precise analogy in Pareus's contention that God's is a threefold book—one section devoted to his providence, another to his universal judgment, and a last section to life everlasting (this section is a "book of life").[65] In its first section, *Lycidas* introduces the question of providence, "Where were ye Nymphs when the remorseless deep/ Clos'd o'er the head of your lov'd *Lycidas?*" (50–51), concluding, as Pareus did, "that one & the same crowne is promised to all that are faythful," this crown "promised not of desert, but of grace, as a reward freely bestowed on them that are constant in faith" (cf. *Lycidas*, 78–84). Here in his first consolation, Milton is no less insistent than Pareus had been: no man is rewarded for good works, which "merit not life" since "all are due to God."[66] In the second section of *Lycidas*, Milton banishes the philosophy that, ascribing all unfortunate occurrences to destiny, is but a "fond dreame" making "fatall periods the cause of all changes and cross-accidents."[67] The stoicism of paganism allows the answer, "It was that fatal and perfidious Bark/ Built in th' eclipse, and rigg'd with curses dark,/ That sunk so low that sacred head of thine" (100–102); but Christianity demands another resolution, which comes through the theme of justice figured by the "two-handed engine" (the two-edged sword)—an instrument not of mortal warfare but of those, like St. Peter, who are invested with the power of the divine word.

64. *A Rebirth of Images*, p. 91.
65. *A Commentary upon the Divine Revelation of the Apostle and Evangelist John*, p. 60.
66. Ibid., p. 545.
67. *Gods Love-Tokens*, sig. B4.

Here again Pareus provides a relevant gloss as he explains that "*Gods wayes* are his counsells and judgments about the Church and the enemies thereof":

> ... though he suffers the godly to be afflicted and ... troubled, and the enemies to bear sway and flourish ... [he is] righteous: ... for in the end he performs his promise to the Saints, in preserving and delivering the Church, and in punishing and destroying their adversaries.[68]

Through his judgments, God weakens Antichrist and brings both the church and her members into the liberty of Christ. This assurance is provided in the third section of Milton's poem, which is modeled on God's "third book" and which contains a vision of life everlasting, achieved for all the faithful by "the dear might of him that walk'd the waves" and emblematized by the "sweet Societies/ That sing, and singing in their glory move" (173, 179–80).

Within Milton's threefold structure, there is prophetical progression, the poem proceeding from Orpheus to St. Peter, to St. Michael, to Christ—from type to type, to manifestation, to the reality. This procession of types, together with the manifestation of Michael (who by most commentators was understood to be Christ) brings Christ to the center of this prophecy, just as he is at the center of John's. And, as in John's prophecy, each visionary panel contains a type of the Last Judgment until it is overwhelmed by the vision of the New Jerusalem. Like its model, Milton's poem is sown in sorrow but culminates in gladness—in a vision of the marriage feast; in this moment, when all things once again center in God and the Lamb, man wipes away the tears.

The promise of Milton's poem, as we have already observed, relates to the building of a new heaven and a new earth, which, in accordance with the idea Milton focuses through the epigraph of his poem (the promise to foretell "the ruin of our corrupted clergy then in their height") and subsequently develops within the boundaries of the invective against the clergy, occurs only when the deceits of the false prophets are wiped away and the church is again purified. This is what is meant, says Richard Bernard, when John speaks of a time when there will be no more crying. Like the

---

68. *A Commentary upon the Divine Revelation of the Apostle and Evangelist John*, p. 369.

Book of Revelation, *Lycidas* is written to assert God's providence in a world where the wicked seem to prosper and the innocent are afflicted with all sorts of punishments, even untimely death. To show, as John does, that "lies, falshod, violence, tyranie, false and franticke opinions, idolatrie and superstition, raign every where," while "truth, righteousenesse, vertue, & all honestie, is trodden under foote, and lieth wounded, maimed, and mangled in the mire of the streates"[69] —to show this is to invite the revolution that will set an upside-down world right side up; and that revolution will occur not by employing the tactics of Antichrist but by manifesting the virtues of Christ. In *Lycidas,* lamentation begins with the "forc'd fingers rude" (3) that pluck berries not yet ripe, a gesture rich in prophetic suggestion and pertinent to the largest objectives of Milton's poem, which are "to root out, and to pull down, and to destroy, and to throw down, to build, and to plant" (Jeremiah 1:10). Consolation comes—in biblical prophecy as in *Lycidas*—not with the promise of judgment executed by a wrathful god but with the promise of resurrection effected by a merciful one. This same promise is at the heart of *Paradise Lost.*

Against the backdrop of poetic tradition, then, *Lycidas* may be usefully studied as a prophecy; but within the context of Milton's canon, it may also be viewed as a prelude poem in the Wordsworthian sense—as a poem that records the history of the poet's mind to the point where his faculties are sufficiently matured that he may enter upon more arduous labors. Indeed, one wonders if Wordsworth's idea of the prelude poem, formulated in his Preface to *The Excursion,* did not derive from Milton himself, who, in an imaginary conversation with Tasso, remembering that he "was *long chusing, and beginning late,*" is made to acknowledge that "there must be essays and attempts . . . before any great work can be brought to perfection"; and acknowledging this, Milton claims that it was in the "unsettled state of mind" from which he wrote *Lycidas* that he "promised a greater work" which years later he accomplished.[70] *Lycidas* is thus a prospect, a particularly lofty one, from which to view Milton's later work: born out of crisis, it

---

69. Bernard, *A Key of Knowledge for the Opening of the Secret Mysteries of St. Johns Mysticall Revelation* (London: Felix Kyngston, 1617), p. 325.

70. *Il Tasso,* pp. 4–5.

reveals much about the poet; and written self-consciously, it reveals much about his art. In the act of writing *Lycidas*, Milton masters the aesthetic that derives from the Book of Revelation, and he here introduces the themes and structures that will come to figure so prominently in the last poems. For this reason, it may be said that *Lycidas* nobly confirms Blake's belief that "the production of . . . youth and of . . . mature age are equal in all identical points."[71] Like *Lycidas*, Milton's epics and tragedy take shape, substance, and strategies from the Revelation model.

Milton's Visionary Forms Dramatic

Perspectives that vie with one another in *Lycidas* are set on a collision course in *Paradise Lost*, where Milton first subverts the heroism of Satan and then, through Christ, undermines the vengeful, wrathful God of orthodox Christianity. As in the Book of Revelation, Christ is at the center; he is the chief pillar upholding the Christian religion and the perfect pattern for the heroism that the Christian warrior—a mental, not a carnal, soldier—aspires to. Even more than *Lycidas*, *Paradise Lost* is an amalgamation of forms and styles; and like the Revelation model, it is a consolidation of all that precedes it, both epic and prophecy. The very forms that are said to have been disjoined after Spenser[72] are by Milton reunited. *Paradise Lost*, its prologue makes clear, is not just an epic but a prophecy, the rhetoric of the proem invoking the one tradition and its pattern of allusion the other. To say that *Paradise Lost* is a composite of forms, however, does not mean that those forms sit comfortably beside one another. Rather, the clash of perspectives in *Paradise Lost* is paralleled by a collision of forms, which is to say that the poem's two containing forms, epic and prophecy, are "countergenres—twinned . . . yet opposite"— joined together by "generic likeness" but held in a state of dynamic tension by an overriding principle of "opposition."[73]

71. *A Descriptive Catalogue*, in Erdman, *Poetry and Prose*, p. 541.
72. See Michael Murrin, *The Veil of Allegory: Some Notes toward a Theory of Allegorical Rhetoric in the English Renaissance* (Chicago: Univ. of Chicago Press, 1969).
73. Colie, *The Resources of Kind*, p. 67.

The affinities between epic and prophecy (both are generic mixtures that attempt to replicate the design of God's universe) are sharply focused by setting Tasso's idea of epic against Richard Bernard's conception of Revelation prophecy. According to Tasso, if God's universe subdues many forms and qualities to an order, so too must the poet's:

I myself think it [variety] decidedly agreeable in the heroic poem and also possible to achieve. For just as in this marvellous domain of God called the world we behold the sky scattered over and adorned with such variety of stars, and as we descend from realm to realm, we marvel at the air and the sea full of birds and fish, and the earth host to so many animals wild and tame, with brooks, springs, lakes, meadows, fields, forests, and mountains, here fruits and flowers, there glaciers and snow, here dwellings and ploughed fields, there desert and wilderness; yet for all this, the world that contains in its womb so many diverse things is one, its form and essence one, and one the bond that links its many parts and ties them together in discordant concord, and nothing is missing, yet nothing is there that does not serve for necessity or ornament; just so, I judge, the great poet (who is called divine for no other reason than that as he resembles the supreme Artificer in his workings he comes to participate in his divinity) can form a poem in which, as in a little world, one may read here of armies assembling, here of battles on land or sea, here of conquests of cities, skirmishes and duels, here of jousts, here descriptions of hunger and thirst, here tempests, fires, prodigies, there of celestial and infernal councils, there seditions, there discord, wanderings, adventures, enchantments, deeds of cruelty, daring, courtesy, generosity, there the fortunes of love, now happy, now sad, now joyous, now pitiful. Yet the poem that contains so great a variety of matters none the less should be one, one in form and soul; and all these things should be so combined that each concerns the other, corresponds to the other, and so depends on the other necesssarily or verisimilarly that removing any one part or changing its place would destroy the whole. And if that is true, the art of composing a poem resembles the plan of the universe, which is composed of contraries, as that of music is. For if it were not multiple it would not be a whole or a plan, as Plotinus says.[74]

Correspondingly, the Book of Revelation, spreading infinitely far and wide, is said to embrace the world in all its variety:

... this book is full of similitudes fetched from every thing: *from heaven,* sun, moone, and starres: *from* the rain-bow, windes, haile, thundering, and

---

74. *Discourses on the Heroic Poem*, tr. Mariella Cavalchina and Irene Samuel (Oxford: Clarendon Press, 1973), p. 205. Cf. Augustine's *City of God* XI.18.

lightening; *from* the ayre, fire, water, sea, rivers, fountaines; *from* the earth, and earth-quakes, Ilands, and mountaines; *from* foules, fishes, beasts, and creeping things; *from* Angels, and men; *from* trees, grasse, greene hearbs; *from* wild wildernesses, and Cities inhabited; *from* warre hosts, and armies, the sword, and battell, horses and Chariots, with triumph and victorie; *from* high callings, Princes, Kings, Priests, & Prophets, Merchants, and sea-men; *from* thrones, crownes, and seates; *from* musicke, and musicians, pipers, trumpetters, harpes, viols, and sound of voices; *from* rayment, long robes, golden girdles, fine white linnen purple, silke, and scarlet. . . .[75]

Underlying these affinities between epic and prophecy, however, are ideological discrepancies, epic poetry recording and celebrating the patterns of history that prophecy, by revising them, seeks to transform. For the epic poet, the historical patterns are drawn as a model for the future; but for the prophet, those patterns are isolated and defined so that they may be altered.

In *Paradise Lost,* where the generic likeness and difference of epic and prophecy are captured within a symbolic structure, epic and prophecy exist in a tension that is dissipated only after epic is overtaken and then subdued by prophecy. Thus, to set Milton's epic within the context of Virgil's, and then to explore the twelve-book structure under its lights, may open *Paradise Lost* to the charge of "hucksterism,"[76] but to set Milton's poem within the context of prophetic tradition is to find in its structure both a statement of poetic intention and a conduit for the poem's meaning, both according with the Miltonic dictum that the great poem is doctrinal to a nation, that it irradiates the morning beam of reformation.

Milton's shift from a ten- to a twelve-book epic has often been noted but seldom explained; and the few explanations offered, however provocative, miss the real point of this structural alteration. One cannot convincingly argue that Milton's shift from one structure to another is prompted by the insistent demands of the Renaissance for an epic in twelve books, for such an argument ignores an important aspect of the epic process: poets who used this form engaged in generic competition with their precursors, claiming to outdo them and then proceeding to do just that by

75. Bernard, *A Key of Knowledge for the Opening of the Secret Mysteries of St. Johns Mysticall Revelation,* pp. 10–11.
76. See, e.g., John T. Shawcross, "The Balanced Structure of *Paradise Lost,*" *Studies in Philology,* 67 (1965), 711.

subsuming, but also expanding, their visions in markedly fewer books than were occupied by the vision of the precursor poet. There are two original models—the classical epic of Homer, composed of twenty-four books that are reduced by Virgil to twelve and by Spenser to six; and the Christian epic of Dante, built upon the one hundred units that are reduced by Ariosto (if we count his four unpublished cantos) to fifty, by Tasso to twenty, and by Camoens to ten. Thus the one tradition or the other provides a model for the different structures of *Paradise Lost,* but what either precedent shows is Milton arresting rather than continuing the process of compression that engaged one poet after another.

Doubtless, Milton invokes the Virgilian model through the final arrangement of his poem, probably not so much to indicate (as is often supposed) that his poem is an imitation of Virgil's, but to suggest, instead, that his poem strikes the same relation with Homer's as did Virgil's. Yet beyond this explanation there is another, deriving credibility from Revelation commentary and relating not so much to the strategies of Milton's epic vision as to its substance, which, in accordance with prophetic tradition, is made accessible through its structure.

Where structure is seen as prophecy, the following premise holds: "A quest for meaningful structures may lead to sudden insight into major themes for the simple reason that these structures embody these themes."[77] Among biblical commentators, the number *twelve* is regarded as "a number of most fulsome universalnesse," being related to the twelve Patriarchs, the twelve sons of Jacob, the twelve Tribes, and the twelve Apostles, and thus

---

77. Maren-Sofie Røstvig, "Structure as Prophecy: The Influence of Biblical Exegesis upon Theories of Literary Structure,'" in *Silent Poetry: Essays in Numerological Analysis,* ed. Alastair Fowler (New York: Barnes and Noble, 1970), p. 64.

This tradition of significance probably bears, too, on Milton's decision to divide *Paradise Regained* into four books. If I am right that the number twelve is chosen because it supports the purpose and theme of Milton's diffuse epic, then it is important to observe with Henry More that the number four, the "All number," "comprehends what reaches to [ten] and the Number [ten] it self [$1 + 2 + 3 + 4 = 10$]." Put differently, the number four is shorthand for the perfection signified by ten and for the apocalyptic hopes signified by twelve; as such it is the appropriate number for a brief epic, especially for one linked in a grand design with *Paradise Lost.* The same numerical tradition, it may be noted, is invoked much later by Blake: four, like twelve, "denotes the Apostolick Church," and twenty-five, "the Church Apostatizing." Significantly, Blake's *Jerusalem*—a poem about the perversion and restoration of Jerusalem (one that

being made to signify "the pure and *Apostolick Church* . . . the state of the new *Jerusalem.*" "The Embleme of the pure church"— the church purged of "false Fundamentals . . . and bad superstructures"—the number twelve, the foundation on which the New Jerusalem rests, anticipates the time "when it shall be again restored to its former purity."[78] From such a perspective, the number twelve encompasses the twelve gates of Jerusalem, the twelve angels at its gates, the twelve tribes written on the gates, the twelve foundations supporting them, the twelve furlongs, and the twelve fruits of the tree of life. The number twelve, then, is the number of Jerusalem and the number for those who, through prophecy, would create it. So pivotal is this symbology in the Book of Revelation that its implications, drawn out in *Paradise Lost,* deserve further attention.

As a symbol for Jerusalem, the number twelve is an emblem for perfect form—the world before the fall and the church before perversion. In the Apocalypse, the number applies specifically to the inner court or temple, a form that has not yet been made irregular and that, if appropriated as a model, can assist in the building up of Jerusalem.[79] Yet metamorphosis, Milton knew, was the one law governing all forms, poetical and institutional; metamorphosis, an effect of the fall, though it did not always change the shape of an experience, did alter its substance. An example was provided for Milton by the "exemplary" epic of Virgil. What did the *Aeneid* represent? We can assume that for Milton it recalled the idea of what for his age it represented—the idea of perfect form; but for Milton, who believed that form was an effect of content, that form matched idea, there was here a certain irony, for the Virgilian epic was a measure of the extent to which the

---

takes from the city its name)—is divided into four books, and each of those books is composed of twenty-five plates. See More, *Apocalypsis Apocalypseos,* pp. 196–97.

By shifting from a ten- to a twelve-book epic, Milton simply shifts the accents of his poem—away from the idea of perfect form (he does not, however, abandon the idea) to the idea of apocalypse, thereby emphasizing the poem's intentions and objectives, its design upon the real world, rather than its achievement as a work of art.

78. See Marlorate, *A Catholike Exposition upon the Revelation of Sainct John,* p. 107; Giffard, *Sermons upon the Whole Booke of the Revelation,* p. 134; and More, *An Explanation of the Grand Mystery of Godliness,* pp. xiii, 196.

79. See both Brightman, *The Revelation of S. John,* p. 71, and Mede, *The Key of the Revelation,* pp. 2–3.

classical epic had, ideologically and structurally, perverted the
Christian epic represented by the Bible. In place of the Bible's
structural intricacies, there were now easy symmetries; and in
place of the refined ethical scheme of Christianity, there were
instead the brutalities of paganism. The very form of poetry that
should, from Milton's point of view, open the gates to Jerusalem
was turned by Homer and Virgil into a great stone set as an
obstacle before those gates, blocking passage and preventing entry.
Thus, if any principle governs the many analogues between *Paradise Lost* and its classical antecedents, it is this: those analogues
invariably point to dissimilitude, and they repeatedly show Milton
reappropriating for poets the office of prophet that Homer and
Virgil abdicated. It had long been recognized that the twelve
Apostles epitomize all the prophets just as, in the Book of Revelation, they are epitomized by the two witnesses—they are the
interpreters of vision and thus the agents through which Christ
builds up the heavenly city, in accordance with the prophecy: "I
am now a building up my *Jerusalem*. I have chosen you [the
prophets] to be some of the Foundation Stones."[80] Restoring to
poets their prophetic office, Milton simultaneously returns to epic
its prophetic design, the labyrinthine structure that finds an archi-
tectural analogue in the mazes on the floors of Gothic cathedrals,
which are meant to be traveled by the pilgrim who will find
Jerusalem at their center (see fig. 6), and literary analogues in both
Chaucer's *Canterbury Tales* and Spenser's *Faerie Queene.*

In prophecy, the way out is the way in: what matters is not the
outer structure but the inner temple; indeed the form of the one is
controverted by that of the other. The pilgrim's journey (and in
Paradise Lost the pilgrims are Adam and Eve and we the readers) is
inward, through the mental spaces of his own psyche, to Jerusalem, the paradise within. The purpose of Milton's epic is not just
to tell an old story but, through that story, to raise Jerusalem in
the mental wilderness through which Adam and Eve—all human
beings in a fallen condition—must travel. This purpose is symbolized by the number twelve, the twelve books that will help man
create Jerusalem and, once created, support and maintain it; and

80. See the prophecy by E. Grey in *A Collection of Prophetical Warnings of the
Eternal Spirit,* p. 93.

this very process, emblematized by the number, is the subject of Books XI and XII of Milton's epic-prophecy.

Once regarded as "an untransmuted lump of futurity,"[81] these books are a vital part of Milton's design. As a summary vision within the poem, they act as commentary on all the others, even as they replicate the pattern of the entire epic. *Lycidas* took its structural model from those who had anatomized the Book of Revelation as a tripartite structure; *Paradise Lost* takes it from those who saw the Apocalypse as a sevenfold stucture (so it was described by David Pareus and so Milton's poem has been explained by Michael Fixler.[82]) This culminating vision repeats the pattern of the entire epic (it is not only the seventh vision but also a sevenfold vision); the prophetical progression operating throughout the epic, encapsulized in Milton's phrase, "From shadowy Types to Truth" (XII.303), is the subject of this vision, which though it may be a brief epic within a diffuse epic is also, and more importantly, a small prophecy within a larger one.

Critics have expressed dismay at Milton's shifting between Books XI and XII from vision to narration without noting that such shifts are common in prophecy. The device Milton employs here is identical with the one employed by Christ as he delivers his prophecy to St. John:

> ... he utters his narration as a chorus, or as an interlocutor in a comedy useth to do his speech, and not by vision only; wherein he opens and explains what could not by vision well have been understood, and therefore gives it by word of mouth.[83]

That Milton attributes the same strategy to Michael is to be expected: Michael was, after all, identified by most commentators with Christ. The pattern that, in this instance, arches over the last two books is the same pattern that dominates the individual visions that comprise Book XI: first there is the vision followed by

81. C. S. Lewis, *A Preface to* Paradise Lost (London and New York: Oxford Univ. Press, 1943), p. 125.

82. See "The Apocalypse within *Paradise Lost*," in *New Essays on* Paradise Lost, ed. Thomas Kranidas (Berkeley and Los Angeles: Univ. of California Press, 1969), pp. 131–78.

83. Goodwin, *An Exposition of the Revelation*, in *Works*, V, 113.

Adam's imperfect interpretation of it; then, accompanying Michael's correction of Adam's imperfect response, there is a fuller, subtler explanation of what the vision means. Book XII breaks the pattern, offering still further amplifications of what these visions contain, Michael now drawing from them their doctrinal implications. Moreover, in accordance with the Revelation model, the biblical visions of Book XI share a common pattern: each portrays, typologically, a conflict between Christ and Satan, dramatizing the struggle that plays itself out in human history and thereby moving the reader, along with Adam and Eve, to the awareness that this battle is not unending, that Christ, at various moments victorious, will be ultimately victorious. This drama of types, informing Book XI, also frames the narration of Book XII, extending from Nimrod, the great Antichrist of history, to Christ, in history, triumphing over Satan on the Cross. There is, finally, a seventh vision, this one extended to the reader, portraying Adam and Eve, repentant, being expelled from the Garden—wiping away their tears, "They hand in hand with wand'ring steps and slow/ Through *Eden* took thir solitary way" (XII.648–49). This vision is both prologue and epilogue to the others: in time it precedes them, but also in time it looks beyond them, beyond Christ's first coming to his second coming, to the time when all things will center in God and the Lamb, when man can wipe away the tears forever from his eyes.

Paradise Lost ends with the same promise that brought consolation to the poet in *Lycidas;* and like *Lycidas,* it draws upon the Book of Revelation for many of its images and most of its themes: it asserts eternal providence by demonstrating that God is just, because he is loving, forgiving, and merciful, these qualities finding their embodiment and manifestation in Christ. It is unsurprising, therefore, that Milton's last epic should be an anatomy of Christian virtues, celebrating in Christ their perfect pattern and through him the moment in which, after trial, they become fully manifested.

Lycidas and *Paradise Lost* reverbertate the prophetic tradition that informs *Paradise Regained* and *Samson Agonistes* as well. The brief epic and the tragedy, both rich in prophetic elements, require more studied attention than the following remarks provide; but then these few observations, however sketchy, draw out the implications of my earlier discussion and point in the direction that new interpretations of these poems might take.

Poets are sometimes their own best critics—and sometimes not. Milton was not, or so it would seem if we set his judgment of his epics against history's evaluation of them: Milton preferred the epic that history has since devalued. In such circumstances, it is better that we ponder what *Paradise Regained* is, rather than proclaim what it is not: it is, most importantly, a poem with its own integrity, yet one that is linked through its prologue to *Paradise Lost* and through its setting to *Samson Agonistes*. We need not here concern ourselves with when these poems were written, for even *if* they were not composed sequentially, they were published that way. Nor can we here concern ourselves with a large-scale interpretation of these poems, though, keeping in mind that Revelation commentary is concerned with how prophecy was written in order to instruct us in how it should be read, we can conjecture about how these poems, once written, were meant to be read.

Paradise Regained, often called a pendant to *Paradise Lost*, has usually been read as if it were a footnote to it; that is, the first epic is treated as a final, definitive vision and the second one as if its every line and episode were to be glossed by the earlier poem. This is, of course, an inference we can make from the fact that Milton uses the prologue of the second poem as a device for linking it to the first. But there is another inference that is possible, especially if we are exploring these poems in the light of prophetic tradition: every new vision is just that, but it is also a commentary on what it succeeds. Thus *Paradise Regained* may be understood as a poem that interprets, rather than as one interpreted by, *Paradise Lost*; and it, in turn, is interpreted by *Samson Agonistes*. These three poems, as integrated as the three prophecies that comprise the Book of Revelation, are, like those prophecies, parts of a multifaceted vision.

Milton's final vision, composed of *Paradise Lost, Paradise Regained,* and *Samson Agonistes,* is, like the Book of Revelation, tripartite in its structure; and Milton's two epics, like John's first two prophecies, are each sevenfold. This pattern, deciphered in *Paradise Lost,* is even more clearly evident in *Paradise Regained,* where a prologue and an epilogue frame (1) the stone temptation,

(2) the banquet temptation, (3–5) the *three* kingdom temptations, (6) the storm temptation, and (7) the pinnacle temptation. *Samson Agonistes,* expectedly, breaks the sevenfold pattern: parodying the Book of Revelation (its open structure), Milton's *tragedy* reverts to the closed form of its Greek models, its vision being not of man's release from the cycles of history but of man's being ground down by them. Such structural continuities unite Milton's last poems in an encompassing vision, but so too do thematic continuities.

For example, in its concluding book, *Paradise Lost* gathers into focus the idea of the Crucifixion, interpreting it only as a promise to be fulfilled somewhere down the corridors of history. In *Paradise Regained,* the meaning of this event is explored with Milton postulating, as Hugh Broughton had done, that instead of precipitating new warfare and further sacrifices the Crucifixion brings an end to them: both, says Broughton, are "ended by our Lords death . . . , and he would destroy Jerusalem that no place of sacrifice should be."[84] Such a view comprehends, with William Perkins, that "to know Christ crucified" is "the most excellent and worthy part of divine wisdome,"[85] but knowing Christ crucified also implies that one comprehends this event metaphorically. The Crucifixion signifies that we must follow Christ into the grave in order to rise with him from it: to follow Christ into the grave is to undertake the mental journey, the one mythologized in *Paradise Regained,* that culminates in the annihilation of selfhood, in donning the garments of the new man. Knowing the Crucifixion also means knowing that Christ and Samson are contrasting figures, Samson hurling down the pillars, going to his death, in order to destroy his enemies, Christ submitting to his death on the cross in order to redeem his. In the words of Perkins, Samson "slue more by his death, then by his life: so Christ . . . saved more by death then by his life."[86]

Thus the very meaning of *Paradise Regained* finds its demonic parody in *Samson Agonistes,* Milton's tragedy showing not a man

84. *A Revelation of the Holy Apocalypse* (London: n. p., 1610), p. 4.

85. *A Declaration of the True Meaning of Knowing Christ Crucified* (London: Printed by John Legate, 1611), p. 2.

86. Perkins, *Lectures upon the Three First Chapters of the Revelation* (London: Printed for Cuthbert Burbie, 1604), p. 272.

releasing other men from the cycles of history but a "hero" binding men down to them. Milton's "tragedy" is just that, showing a false apocalypse, resulting from a commitment to "mortal fight" (1175), and contrasting with the true apocalypse whose harbinger is Christ and which comes only when mankind, undergoing the experience of self-annihilation, toppling the Antichrist who has enthroned himself within the temple of the mind, begins to build, through mental fight, a Jerusalem in England's green and pleasant land. Samson is a type of those apocalyptic angels who fall from the divine vision; Christ, and Milton with him, a type of the Mighty Angel who restores to mankind the Everlasting Gospel.

The restoration of the Word, the restoration of the forms that would contain it—this is the undertaking of all prophets and the purpose of all their prophecies. Accordingly, prophets are not the authors of single poems but the shapers of large visions that would contain them all, their own and those of others. Insofar as any prophet (or any poet who aspires to be one) is the maker of a definitive vision, that vision is the canon and not a single poem within its boundaries; and insofar as that vision bursts into clarity, it does so progressively, *prophetically*. There is reciprocity, interdependency, among poems—those within the canon and those invoked as a context for it: one poem, or a whole collection of them, opens the way into what succeeds it, but then the later poem often rolls away the obscurities from the precursor poems, sharply focusing their meaning, on occasion doing this by posing against them an alternative or contending perspective, or sometimes by creating for them a subsuming perspective.

Lycidas contributes meaning to *Paradise Lost,* as do many other poems and polemics that precede the epic. However, whereas *Lycidas* vies with the other poems in the Edward King memorial volume, *Paradise Lost,* taking as its context the Book of Genesis, develops biblical themes and details the theology that in *Paradise Regained* Milton will seek to revise. Itself a subsuming structure, *Paradise Lost,* in turn, serves as a gateway into the brief epic and the tragedy; yet these poems are much more than recapitulations of the diffuse epic, and certainly they are not redactions of one another's visions. In no case does the perspective of one poem replicate that of the other: the diffuse epic is a focusing of the orthodoxies that it proceeds to demolish; the brief epic is a formulation of a new system of religion, more perfect and enduring than the one it supersedes, yet one that is tested against the contrary vision of Milton's tragedy. Or, to make the same point differently: just as the various perspectives of *Paradise Lost* clash with one another, so too do the different perspectives that emerge from *Paradise Regained* and *Samson Agonistes*. Within *Paradise Lost,* two systems of religion—that of Christian orthodoxy and Milton's own—meet head on; and when Milton's poems are set side by side—either the two epics or the brief epic and tragedy—spiritual states face one another in an eternal enmity. Yet the fact that *Paradise Regained,* having shown how the paradise within may be achieved, is complemented by a tragedy that shows how it may be lost, and the effects of its being lost, should not be construed to mean that Milton's faith in, or hopes for, an outward apocalypse are abandoned. Rather, because his faith has been so deeply challenged and because his earlier hopes have been so completely dashed, Milton distances apocalypse in the future, making it contingent upon the spiritual man's rising up against the natural man and thereupon establishing for himself and his society a new system of values.

Waiting for apocalypse—that is Milton's posture both when he completed *Lycidas* and *Paradise Lost* and when he published his brief epic "to which is added" *Samson Agonistes.* That is also the posture from which Milton's successors, Romantic ones and modern ones, have written their greatest poems. In this sense, it may be said that Milton's poetry, restoring the tradition of prophecy to perfection and then delivering that tradition to future generations of writers, looks beyond itself with forward gaze. Yet there is a sense in which Milton's poetry looks behind itself as well.

However much Morton Bloomfield, in his astute commentary on *Piers Plowman,* wished to claim Langland's poem as an example of the apocalyptic mode, he retreated from that desire, explaining that "One must . . . accept as genres only literary forms defined as such before the time of the composition of the work being considered. . . . The chief objection to taking the form of *Piers* to be an apocalypse," Bloomfield concludes, "is that it is doubtful whether such a literary form existed."[87] Bloomfield's supposition

87. Piers Plowman *as a Fourteenth-Century Apocalypse*, pp. 9, 10.

tends to confirm the popular belief that the eighteenth century began the research into prophecy that flowered in the nineteenth century; yet it also ignores the fact that Renaissance commentators registered no doubts about the generic status of prophecy, tracing their understanding of the Revelation prophecy as a finely formed genre to St. Augustine, Nicolaus Collado, and Gorran and then claiming it as the prototype for all true prophecy. From the mid-sixteenth century onward, John's Apocalypse had the same status in relation to other prophecies as Virgil's epic had in relation to other epics: though not the first, it was the best example of its kind, epitomizing the genre and yielding the aesthetic that, attributable to Christ, had for the Christian poet even more authenticity than did Aristotle's aesthetic formulated in his *Poetics.*

The status of John's Apocalypse during the Middle Ages probably bears reexamination, and its influence on Renaissance poets and poetics is a matter for further inquiry. Does the same Book that has been said to structure Book I of *The Faerie Queene* contribute to the structure of the poem as a whole? Does the Book described as a comedy and a tragedy inform Shakespeare's idea of tragi-comedy? What is its impact on plays like *Antony and Cleopatra* and *King Lear*? To what extent are poets like Sidney and Chapman—or poets like Donne and Herbert who are usually identified with another tradition of poetry—indebted to the visionary tradition described here? The elements of prophetic tradition are to be found everywhere in Milton, in the efforts of his left hand no less than in the achievements of his right hand. Yet the presence of many of these same elements in his precursors makes Milton a less singular poet, though such a recognition should not be allowed to blur Milton's singular achievement: the great consolidator of prophetic tradition, Milton is also its most distinguished purveyor.

There is no more evident link between the tradition of prophecy, *the Milton tradition,* and the Romantic poets than their eagerness to elevate historical figures, Milton and themselves, into the eschatological position of apocalyptic angels. This constellation of poets, whose greatest star is Milton, regarded themselves as the spiritual men who would usher in a new order and a new age: like their precursor, they saw it as their calling to embody in themselves the spiritual life of the new age and, at the same time, to lead the pilgrimage toward it. The correlative to the centuries-old tradition of historicizing Antichrist, of seeing him in Pope or High Priest, in Monarch or Ruler, is the historicizing of Christ, which involves the belief that he will reign over the new age in spirit, through the apocalyptic angels (the poets and prophets) who, as "Authours," are "guides and Captains"—Christ's emissaries effecting the reformation of mankind.[88] For Blake and for the other Romantics, Milton is a type of the *renovator mundi,* a liberator rather than an oppressor, who, like other such figures, appears under a number of guises—as *Corrector, Reparator, Reformator.* Milton, for these poets, is the great prophet who stands between the ancient and the modern world.

It has been said that "prophecy was . . . one of the bonds between medieval and Renaissance thought"; but whether, after the Renaissance, it ceased to be important, "except on the fringe of modern civilization," is another matter.[89] From the standpoint of literary history, prophecy is a link between Milton's poetry and Sidney's poetic, and an absolute bond between Milton's poetry and that of Chaucer, Langland, and Spenser—their poetry, in its generic mixtures, rhetorical strategies, and labyrinthine structures, finding major analogues, if not a primary source, in prophetic tradition. But prophecy is also the bridge thrown up over time, uniting Milton with Romantic poets and modern ones. Not only is prophecy kindling for Romantic poetry; it is "the main fuel of the 'inclusive' flame that is American poetry."[90] From the perspective of literary history, Milton may thus be seen at the center of a poetic tradition that, extending from the Middle Ages into the modern world, also reaches beyond national boundaries to form cultural ones.

---

88. Mede, *The Key of the Revelation,* p. 82.

89. Reeves, *The Influence of Prophecy in the Later Middle Ages,* p. 508. For a provocative discussion of how this tradition, secularized, impinges upon Romantic poetry, see M. H. Abrams, *Natural Supernaturalism: Tradition and Revolution in Romantic Literature* (New York: W. W. Norton, 1971).

90. Glauco Cambon, *The Inclusive Flame: Studies in Modern American Poetry* (Bloomington: Indiana Univ. Press, 1965), p. 52. Two studies related to the concerns of this essay, but appearing too late to be taken into account, are William Kerrigan's *The Prophetic Milton* (Charlottesville: Univ. of Virginia Press, 1974) and Austin C. Dobbins's *Milton and the Book of Revelation,* Studies in the Humanities, No. 7 (University: Univ. of Alabama Press, 1975).

Blake Encountering Milton:
Politics and the Family in
Paradise Lost *and* The Four Zoas

JACKIE DISALVO

A study of poetic influence presumes a theory of history. And no poet was more conscious of influence than William Blake, who made the "enormous work" of understanding his roots the articulate center of his major poems. Two sources stand out above all others—the Bible and John Milton—and not simply because biographical accident makes Blake a Christian and an Englishman. Without subjectivity or parochialism, Blake places the question of his sources at the center of an epic of the entire human race, making the comprehension of his relationship to the Bible and Milton a path to the comprehension of universal history.[1]

1. The Blake-Milton relationship is a focus of increasing critical attention. Some noteworthy studies which deal with the subject are: (1) Harold Bloom, *The Anxiety of Influence: A Theory of Poetry* (New York: Oxford Univ. Press, 1973); (2) Leslie Brisman, *Milton's Poetry of Choice and Its Romantic Heirs* (Ithaca: Cornell Univ. Press, 1973); (3) Florence Sandler, "The Iconoclastic Enterprise: Blake's Critique of Milton's Religion," *Blake Studies*, 5 (1972), 13–57; (4) Joseph Anthony Wittreich, Jr., "Opening the Seals: Blake's Epics and the Milton Tradition," in *Blake's Sublime Allegory: Essays on The Four Zoas, Milton, Jerusalem*, ed. Joseph Anthony Wittreich, Jr., and Stuart Curran (Madison: Univ. of Wisconsin Press, 1973), pp. 23–58, and also his article, "'Sublime Allegory': Blake's Epic Manifesto and the Milton Tradition," *Blake Studies*, 4 (1972), 15–44. I myself have already published one relevant essay, "William Blake on the Unholy Alliance—Satanic Freedom and Godly Repression in Liberal Society," *The Wordsworth Circle*, 3 (1972), 212–22, which deals with the relationship of Blake and Milton to the development of the bourgeois state. I am at work on an additional essay, which will complement the present one, on their relationship to the historical origins of the family.

For Blake humanity is its history. In *The Four Zoas,* the story of Albion the Eternal Man's "Fall into Division & his Resurrection to Unity" (4:4),[2] Blake recounts the social, cultural, and psychological history of the human race from its dim origins recorded in ancient myth to its present struggles and apocalyptic possibilities. That epic makes continuous, overlapping reference to the Bible and to Milton because Blake has identified in them the two crucial events in human development. The first event is expressed in both the Bible and ancient myth as a loss of paradise; it marks the transformation of tribal society into "civilization," and Blake anticipates Frederick Engels's identification of that transformation with *The Origin of the Family, Private Property and the State.*[3] Blake takes his rendition of the fall, not only from ancient sources, but from Milton's *Paradise Lost* because he finds there the echo of a second great human catastrophe, deepening the direction of the first. Because the revolution made by the English bourgeoisie in the seventeenth century built upon the institutions forged in the ancient patriarchal revolution, Milton could find no better symbol to express that revolution than the myth of a primal human catastrophe. In the life of collective humanity, as in those toy boxes with collapsible bottoms, one fall prepares for the next.

Milton becomes the key to all human history and human consciousness because it was the seventeenth-century English bourgeoisie that first wrapped history in a ball and rolled it toward the overwhelming questions of human development. There is no society in the world today that is not being defined by its relation to the values and institutions of Milton's England. As a spokesman of the Puritan revolution, Milton articulated the values that enabled mankind to liberate itself from the shackles of feudalism, creating at the same time new fetters in their stead.[4] Blake turns

2. All Blake quotations are from *The Poetry and Prose of William Blake,* ed. David V. Erdman, rev. ed. (Garden City, N.Y.: Doubleday, 1970). Citations are usually to page and line number of Blake's manuscript; with short poems the reference is to the page of the Erdman text.

3. See Engels in the edition by Eleanor Leacock (New York: International Publishers, 1972). For the link between ancient history and the myth of paradise, see Joseph Campbell, *The Masks of God: Occidental Mythology* (New York: Viking Press, 1964), and George Thomson, *Studies in Ancient Greek Society: The Prehistoric Aegean* (London: Lawrence and Wishart, 1949).

4. See my essay, "'The Lord's Battells': *Samson Agonistes* and the Puritan Revolution," *Milton Studies,* 4 (1972) 39–62, and my article mentioned in n. 1 above.

to Milton for his espousal of freedom but also for his expression of its bourgeois limitations. Milton gave otherwise invisible, unconscious ideological assumptions and psychological experiences a concrete form, and thus resembles the prophet Los who, in *Jerusalem*, gives "a body to Falshood that it may be cast off for ever" (12:13). Whereas commentators such as A. J. A. Waldock attack Milton's poetry for its inconsistencies, Blake is indebted to Milton's epic for its exposure of the contradictions at the heart of our culture.[5] Milton's art has not failed, but succeeded so brilliantly in expressing those fundamental dilemmas that Blake's struggle to transform society can take the form of a struggle to transform Milton's myth.

Within this broad context, I will explore Blake's encounter with Milton, focusing on only one institution whose conflicts Blake found captured in *Paradise Lost*—the bourgeois family. In *The Four Zoas* Blake reads Milton's epic, on one level, as a record of the collective trauma suffered by the middle class with the capitalist transformation of the family. Blake's clarity here arises from the fact that he views middle-class family values from the vantage of another class and another era, and thus sees them, in "The Garden of Love," encroaching for the first time upon other modes of experience:

> I went to the Garden of Love
> And saw what I never had seen.
> A Chapel was built in the midst,
> Where I used to play on the green.

(p. 26)

Seeing the chapels, the factories, and the mind-forged manacles of the bourgeois family where they never had been, Blake comprehends them as part of a common system, whose historical limitations he grasps, challenging its assumptions and prophesying its end. Struggling, as so many of his characters do, to utter the voice of man, Blake articulates the working class's anguish at the horrors of nineteenth-century capitalism, which would swallow it into the vortexes of bourgeois ideology.

When, in *Milton*, Blake challenges the Puritan bard to criticism and self-criticism, he has him reject two errors of his "Spectre,"

---

5. *Paradise Lost and Its Critics* (Cambridge: Cambridge Univ. Press, 1947).

or false consciousness: his "selfhood" (bourgeois individualism)
and his sexism (his domination of women). In *Jerusalem* Blake
identifies both the denial of the community and the repression of
the individual with the patriarchal family:

> Is this thy soft Family-Love
> Thy cruel Patriarchal pride
> Planting thy Family alone,
> Destroying all the World beside.
>
> A mans worst enemies are those
> Of his own house & family . . .
> (27:77–82)

Henry Crabb Robinson reports a pertinent conversation in which
Blake announced, "I saw Milton in Imagination. And he told me
to beware of being misled by his *Paradise Lost*. In particular he
wished me to shew the falsehood of his doctrine that the pleasures
of sex arose from the fall—the fall could not produce any pleasure." "And then," Robinson continues, "he went off upon a
rambling state of a Union of Sexes in Man as in God—an androgynous state—in which I could not follow him."[6] In *The Four
Zoas* Blake performs that service of rewriting *Paradise Lost,* eliminating those errors with regard to sex and the family deriving from
Milton's "Spectre."

In examining both poems we find that Blake and Milton seem
to agree in associating Eden with erotic fulfillment and the fall
with the advent of sexual alienation. Milton presents Adam and
Eve "Imparadis't in one anothers arms/ The happier *Eden*" (*PL*
IV.506–7). Sexual communion touches the essence of paradise,
functioning as a kind of sacrament of universal harmony. The
lovers' intense unity, "one Flesh, one Heart, one Soule"
(VIII.499), is part of their loving interaction with the cosmos itself
through the medium of their heightened sensibilities. All nature
participates in their love-making as "on their naked limbs the flourie
roof/ Showrd Roses" (IV.772–73), and their erotic sensitivity
extends to an Eden personified as a living, breathing body
(IV.133–63, 215–48). Blake calls this paradise of unfallen eroticism Beulah, the "married land," emphasizing the same dual

---

6. *Blake Records*, ed. G. E. Bentley, Jr. (Oxford: Clarendon Press, 1969), p. 544.

harmony of human beings with each other and their environment. Similarly he portrays Los and Enitharmon both as primal lovers and as the mythic representatives of the relationship between the human subject and the material world "in those mild fields of happy Eternity/ Where thou & I in undivided Essence walkd about/ Imbodied. thou my garden of delight & I the spirit in the garden" (84:4–6).

The immediate consequence of the fall, for both Milton and Blake, is the degeneration of sexuality. When Blake cries in *Jerusalem* that "Shame hath divided Albion in sunder!" (21:6), he is echoing Milton's dramatization of fallen love. Consciousness, which once expanded in the exultation of love, now appears only as a barrier that must be obliterated by intoxication (*PL* IX.1008), as the teasing, flattering lovers draw each other against the brakes of each other's wills. The subjects of human communion are reduced to the objects of each other's hunger, and Adam even acknowledges that it is prohibition, more than desire, that arouses him (IX.1024–26). This perversion, the conjunction of desire and denial, has turned the lovers against their own bodies, of which they are now ashamed (IX.1093–94); against each other; and, in a general shriveling of their sensuous capacities, against the environment, which is transformed from a cosmic body embraced in love to a hiding place for the naked human spirit, crouching within the walls of its own skin (IX.1084–90).

Recapitulating these splits dramatized by Milton, Blake asserts that the paradise lost was man's own unrepressed material life "In Eden; in the Auricular Nerves of Human Life" (4:1). The fall, Milton's "agonie of love till now/ Not felt" (IX.858), becomes in the subtitle to Blake's poem "The Torments of Love and Jealousy in the Death and Judgment of Albion . . . . " Blake, however, goes beyond Milton in asserting that man's alienation from his body is not just a result of the fall; it is the fall itself. Man's desires have become hostile forces, "secret monsters of the animating worlds . . . " (82:7), with which he is at war. His senses have shrunken and turned inward till "bones of solidness froze over all his nerves of joy" (54:14), and the world, cut off thereby from the grasp of human consciousness, has become alien and opaque: "Thy roses that expanded in the face of glowing morn/ Hid in a little silken veil scarce breathe and faintly shine" (81:33–82:1).

Finally, as with Milton's lovers, a veil is draped over the genitals to hide their newly discovered shame. The bars on the gates of paradise are the barriers to genital intercourse:

> Three gates within Glorious & bright open into Beulah
> From Enitharmons inward parts but the bright female terror
> Refusd to open the bright gates she closd and barrd them fast
> Lest Los should enter into Beulah thro her beautiful gates . . .

                                                                            (20:4–7)

All this amounts, for Blake, to a "Fall into Division" (4:4). This division is, first of all, an alienation of the sexes, of Tharmas and Enion, Los and Enitharmon, Luvah and Vala, Urizen and Ahania, who are torn apart by their conflicts with their own forbidden desires. *The Four Zoas* opens upon Tharmas and Enion reenacting the agonies of Adam and Eve who "in mutual accusation spent/ The fruitless hours" (*PL* IX.1187–88). Torn from each other by the conflicting demands of denial and desire, Enion cries, "Once thou wast to Me the loveliest son of heaven—But now/ Why art thou Terrible and yet I love thee in thy Terror"; and Tharmas replies in despair, "my Emanations are become harlots . . . O Enion thou art thyself a root growing in hell/ Tho thus heavenly beautiful to draw me to destruction" (4:19–20, 35, 38–39).

The division of the sexes, and the alienation of one's own sexuality, involve finally a self-division. Enion splits off from Tharmas and, in doing so, divides Tharmas against himself, creating his "Spectre" (5:15–16). In fragmenting each Zoa into a Spectre, Blake dramatizes the psychological schizophrenia of Christian doctrine as in St. Paul:

For I do not the good which I want but the evil I do not want is what I do. Now if I do what I do not want it is no longer I that do it, but sin which dwells within me. . . . For I delight in the law of God in my inmost self, but I see in my members another law at war with the law of my mind. . . . the law is spiritual but I am carnal.

                                                                   (Romans 7:15–24)

Blake's world-view eschews this idea "that Man has two real existing principles: Viz: a Body & a Soul. That Energy. calld Evil. is alone from the Body. & that Reason. calld Good. is alone from the Soul" (*The Marriage,* plate 4); and here Blake's analysis diverges from Milton's.[7] Although he bases his own interpretation of human fulfillment and misery on Milton's depiction of paradise and the fall, Blake rejects Milton's assertion that the cause of "all our woe" is sin. Attributing that error to Milton's own Spectre, Blake builds his analysis on the cracks and contradictions in Milton's story.

If we examine Milton's reasons for the loss of Eden, it seems at first that the passage from a world of pleasure to one of sorrow and toil, of sexual neurosis, alienation from nature, and the battle of the sexes, is just an arbitrary punishment for an act of primal naughtiness in which the first children broke a paternal command and dipped into the divine cookie jar. However, looking more closely, we find that the prohibition against the fruit of the Tree of Knowledge was not God's "Sole command"; rather, Milton portrays the fall as a breach of three separate laws written into the structure of Eden: (1) the obligation to restrain sexual desire, (2) the need to maintain a sexual hierarchy, (3) an obligation of absolute filial obedience to these and any other rules laid down by the "Almighty Father." Since these assumptions are precisely those upon which the bourgeois family is built, they lead us into the heart of the contradictions within Milton and his culture.

Christopher Hill notes that "Adam's fall was not due to pride or intellectual curiosity, as it well might have been if Milton had followed Genesis and the commentators. It was due to love, love for a woman."[8] In having Adam "fondly overcome with Femal charm" (IX.999), Milton builds into his epic what some critics have considered a contradiction. Adam loses Eden by trying to preserve that very unity which was its essence. "Flesh of Flesh,/ Bone of my Bone," he cries at the moment of his fall, "How can I live without thee?" (IX.914–15, 908).

This contradiction is built into Milton's attitude toward sexual love. On the one hand, he celebrates "the Rites/ Mysterious of

7. For Blake's attitude towards the matter-spirit dualism, see Stuart Curran, "Blake and the Gnostic Hyle: A Double Negative," *Blake Studies*, 4 (1972), 117–33. Milton, it has been noted, leans towards a less dualistic view in his prose, particularly his *De Doctrina Christiana*. See, for example, Denis Saurat, *Milton, Man and Thinker* (London: J. M. Dent, 1925), pp. 116–18, and Arthur Sewell, *A Study in Milton's Christian Doctrine* (London: Oxford Univ. Press, 1939), pp. 180–81.

8. *The World Turned Upside Down* (New York: Viking Press, 1972), p. 322.

connubial Love" (IV.742–43); on the other, he has Raphael warn
Adam, "in loving thou dost well, in passion not" (VII.588). Milton
alternately elevates sexual love to a holy passion and denigrates it
as the activity of "Cattle and each Beast" (VII.582). When the
forbidden fruit turns out to be an aphrodisiac, it suggests that the
divine bans were always against eroticism. The schizophrenic,
fallen consciousness of Adam and Eve reflects that of Milton
himself.

Adam's failure to put love in its "proper" place, moreover,
involves not only excessive carnality, but excessive affection, an
overestimation of Eve—a failure to put Eve in her place. Thus
Christ chastises him, "Was shee thy God, that her thou didst
obey? . . . that to her/ Thou did'st resigne thy Manhood" (X.145,
147–48). In her article on kinship patterns in *Paradise Lost* Marcia
Landy shows that Milton has laid out a whole system of sexual
subordination.[9] Adam and Eve were "Not equal, as thir sex not
equal seemd . . . / Hee for God only, shee for God in him" (IV.
296, 299). Eve's fall will therefore take on an aura of conscious
rebellion against male domination. Seduced by one who has succeeded in "ventring higher then my lot" (IX.690), she justifies her
act, "for inferior who is free?" (IX.825).

Blake puts his finger on Milton's dilemma when he has Enion
cry, "Can Love seek for dominion?" (41:12). The problem was
implicit in the Puritan conception of marriage, of which William
Haller says:

> Though the wife was bound to obey the husband, the husband was bound
> to love the wife, and each was to render without restraint or difference what
> was named "due benevolence" to the other. It was this relationship of love
> and obedience, reciprocal, inseparable, exclusive and unique, which made
> marriage in truth, the image of nothing less than Christ's relation to his
> Church.[10]

In the myriad sermons and conduct books wherein the Puritans
defined their nuptial ideals, they harped precisely upon this compatibility of love and dominion. Given such doctrines, Levin L.

---

9. "Kinship and the Role of Women in *Paradise Lost*," *Milton Studies*, 4 (1972),
3–18.

10. "Hail Wedded Love," *ELH*, 13 (1946), 84.

Schucking remarks in *The Puritan Family,* Eve appears as a dramatization of the chapters entitled "Feminine Weakness."[11] This
denigration of women was a Christian tradition taken from St.
Paul, for whom the husband is head of the wife (I Corinthians
11:3). However, when the medieval fathers denounced "filthy
woman, filthy matter," they did so as an encouragement to
celibacy. What is new in the seventeenth century is the attempt to
reconcile the doctrine of feminine inferiority with the elevation of
marriage.

In addition, it had been assumed formerly that love and marriage might be incompatible. The Jewish patriarchs took wives to
beget sons—hence, biblical marriage-deals of incredible complexity. Greek mythology reveals a world of erotic adventure, but
not of sentimental monogamy, and the great Athenians exalted a
"love" which was both extramarital and homosexual. In the rules
of medieval chivalry, love is by its nature adulterous. C. S. Lewis
argues that the association of love with marriage only begins in the
sixteenth century with Shakespeare and Spenser leading their
lovers to the altar rail in what is now the ultimate happy ending.[12]

Milton and the Puritan preachers reflect this same historical
phenomenon. Although the Anglican wedding ceremony listed
three objects of marriage—the procreation of children, the relief of
concupiscence, and "the mutual help and comfort that one ought
to have of the other"[13] —the ministers now emphasized the last:

> They exhorted the young to choose helpmeets with godly companionship as
> the chief end to be desired. . . . They exhorted parents not to interfere with
> such promptings in the hearts of their children. A wife they said was to be
> regarded not simply as a bedfellow or a servant, but as a spiritual equal and
> companion. The later preachers especially dilated upon the joys of spiritual
> union of the flesh, and upon the misery of those who, coupled in body, were
> divided in soul. The most enthusiastic went so far as to say that husbands and
> wives, in communing with one another, came nearer to communion with God
> himself.[14]

11. *The Puritan Family* (New York: Schocken, 1970), p. 111.

12. *The Allegory of Love: A Study in Medieval Tradition* (London: Oxford Univ.
Press, 1953).

13. William and Malleville Haller, "The Puritan Art of Love," *Huntington Library
Quarterly*, 5 (1942), 239.

14. Haller, "Hail Wedded Love," pp. 84–85.

These conceptions, traced back to the Edenic marriage of Adam and Eve, pervade Milton's epic. However such views also underlie his *Doctrine and Discipline of Divorce*, where, quoting Paulius Fagius, he argues *"that indisposition, unfitnes or contrariety of mind, arising from a cause in nature unchangeable, hindring and ever likely to hinder the main benefits of conjugall society, which are solace and peace, is a greater reason of divorce then naturall frigidity"* (*CM*, III, ii, 388).

The problem is that if these ideals are taken seriously, every marriage will appear to be hindered by "a contrariety of mind arising from a cause in nature unchangeable"—namely the intellectual inferiority of all women. Milton faced this dilemma in his own marriage to Mary Powell when his high hopes for "the cheerful conversation of man with woman" were dashed by his discovery that the "bashfull mutenes of a virgin" in fact could reflect an "unlivelines and naturall sloth" (*CM*, III, ii, 394) and, he might have added, an inferior education. When Milton banished Eve from angelic instruction he failed to understand that with women rendered defective in Reason, real communion is impossible, and all sexuality is degraded.

This is the hidden contradiction in Edenic love. Eve's love for Adam is a mixture of dependency and self-hatred; Adam's love for Eve is perverted by superiority and arrogance. Raphael recommends self-esteem to Adam ("weigh with her thy self;/ Then value" [VIII.570–71]), but Eve must repudiate her own image in the pool and acknowledge that her beauty is "excelld by manly grace" (IV.490). Her fall, therefore, is an attempt both to restore her own injured self-love, "so to add what wants/ In Femal Sex," and "the more to draw his Love" (IX.821–22). Like so many women after her, Eve finds herself in an inferior position that renders her dependent on Adam for her very identity, at the same time that it makes her feel unworthy and insecure in his love. Caught in this double bind, she has to destroy the relationship in order to save it.

Adam, on the other hand, finds his feelings torn between desire for a companion and contempt for an inferior. His fall reflects the experience of Everyman who passes from idealization of a woman as a goddess to contempt for her feminine limitations, spurning his earlier love as mere lust for a beautiful object. But Adam should

have anticipated this; for he had, after all, refused for that reason
to find a companion among the animals, complaining, "Among
unequals what societie" (VII.383).

"Among unequals what society . . . ?"; "for inferior who is
free?"—these lines which needle Milton's poem become, in effect,
the center of Blake's recreation of it in *The Four Zoas*. Ruled by
the patriarchal Urizen under the codes of male supremacy, the
poem captures the agony of a world divided between phallic
aggression and feminine passivity. The "male forms without female counterparts" are "Cruel and ravening with Enmity & Hatred
& War" in their obsessive "Domineering lust" (85:19—20, 31). The
females are cunning in their subservience, "for we are weak wom-
en & dare not lift/ Our eyes to the Divine pavilions" (56:3—4).
Urizen, like the other Zoas, casts off his wife, Ahania, rejecting
emotion for power:

> Shall the feminine indolent bliss. the indulgent self of weariness
> The passive idle sleep the enormous night & darkness of Death
> Set herself up to give laws to the active masculine virtue [.]
>
> (43:6—8)

In response the females seek to control the men through manipula-
tion and through the passive aggression of sexual withdrawal.
Enitharmon declares Los, her master, "Created for my will my
slave tho strong tho I am weak," for "The joy of woman is the
Death of her most best beloved/ Who dies for Love of her/ In
torments of fierce jealousy" (34:46, 63—65).

Blake's critique of sexual inequality links the sexual politics of
male domination to the very differentiation of male and female
roles.[15] Milton had assumed that sex roles were created in Adam
and Eve, "For contemplation hee and valour formd/ For softness
shee and sweet attractive Grace" (IV.297—98). Blake, however,
turns the patriarchal myth of woman created out of man into a
symbol of the fragmentation of humanity, through the separation
of the feminine into a separate being:

> And Many Eternal Men sat at the golden feast to see
> The female form now separate They shudderd at the horrible thing

---

15. For Blake's attitude toward the female role, see Irene Tayler, "The Woman
Scaly," *Bulletin of the Midwest Modern Language Association*, 6 (1973), 74—87.

> Not born for the sport and amusement of Man but born to drink up
> all his powers
> They wept to see their shadows they said to one another this is Sin . . .
>   (133:5–8)

For "Man," as Blake told Henry Crabb Robinson, was originally androgynous, "a Union of Sexes in Man as in God."[16] In *Jerusalem*, Blake recounts the catastrophe in which "The Feminine separates from the Masculine & both from Man,/Ceasing to be His Emanations, Life to Themselves assuming!" and cries, "O Vala! Humanity is far above/ Sexual organization . . . " (90:1–2; 79:73–74).

In their vision of the fall in *The Four Zoas*, the Eternals reveal the cause of this "Sexual Organization": "In families we see our shadows born" (133:21). We can only really comprehend sexual repression and the division of the sexes in the context of the patriarchal family, and the profundity of *Paradise Lost* lies in the fact that we are always simultaneously aware of Adam and Eve as siblings as well as spouses, whose every conjugal embrace takes place under the eyes of a hovering parent. We are thereby forced to consider the connection between the relationship of parent to child and the adult forms of marriage and love.

Much has been written about Milton's transformation of the epic, replacing an ideal of active or military heroism with one of spiritual heroism. We may now note that he does so by telescoping an entire cosmic drama into the everyday conflicts of domestic relations. A child rebels against a parental command; she gets her brother to share her naughtiness; they both are caught and punished. A lover is torn between his father and his wife. A disobedient son is disinherited, while an obedient son is appointed heir. A young couple is banished from the parental estate. The message seems to be that the struggle for psychological integrity within the patriarchal family is heroism enough.

Milton's contradiction may now be focused more sharply. If we actually examine his praise of "Wedded Love," we find that Milton has linked in those two words two very different phe-

---

16. In the awkwardness of the present moment in the transformation of the language of sex, I will go along with Blake in using "Man" to refer to the species and not just the male.

nomena—on the one hand, "love" as an experience of being-at-one-with-the-world, and on the other hand, the social institution of patriarchal monogamy:

> Haile wedded Love, mysterious Law, true source
> Of human ofspring, sole proprietie,
> In Paradise of all things common else.
> By thee adulterous lust was driv'n from men
> Among the bestial herds to raunge, by thee
> Founded in Reason, Loyal, Just, and Pure,
> Relations dear, and all the Charities
> Of Father, Son, and Brother first were known.
>
> (IV.750–57)

In this celebration of marriage Milton identifies it with the end of sexual freedom, with private property and male domination, the very characteristics condemned by Blake.

Contrastingly, in *The Four Zoas*, marriage is shown as the opposite of love. The fall of the Zoas and their female emanations is also a wedding:

> And Los and Enitharmon sat in discontent & scorn
> The Nuptial Song arose from all the thousand thousand spirits[.]
>
> (13:19–20)

The poem begins as Enion's imposition of monogamy causes Tharmas's fall: "Lost! Lost! Lost! are my Emanations Enion O Enion . . ./ Why hast thou taken sweet Jerusalem from my inmost Soul" (4:6,10). Connecting monogamy with the same selfish individualism as private property, Blake makes the nuptial song a song of war, slavery, and human misery.

The stern chastity of marriage, according to Blake, arises not from love but from jealousy and Urizen's patriarchal reign of repression:

> . . . I whose labours vast
> Order the nations separating family by family
> Alone enjoy not I alone in misery supreme
> Ungratified . . .
>
> (121:15–18)

The problematic relationship of Adam and Eve must similarly be seen in the context of divine patriarchy. By centering his epic around an incident of feminine and filial rebellion Milton took on the politics of the family. Although he condemned human beings, not the "divine" order, some unrelinquished ties to the devil's party enabled him to portray the conflicts in patriarchy with sufficient clarity that the poem's triumphant moments remain, not with God, the validator of hierarchy, but with a Satanic son and a rebellious woman who cut through righteous pretenses to the realities of power—that "great Forbidder, safe with all his Spies/ About him" (IX.815–16).

The Puritans made the patriarchal family the center of their social order. "The household," Christopher Hill writes, "was almost a part of the constitution of the state."[17] Thus in 1641 a Puritan preacher urged Parliament, "First reform your families, and then you will be fitter to reform the family of God."[18] The father became a magistrate and, as lay piety replaced Catholic ritual, a minister within his own home. Thus William Gouge wrote, "A family is a little Church and a little Commonwealth whereby tryal is made of such as are fit for any place of authority. . . ." [19] And Richard Sibbes commented that "the word *Father* is the epitome of the whole Gospel."[20]

In order to understand the importance of the family, we must examine the broader social picture. The basic unit of feudal society had been the manor. Authority was vested in the lord, who controlled the land by custom and military might, and ruled it through his intermediaries, his bailiffs and clergy. The peasants labored communally on the lord's fields, as well as on their own plots scattered throughout the common fields. The family was therefore immersed in larger units. The peasant's life centered about the village and the parish church, which administered education, welfare, and even justice. The noble's family was lost in the large castle retinue of soldiers, guests, kin, entertainers, and animals.

Marriage was primarily an economic affair. For the serf it was a means of transferring land and begetting fellow laborers to till it.

17. *Puritanism and Society in Pre-Revolutionary England* (New York: Schocken, 1964), p. 448.
18. Quoted by Hill, p. 444.
19. *Domesticall Duties* (London, 1622), pp. 16–17.
20. *Works*, ed. A. B. Grosart (Edinburgh, 1862–64), V, 25.

The nobility married in order to unite adjacent estates, forge diplomatic ties, and extend their rule. With such weighty matters at stake, marriage could not be left to the vagaries of human emotions, which were accommodated, in any event, through the double standard and a tolerant attitude toward illegitimate children. Peasant morality, sanctioned by church custom, held that children were legitimized once marriage ensued. Thus, for all the rantings of the celibate clergy, there was in medieval society, as any reading of Chaucer will indicate, a tolerance of sexuality as part of the weakness of all flesh and a pragmatic attitude toward the marriage vow.[21]

Moving from Chaucer to Milton one notices a drastic change. This alteration in morals reflects the new conditions of the middle class. The middle-class farm and workshop has separated itself off from the communal production of the manor; it has hedged in its private property and established the "household" as the basic social unit, including the nuclear family as well as those servants and apprentices bound to it in the family economy. "Who anywhere," asks a London preacher in 1608, "but is of some man's family and within some man's gates?"[22] The answer would be only the poor, day laborers, vagabonds, and those still able to eke subsistence out of little cottage plots after the enclosure of private property robbed the peasantry of access to the forests and fields while destroying the village economy.

Within this new system, the father as the owner of the property, the householder, is quite literally the boss of those within his walls. His relationship to his family, as to his apprentices, is determined by the family economy. When the Puritan preachers exalt the authority of "fathers," it is to these "chief fathers, ancients and governors of the parish,"[23] that they refer, not to every biological sire. These alone voted, paid taxes, directed the parish, and administered the poor laws. Moreover, as feudal so-

21. For discussion of the different sexual ethos of the noble, peasant, and middle classes, see Sheila Rowbotham, *Women, Resistance and Revolution* (New York: Random House, 1974); and Eli Zaretsky, "Capitalism, the Family and Personal Life," *Socialist Revolution* (Spring, 1973), 69–126.

22. In Keith Thomas, "Women and the Civil War Sects," in *Crisis in Europe, 1560–1600*, ed. Trevor Aston (Garden City, N.Y.: Doubleday, Anchor, 1967), p. 332.

23. William Stoughton, *An Assertion for True and Christian Church-Policie* (London, 1604), pp. 205–47.

ciety broke down in this period before the development of police departments, public schools, and the welfare state, all these functions of the community fell upon the household. In 1659, for example, the Mayor of London sought to prevent civil disturbances by charging all heads of households with responsibility for policing their dependents. Eve is not far off in attacking her "Almighty Father" as a kind of domestic cop. The power of fathers increased proportionately to the atomization of the society. Thus Christopher Hill writes, "In the great conflict of our period between the ethos appropriate to a society composed of feudal households, and the ethos appropriate to an individualistic society, the Puritan emphasis on the duties of small householders played an important part."[24]

These changes in the functions of the family are behind the alterations in family relationships. The relationship of husband and wife ceases to be a mere formality for linking family names and becomes the crux of the day-to-day activities of the household economy. This change requires a new stability, leading to an emphasis on voluntary marriage and compatibility, and a condemnation of child marriages, adultery, and the double standard, which, in any case, would squander the family capital on mistresses and bastards.

Over this new economic partnership the preachers raised the banner of "love," by which they meant, not the unpredictable flux of emotion, but a voluntary commitment to cooperation and harmony. Woman, moreover, is redefined from a breeder of heirs to a "help-meet." Declaring her a "spiritual equal," the preachers condemn such abuses as wife-beating. In fact, as Alice Clark documents, the new economic conditions often resulted in actual diminution of woman's social power.[25] Aristocratic women had been able to inherit land and consequently could at times wield a great deal of power; and outside marriage some women could rise through the Convent to positions of leadership, as had the founders of the great medieval orders. In artisan households, women could share and inherit their husbands' trades; and peasant wom-

24. *Puritanism and Society*, pp. 463–64.
25. *The Working Life of Women in the Seventeenth Century* (New York: A. M. Kelley, 1968).

en, an integral part of agricultural production, probably had some say thereby in family affairs.

The middle-class woman, however, is now forbidden to own property, squeezed out of the skilled trades, denied an education; and she sees even her traditional service functions, such as medicine and education, usurped by professions she is not allowed to enter. In short, she has no economic alternative but marriage, in which she is pushed into the kitchen and the nursery to perform those unprofitable—and therefore little-valued—functions without which, however, the household economy could not survive. Moreover, as journeymen and peasants lose their independence and become wage laborers outside the family economy, their wives are forced onto the poor rates and into the sweated trades of the clothing industry where they can no longer earn enough to support themselves. For the first time, according to Clark, one gets the notion of a woman being supported by a man; formerly, she was an economic asset, providing the family's subsistence from her cottage garden. Eventually, as production is moved from the home and as the middle class can afford more servants, it becomes a status symbol to have an idle wife, the bourgeois ideal of womanhood then becoming that ornament and plaything known as femininity.

This sexual division of labor is the basis for the differentiation of masculine and feminine roles that Milton will acclaim and Blake condemn. Adam and Eve are linked in a typical Puritan household, with its family economy and piety. Although they work together, Adam is clearly the master; he is educated and functions in the larger world, while Eve is primarily relegated to the boudoir and the kitchen where she waits upon his angelic guests. It is of great significance, therefore, that Milton makes the immediate cause of the fall Eve's assertion of her right to go off and work on her own. For it was precisely the loss of that right, according to Clark, that transformed the character of women so that we pass in a brief half century from the vital and intelligent women of Shakespeare to the coy insipid females that will dominate literature from the moment of Eve's surrender until the feminist rebellion of the nineteenth century.[26]

26. Ibid., p. 3.

It is this socially imposed inferiority, dividing humanity into
"active masculine virtue" and "indolent feminine bliss," that
Blake identifies as the source of human misery in love and in the
family. Not only does it lead to the degeneration of the male into
a petty tyrant, but it also leads women, denied creative self-
expression in the world, to turn their passivity into a perverse
power through sexual denial and maternal domination—the horrors of "Female Will." Therefore Blake prophesies that the return
of Albion to Eden will involve the return of the female to the
unity and equality of participation in communal work:

> Then Enion & Ahania & Vala & the wife of Dark Urthona
> Rose from the feast in joy ascending to their Golden Looms
> There the wingd shuttle Sang the spindle & the distaff & the Reel
> Rang sweet the praise of industry . . .
>
> (137:11–14)

An equally important transformation of the family can be
traced to a general change in the evaluation of work. Milton
reflects this fact in the two attitudes towards labor that he
explicates in Eve's argument with Adam. She supports her demand
for independence in the terms of a good bourgeoise, contending
that it will increase their production:

> For while so near each other thus all day
> Our taske we choose, what wonder if so near
> Looks intervene and smiles, or object new
> Casual discourse draw on, which intermits
> Our dayes work brought to little . . .
>
> (IX.220–24)

Milton had broken with the tradition that made all work a consequence of the fall. However, he still adheres to a concept of Eden
as primarily pleasure and has Adam reply:

> Yet not so strictly hath our Lord impos'd
> Labour as to debarr us when we need
> Refreshment, whether food, or talk between,
> Food of the mind, or this sweet intercourse
> Of looks and smiles . . .
> Love not the lowest end of human life.

> For not to irksom toile, but to delight
> He made us . . .
>
> (IX.235–43)

Since Max Weber published his profound study, historians have substantiated the link between *The Protestant Ethic and the Spirit of Capitalism.*[27] Whereas medieval ethics centered around the idea of the common good and a social morality, there now develops an individualistic ethos of self-control, hard work, and sober, austere living. As this "godly discipline" becomes a sign of the Elect, so the accumulation of wealth which it facilitates becomes a mark, not of worldliness, but of righteousness:

> . . . industry and diligence in a lawful and warrantable vocation and calling, in order to gain a competent provision of earthly things for our children and relations is not condemned in sacred writ . . . but commended. . . . Grace in a poor man is grace and 'tis beautiful but grace in a rich man is more conspicuous and more useful.[28]

Underlying this development is a vast social and economic revolution. Under the feudal form of production, there was little trade, and therefore little means for exchanging or investing a surplus. Whatever was produced had to be immediately consumed, hence the opulent hospitality of the nobility and the seasonal festivities of the peasantry. The aristocracy was freed from the need to labor and maintained a lifestyle based on leisure and consumption, and there was no motivation for the peasant to work harder, since the gain would not be his. Consequently he enjoyed an easygoing workday, with neither a time clock nor a supervisor; one's labors could be interspersed with village gossip, enjoyment of nature, courtship, or the play of children. Life was hard, threatened by natural catastrophe and coarsened by the bruteness of peasant labor; but it was whole, with its wholeness rooted in the material character of this undifferentiated working day.

The creation of markets and capitalist agriculture and the drive to accumulate capital for investment replaced this lifestyle with

27. In addition to Hill, see also R. H. Tawney, *Religion and the Rise of Capitalism* (New York: NAL, 1954).
28. H. Peter, *Good Work for a Good Magistrate* (London, 1655).

the work ethic of the Puritan bourgeoisie. In presenting the fall as a passage from a world of "pleasant labours" to one of unrelenting toil, Milton captures the sense of human catastrophe that accompanied the rise of capitalism, the passage from a world in which production exists for humanity to one in which humanity exists only for production. Milton's "Eternal Father" is also "the great Work-Maister" (III.696), the model for Blake's Urizen, the slave-master "Petrifying all the Human Imagination into Rock & Sand" (25:6).

The Puritans proposed a complete "reformation" of the human personality. What they sought to achieve was the continuous and unrelenting subordination of the vagaries of human impulse to the "godly discipline" of productive activity. The institution for achieving this reformation was the family. We might, therefore, reflect upon the significance of Milton's presenting the loss of paradise as a loss of childhood.

Phillip Aries argues that growing up took on a new character at about this time. In the large medieval households and in the village community, children grew up alongside adults without special notice.[29] Ages are not observed; clothing is not different; even games are shared. Childhood is a biological, rather than a social, phase; and, as soon as they are physically capable, children are apprenticed to someone who will initiate them in their adult roles. When the middle-class family withdraws from this community, it also becomes more child-centered. Children are no longer farmed out to wet nurses and masters but, remaining in their families, become the subject of a new attention which reflects the economic needs of the bourgeoisie. A noble's child, who only had to inherit the family name, just needed to learn the appropriate protocol from his peers, and the peasant's education was labor, but the sons of the bourgeoisie will rise through industry and skill. Unless they are trained in the economic virtues of thrift and rationality, they might squander the hard-earned family capital through loose living, unwise investments, or improper management. Puritans like the Miltons sent their children to school and carefully supervised their progress. And this emphasis on education, Ivy Pinchbeck notes, reflected more than just a concern for

29. Phillip Aries, *Centuries of Childhood* (New York: Random House, 1965).

knowledge; it was a testimony to a growing awareness of the desirability of "moulding the man."[30]

The goal of the Puritans' upbringing was "breaking the will"[31] of the child. They considered the infant completely corrupted by original sin, evidenced in what they appropriately called its *idle* affections:

> The young child which lieth in the cradle is both wayward and full of affections; and though his body be but small, yet he hath a great heart, and is altogether inclined to evil. . . . If this sparkle be suffered to increase, it will rage over and burn down the whole house.[32]

In order to suppress the child's will, it will be swaddled so tightly that it cannot move, deprived prematurely of the maternal breast, and, if it protests, left to cry itself to exhaustion. The growing child will, furthermore, be denied too great familiarity with its parents, forbidden children's games and stories, threatened into silence, and trained to a routine of disciplined productivity. (Locke once remarked that it pained him to see a child, above the age of three, idle!)

Christopher Hill contends that in trying to reorient human instincts from the pursuit of pleasure to the tyranny of production, "the preachers knew what they were doing. Their language is revealing. They were up against 'natural man'."[33] Morality is no longer turned only against antisocial behavior; now every motion of the human organism must be scrutinized lest it prove idle or indulgent. Like Milton, laboring ever in his taskmaster's eye, the child is raised in fear of the constant superintendence of his parents and God, the Super-foreman. A seventeenth-century teacher's manual advises:

> A close watch must be kept on the children, and they must never be left alone anywhere. . . . this constant supervision should be exercised gently and

30. Ivy Pinchbeck and Margaret Hewitt, *Children in English Society*, 2 vols. (Toronto: Univ. of Toronto Press, 1969), I, 297.

31. On "breaking the will," see Pinchbeck, *Children in English Society*, p. 274. Other works on Puritan child-rearing include those by Phillip Greven, *Child-Rearing Concepts 1628–1861* (Itasca, Ill.: Peacock, 1973), and G. Rattray Taylor, *The Angel-Makers* (London: Heinemann, 1958).

32. John Dod and Richard Cleuer, *A Godlye Forme of Household Gouernment* (London, 1630), sig. S8–S8ᵛ.

33. *The World Turned Upside Down*, p. 262.

with a certain trustfulness calculated to make them think one loves them. . . .
this will make them love their supervision rather than fear it.[34]

And John Bunyan writes of the effect upon him of a sermon
denouncing games:

When I was a child of nine or ten years old these things did so distress my
soul, that then in the midst of my merry sports and childish vanities, amidst
my vain companions, I was often much cast down and afflicted in my mind
therewith; yet I could not let go of my sins.[35]

It is in this context that we can understand how Milton can rest
the entire human tragedy upon a breach of paternal authority.
When we first see his patriarchal God, he is a divine overseer
spying upon his children as he "bent down his eye,/ His own
works and their works at once to view" (III.58–59). Milton's
obsession with the theme of temptation is also hereby explained;
the human organism, with its rhythms perverted to the requirements of inordinate labor, is continually tempted to return to its
natural pace and desires. Thus, Adam and Eve, like the infant
child, are never really innocent but must be hemmed in with
constant warnings and prohibitions. God must "place within them
as a guide/ My Umpire *Conscience*" (III.194–94) because their
unfallen impulses cannot be trusted. When Raphael admonishes
Adam to follow Reason, he underlines this same idea that a
psychic faculty must be developed which will serve as a mental
referee between the ways of God and man, of parent and child, of
desire and artificial restraint. It is this notion of Reason, as
bourgeois repression, that Blake attacks in plate 5 of *The Marriage
of Heaven and Hell:*

Those who restrain desire, do so because theirs is weak enough to be
restrained; and the restrainer or reason usurps its place & governs the
unwilling. And being restraind it by degrees becomes passive till it is only the
shadow of desire. The history of this is written in Paradise Lost. & the
Governor or Reason is call'd Messiah.

Students of Puritan psychology have supported Blake's association
of this repression with the creation of a divided self:

34. In Aries, *Centuries of Childhood*, p. 255.
35. Quoted in J. R. Green, *A Short History of the English People* (New York:
Harper, 1895), p. 45.

These Puritanical parents were not only severe, but what may be more psychologically important, they were extremely demanding. . . . Demanding supervision tends to create the schizophrenic (or "split") type of personality . . . that is, the child constructs a screen personality which satisfies the parents' demands, while continuing to live its own life in fantasy behind the screen.[36]

Blake suggests that Milton portrays a single personality, split into Reason and Desire, in the characters of Christ and Satan. Christ's entire identity revolves about his "Filial obedience" (III.269). This filial piety, however, goes beyond mere obedience, becoming a masochistic willingness to be sacrificed by the father and reconstructed as a "Divine Similitude" (III.384), worthy of inheriting his power. This process, on a psychological level, is the essence of Puritan child-rearing.

This portrayal of Christ as a self-sacrificial son is an emphasis of Protestant theology developed by Luther, which, significantly, has been directly traced to Luther's experience growing up in a bourgeois family.[37] Luther's father was a dispossessed peasant who advanced from holding a small miner's claim to becoming an owner and employer. He hoped to secure his new class status by having Martin become a lawyer, so he submitted the boy to harsh and constant discipline. Martin revolted, joining a monastery, but, according to Erik Erikson, he was torn all his life between the conflicting demands of obedience and rebellion. Unable to believe in God as a loving Father, Luther, after several nervous outbreaks, sought salvation in the idea that God's love is shown in his wrath. He concluded that the Christian must therefore internalize Christ, the suffering son, as part of his own personality. This psychological "conversion" puts a lid on one's guilt for feeling unloved and, at the same time, one's hatred for the tyrannous Father-God. In Luther's case, the suppressed rage could be redirected at that international patriarch, the Holy Father in Rome. His Protestant consciousness never fully relinquished the ambivalent attitude toward authority, however, as was evidenced in his support for vicious repression of the revolutionary peasantry. The mechanism of Protestant child-rearing creates exactly this double

36. Taylor, *Angel-Makers*, p. 318.
37. Erik Erikson, *Young Man Luther* (New York: Norton, 1958), pp. 201–22.

bind, ensuring that individual assertiveness, crippled by early oppression, finds its outlet finally by allying itself with the established powers.

Luther's theological and psychological solution was neurotic; it
maintained rather than resolved his conflicts. Thus, later in life
these recurred in his hallucinations of devils who made excre-
mental attacks on him. Erikson interprets these episodes as the
revival of Luther's battle against paternal repression, at the time
when Luther had, ironically, become all that his father wished him
to be, powerful, influential, a kind of super-lawyer. Erikson concludes that "Luther's use of repudiative and anal patterns was an
attempt to find a safety valve when unrelenting inner pressure
threatened to make devotion unbearable and sublimity hateful—
that is when he was again about to repudiate God in supreme
rebellion. . ."[38]

Satan, Norman O. Brown has argued, dominated the consciousness of Puritans.[39] Just at the time when science was driving the
demons out of nature they were establishing an expanding empire
in the psyche. William Haller notes that the central metaphor of
Puritan sermons was the battle between God and Satan raging
within every Christian soul.[40] Schizophrenia had become the
normal condition of the human psyche. It is in this sense that we
can understand Milton's Satan. If the characters of Christ and
Adam appear somewhat stiff, it is probably because they, like the
screen personalities children put up to please their parents, are
dramatizations of the ideals of the conduct books. The psychic
reality underlying those ideals is revealed in Satan and his impo-
tent rage. He is defined as one who rejects "feign'd submission"
(IV.96), rebels against patriarchy, and denies the paternity of God,
claiming the devils "self-begot, self-rais'd/ By our own quick'ning
power" (V.860–61). His static anger, Blake's rage of ice and snow,
is the other side of a paternal "love" that is expressed in prohibition, temptation, and punishment.

The repression of children is a central theme for Blake who, in
Songs of Experience, already draws the links among capitalist
exploitation, Puritanical religion, and parental oppression. In "The
Garden of Love," a chapel has been built "Where I used to play on

38. Ibid., p. 247.
39. *Life Against Death,* pp. 202–33.
40. *The Rise of Puritanism* (New York: Columbia Univ. Press, 1938), pp. 150–52.

the green./...And Priests in black gowns, were walking their rounds,/ And binding with briars, my joys & desires" (p. 26). "The Chimney Sweeper" has been sold to labor by parents who "are gone to praise God & his Priest & King/ Who make up a heaven of our misery" (p. 23). In "A Little Boy Lost," the essence of patriarchal "love" is revealed as a sadistic demand for human sacrifice:

> The weeping child could not be heard.
> The weeping parents wept in vain:
> They strip'd him to his little shirt.
> And bound him in an iron chain.
>
> And burn'd him in a holy place
> Where many had been burn'd before . . .
>
> (p. 29)

Blake expands his analysis of this psychological sacrifice of humanity in *The Four Zoas* where the patriarchal Urizen announces:

> For labourd fatherly care & sweet instruction. I will give
> Chains of dark ignorance & cords of twisted self conceit
> And whips of stern repentance & food of stubborn obstinacy . . .
> Go forth sons of my curse Go forth daughters of my abhorrence . . .
>
> (68:21–23, 27)

Blake reads in Milton's Puritan myth the workings of the repressive family. In Blake's version, Los, in "Love of Parent Storgous Appetite Craving" (61:10), crucifies his son Orc on a mountain of obdurate rock, a symbol of stern, hard-hearted parental discipline. Orc is simultaneously the crucified Christ and the rebellious Satan, reuniting the split aspects of the Miltonic psyche. His sacrifice is revealed as the source, not of salvation, but of the fall; from the place of his crucifixion grows Satan's "Tree of Mystery." Its spirit of prohibition is the cause of the crucifixion in every man. Its "Mystery" is the theological justification for repression in the family expressed in Milton's Lutheran doctrine of Atonement, bidding children to sacrifice themselves to their father's tyranny and providing the psychological underpinnings for a society in which a whole class of chimney sweepers is sacrificed to its employer's greed.

It is because Milton's epic reflects this larger psychological and social conflict in bourgeois society and in the bourgeois family that Blake's ideological attack on his society can be posed as a struggle to reconstruct the categories of Milton's myth. Blake seems, however, in one aspect to fall under the shadow of Milton's patriarchalism, for, although he blames the fall on the "Father of Jealousy," he also identifies it with "Female Will," crying out against having been "Woman-born/ And Woman-nourishd & Woman-educated & Woman-scorn'd" (*Jerusalem*, 64:16–17), in passages which make Milton's misogyny seem pale. In fact, there is no real contradiction between Blake's call for the liberation of women and his castigation of "Female Will," which, closely examined, is an attack not on woman but on the role of the mother—bearer, nourisher, and socializer—under patriarchy.

Returning to Milton's patriarchal myth, we find that it seems to eliminate the mother completely from the "Charities/ Of Father, Son and Brother" (IV.756–57) on which the family is built. The significance of this emphasis on the creative role of the Father-God, and the idea, which Freud was to find so "peculiar and singular,"[41] of the birth of the first woman out of the body of a man, might be dismissed as implicit in the biblical sources. It was, however, exactly this denigration of woman's role which the Puritans stressed in the Genesis text. (One contemporary had to remind them that she wasn't taken "out of his foote to be trod upon.")[42]

Milton's attitude toward woman in *Paradise Lost* is contradictory. On the one hand, the mother is completely suppressed in his patriarchal ideology; on the other hand, the poetic center of his epic is a nostalgia for the tranquility and unity of the mother-child relationship. The myth of fulfillment is built on the association of Eden with Eve, and both with a maternal benevolence ministering to the sensuous needs of children: "Whatever Earth all-bearing Mother yields . . . [she]/ Heaps with unsparing hand . . ." (V.338, 344). Eden is constantly associated with the maternal breast and the maternal womb. The bower in which Adam

41. Letter to C. G. Jung, Dec. 7, 1911, quoted by Theodor Reik, *The Creation of Woman* (New York: Braziller, 1960), p. 74.
42. *The Women's Sharpe Revenge* (London, 1640), p. 77.

and Eve make love is so womb-like that the sexual act seems to be a return to prenatal harmony.

Lest it be thought that we are imposing an overly Freudian view, we might note that it is Milton himself who parodies the incestuous aspects of the relationship of Adam to "our General Mother" with the full-blown Oedipal relations of Satan, Sin, and Death. The Genesis story of birth from the male is paralleled in the birth of the very first woman out of the head of Satan as he conceives his first anti-patriarchal thought; the woman's name, of course, is Sin. The "sin" involved can, I think, be read as a Freudian inversion of Mother-Son to Father-Daughter incest. At any rate, it is followed by the birth of Death, an embryonic horror who rapes his mother, engendering a pack of monsters who are caught in a continuous cycle of birth and return to the womb.

We have remarked that Satan is frozen in eternal rage against the Father; his anger is also linked to his relationship with the mother. In that marvelous passage in which he first comes upon Eve alone in the garden, Satan is lifted momentarily to a vision of pastoral delight:

> The smell of Grain, or tedded Grass, or Kine,
> Of Dairie, each rural sight, each rural sound;
> If chance with Nymphlike step fair Virgin pass . . .
>
> That space the Evil One abstracted stood
> From his own evil, and for the time remain'd
> Stupidly good, of enmitie disarm'd . . .
> But the hot Hell that always in him burnes,
> Though in mid Heav'n, soon ended his delight,
> And tortures him now more, the more he sees
> Of pleasure not for him ordain'd: then soon
> Fierce hate he recollects . . .
>
> (IX.450–53, 463–71)

For a moment Satan makes contact with that deeper self which existed before that first relationship with the mother was perverted and destroyed. If Adam's wife has suddenly been transfigured to a Virgin Madonna, it is because the fear of incest divides her, like all women, into the dichotomy of Virgin and Whore. Satan approaches her with childlike innocence, "with rapine sweet bereav'd" (IX.461), but the experience of prohibited gratification turns this vision of pleasure into the rage of frustration.

Blake has captured these incestuous undertones of Milton's poem, contending that fixation in rage against the Father and nostalgia for the mother are the complementary components of patriarchal psychology. He distinguishes Beulah from Eden in order to show that the "moony sleep" of infantile sexuality, as well as the Urizenic denial of pleasure, can render the human being passive, and propel a fall into Generation. For instance, Vala, the Eternal Mother, is herself a tyrannical character, for attachment to the lost pleasures of childhood and sexuality can so drain creativity that people remain infantile, never fully born, never fully human. Thus Albion recounts in one version of his fall:

> Among the Flowers of Beulah walkd the Eternal Man & Saw
> Vala the lily of the desart. melting in high noon
> Upon her bosom in sweet bliss he fainted   Wonder siezd
> All heaven they saw him dark. they built a golden wall
> Round Beulah . . .

> (83:7–11)

We can comprehend these tensions better when we analyze the relationship to the mother in the bourgeois family. For one thing, the sexual division of labor and the isolation of the nuclear family make the young child completely dependent on its mother, enabling sexual and emotional fixation. That total early attachment, however, will be ultimately and increasingly subordinated to the authority of the father. Thus, when Luther records a childhood trauma in which his mother beat him for taking one nut, Erikson speculates that his father intervened between mother and child, forbade her maternal affection, and forced her to be an agent of his discipline.[43] This pattern, exemplified in the actions of Los who tears Orc from the bosom of Enitharmon, was common in Puritan child-bearing. For instance, John Robinson writes in his treatise "Of Children and their Education":

Children, in their first days, have the greater benefit of good mothers, not only because they suck their milk, but in a sort, their manners also, by being continually with them, and receiving their first impressions from them. But,

43. *Young Man Luther*, pp. 67–73.

afterwards, when they come to riper years, good fathers are more behoveful for their forming in virtue and good manners, by their greater wisdom and authority, and ofttimes also, by correcting the fruits of their mother's indulgence, by their severity.[44]

The child in the bourgeois family, as Erikson explains, will indeed experience the loss of a maternal paradise:

Puritanism, beyond defining sin for full-blooded and strong-willed people, gradually extended itself over the total sphere of bodily living, compromising all sexuality, including marital relationships—and spreading its frigidity over the tasks of pregnancy, childbirth, nursing and training.[45]

G. Rattray Taylor makes a similar observation:

However, the main significance of weaning and feeding disturbances is not the amount of frustration immediately produced, but the total effect on the child's relationship with its mother. A mother who continually frustrates, however loving she may be in reality, seems to the infant to be unloving.[46]

The result of this trauma, Taylor argues, is just that unconscious obsession to return to the mother and satisfy those ungratified longings to which Blake attributes the triumph of Vala.

This frustration is, moreover, intensified by the fact that the mother, herself under the father's tyranny, is often made responsible both for rebuking the child and for casting him out from those "Short pleasures" (IV.535) of infancy; as Schucking remarks, "so delicately minded a writer as Rogers can find no better way of describing the spiritual harmony and agreement of husband and wife than the following: 'she holdes not his hand from due stroakes, but bares their skins with delight, to his fatherly stripes.' "[47] Finally, we cannot ignore the point made by Taylor that women, as domestic slaves, tend to become the perfect perpetuators of a slave mentality:

. . . it is not difficult to appreciate that women deprived of almost every other outlet for constructive and manipulative activity, and themselves dominated by their husbands, must have found in the domination of their children

44. In *Child-Rearing Concepts*, p. 11.
45. *Childhood and Society* (New York: W. W. Norton, 1963), p. 293.
46. *Angel-Makers*, p. 330.
47. *The Puritan Family*, p. 75, quoting from Daniel Rogers, *Matrimoniall Honour* (London, 1642), p. 299.

an outlet for their pent-up frustrations. Here, I suspect, is an important social mechanism by which the frustrations of one generation are, as it were, amplified in the course of being transmitted to the next.[48]

The mother passes on her slavery; the angry child hoards his rage until he can express it as a tyrannical father. It is precisely this "bloody chain," this "chain of jealousy," that Blake has viewed with such horror. The essence of his state of Generation is the chain of generations. He has discovered the family as the institution by which the human race is re-created in the fallen image of its parents, by which each newborn child is socialized to cramp its potential into the narrow confines of capitalist society. Los and Enitharmon are born of the conflict between Tharmas and Enion and, "link'd in the marriage chain," repeat their tragedy. History is bound up by the stony laws of Urizen's social institutions, but also by each generation's internalizing the entire horror of social relations in its character structure.

The key link in this chain is patriarchal dominance and the sexual division of labor, which leads finally to the split between home and work, reproduction and production, feminine and masculine, infancy and adulthood. There is a fundamental divide in the experience of every human being (different for the sexes) in such a society: one passes from the dominance of "feminine" values (emotion, caring) to the dominance of "masculine" values (self-reliance, toughness). There is a chasm that separates one permanently from the spontaneity of childhood, a finishing off of the "Auricular Nerves of Human Life" and a transformation of the body from an organ of experience into an instrument of production. This division of roles also destroys the fraternal relations of brother and sister, at once implanting a pattern of inequality and forcing each to pursue a lost potential through the clumsy refitting of the marriage bond.

Furthermore, fixing all affection and nurturance solely on the biological mother in infancy creates a desperate predilection for the security of monogamy and the desire to have all one's needs gratified by a single mother-substitute. Caught up in these infantile

48. *Angel-Makers*, p. 316; Taylor also mentions that in Blake's period women such as Mrs. Pennington, Mrs. Chapone, Mrs. Sherwood, Miss Edgeworth, and Mrs. Trimmer are the leading moralists, publishing books on the proper conduct for women and children which run through several editions.

patterns, marriage becomes a jealous and possessive relationship, exclusive of all other ties of fraternal love. And, in order to ensure this monogamous orientation, upon which the property system as well as patriarchy depends, the child must be trained to discipline its desires. In doing so, it becomes that Human Zero, perfectly malleable to the needs of capitalist society, the repressed child placing itself either, as a wage slave, into the path of "feminine" subservience or into the tyrannical role of the patriarchal boss. Therefore, Blake prophesies that a full revolution will have to tear down, along with the norms of class oppression, the patterns of family oppression as well. Then the oppressed will no longer have to crucify the psyches of their children:

> But Los loved them & refusd to Sacrifice their infant limbs
> And Enitharmons smiles & tears prevaild over self protection
> They rather chose to meet Eternal death than to destroy
> The offspring of their Care & Pity . . .
>
> (90:50–53)

Having shown how Milton provided Blake with an insight into the family structure and character structure of the rising bourgeoisie, we must now consider its implication for the society as a whole. First of all, we should realize that the patriarchal discipline which turned bourgeois sons into sober employers also had consequences for their employees. For, as Gouge wrote, the family was "a school wherein the first principles and grounds of government and subjection are learned."[49] Discipline within the household is a two-headed monster, providing, on the one hand, for the psychological transformation of the bourgeoisie and, on the other hand, for the compulsory discipline of its servants and apprentices. "Calvinism," Michael Walzer writes, "brought conscience and coercion together."[50] The fall, Calvin argued, had been not only a spiritual but a political disaster, leaving human affairs in such disarray that only Christian "reformation," permanent and unrelenting discipline, could prevent a fall into total anarchy. This discipline was to be found in the self-imposed subordination of the Elect to a divine order of subordination, systematic labor, and sober living, all of which dovetailed nicely with the real interests of the rising middle

49. *Domesticall Duties*, pp. 16–17.
50. *Revolution of the Saints* (New York: Atheneum, 1968), p. 47.

classes. Calvin, realizing that only the elite would espouse this ethic, argued that they should maintain the social order, imposing their God-given authority on the unregenerate masses by any means necessary. This justification of class rule, of course, included the authority of the patriarchal employer over his employees. Thus, Christian paternalism provided the obvious advantage of backing up the economic power of these new masters with religious sanctions. As Henry Bullinger admitted in his work on household governance,

... the good man of the house, by planting godliness in his family, doth not a little advance and set forward his private profit and own commodity; for wicked servants are for the most part pickers and deceitful; whereas all the godly are faithful whom in his absence he may trust to govern his house.[51]

This idea of paternal authority within the household can also be seen as a corollary to the bourgeois disregard for the community. When they abolished the church courts and censors, they also did away with the whole fabric of rights and responsibilities through which feudal society had tried to ensure the preservation of its members. Before the split of capital from labor and the abrogation of feudal rights to the land, survival was not dependent on having either property or a job. The peasant's means of subsistence was ensured by his right to work a plot on the domain, hunt in the forest, and graze animals on the village commons. In times of trouble, the people relied on the collective resources of the community and the church. The monasteries dispensed welfare, and guilds looked after artisans. Suddenly, under the onslaught of rising capitalism, this all begins to crumble. Land is enclosed by farmers producing for the market, and thousands of peasants are dispossessed. A world of mutual and overlapping rights to the land is replaced by a world divided into those men of property who can support their families and the landless poor who cannot. Marx recapitulates this ugly history in *Capital:*

They were turned en masse into beggars, robbers, vagabonds, partly from inclination, in most cases from the stress of circumstances. Hence ... throughout Western Europe a bloody legislation against vagabondage. The fathers of the present working class were chastised for their enforced transfor-

51. *The Decades of Henry Bullinger,* 3 vols. (London: Parker Society, 1849–52), I, 258

mation into vagabonds and paupers. Legislation treated them as "voluntary" criminals and assumed that it depended on their good will to go on working under the old conditions that no longer existed.[52]

From this individualistic bourgeoisie came an individualistic ethos; those whom they destroyed they also condemned. Similarly Milton, unable to find a social analysis of the failure of the revolution to establish a just society, as, for example, Gerrard Winstanley did, is only able to blame tyranny on its victims:

> . . . yet know withall,
> Since thy original lapse, true Libertie
> Is lost, which always with right Reason dwells
> Twinn'd, and from her hath no dividual being:
> Reason in man obscur'd, or not obeyd,
> Immediately inordinate desires
> And upstart Passions catch the Government
> From Reason, and to servitude reduce
> Man till then free. Therefore since hee permits
> Within himself unworthie Powers to reign
> Over free Reason, God in Judgement just
> Subjects him from without to violent Lords.
>
> (XII.82–94)

When Milton must explain political oppression, all he can come up with in the end is sin, and the sin, "passion." It is this ethic, rationalizing all the injustice of history by the failure of self-control, proclaiming the cruel and unusual punishment of death for an impulse of childish hunger, that makes Milton's God so offensive. He speaks in the clearly distinguishable tones of the self-righteous English bourgeois pouring scorn on the heads of those they have ruined: "whose fault?/Whose but his own," God carps; "Ingrate, he had of mee/ All he could have" (III.96–98).

The ideology of the bourgeois family made people completely responsible for their own survival. The bourgeoisie hedged in their property; and then, from the comfortable vantage of their hearths, they condemned those they had locked out for failing by their standards of domesticity. Almsgiving was no longer advanced as a Christian virtue; rather the preachers blessed the selfish accumulation of wealth. Thus Henry Bullinger wrote:

---

52. Karl Marx, *Capital*, 3 vols. (New York: International Publishers, 1967), I, 734.

No parcel of God's law doth bind thee to distribute to other men the wealth which thou thyself doth need as much or more than they. It is sufficient for thee to provide that they of thine own household be not a burden to other men's backs.[53]

The wealthy household was, therefore, a sign of election; William Temple could still assert that the man who could not provide for his family was "worse than an infidel."[54]

The bourgeoisie passed Poor Laws that made indigence a crime and accompanied relief with the punishment and shame of the workhouse. They destroyed the institutions through which the Elizabethans had tried to care for orphans, and made the lives of illegitimate children a torture as an example to their unregenerate mothers. When the children of the poor starved, it was convenient to condemn them for having children.

The monogamous sexual standards of the middle classes, we have seen, were linked to their economic interests. They were concerned with the orderly transmission of family property, unwilling to squander their capital on bastards, to disrupt the family economy with adultery, or to waste time on erotic pleasure. "It was," Christopher Hill writes, "especially in sexual behaviour that the standards of the bourgeoisie differed from the aristocracy." [55] At the same time, he argues, it distinguished them from the lower classes who lacked the resources to establish stable monogamous families, who rarely could even afford the marriage license. (One in three seventeenth-century brides is reported to have come to the altar pregnant.)[56] The bourgoisie blamed the conditions of the poor on their morals, when clearly the reverse was true. Like contemporary politicians, they watched procreation among the lower classes with their eyes on the poor rates. They harangued about how "the poor when their bellies were filled . . . fell to lust and concupiscence and most shamefullie abused their bodies and brought forth basterdes in such quantity that it passed belief." [57]

53. *Decades*, III, 32–33.
54. In Hill, *The World Turned Upside Down*, p. 265.
55. *Puritanism and Revolution* (New York: Schocken, 1964), p. 372.
56. P. E. H. Hair, "Bridal Pregnancy in Rural England," *Population Studies*, XX (1967), 233–43.
57. *Records of the City of Norwich 1570*, ed. John Cottingham Tingey and Rev. William Hudson (Norwich: E. Burgess, 1898), p. 344.

It was a peculiar logic; like Adam and Eve, the poor overvalued their appetites, and so they deserved to starve.

Out of the conditions of the lower classes arose an alternative ethic. Since their women were often forced to be independent, it was natural that they should accept equality of the sexes; since there was no property to be passed on and no gain to be had from delayed gratification, they demanded sexual enjoyment; since they had no individual wealth, they espoused communal cooperation:

> The middle class . . . had found the Protestant ethic, the dignity of labour and hatred of idleness written in their hearts; the environment in which they lived and worked had put it there. Not so cottagers, casual labourers. Labour is one thing for small masters whose wealth is directly related to their labour: if they do not work, neither shall they eat. But the wage labourer works in part, at least, that another may eat. So long as he gets his wages, he is not interested in what he produces or how much. The inner voice speaks differently to communities drawn from the lower classes. Idleness is not a sin; adultery is no sin to the pure of heart. Love is more important than faith. [58]

Hill brilliantly documents all this in his history of the lower-class Protestant sects of the seventeenth century. Ranters, like the amazing Abiezer Coppe, decry the "stinking family duties" of the middle class in language that anticipates Blake.[59] "The Pharisee in man," Coppe says, "is the mother of harlots and being the worst whore cries 'Whore' first."[60] Coppe records a marvelous story in which he came upon a poor vagabond in an open field and then was torn apart in an interior battle between his two consciences, the true Christian one urging generosity while "the WELL-FAVORED HARLOT" argued like a Puritan:

> It's a poor wretch, give him 6d; and that's enough for a squire or knight to give to one poor body. Besides, (saith the holy Scripturian whore) he's worse than an infidel who provides not for his own family. True love begins at home etc. Thou and thy family are fed, as the young ravens, strangely. Though thou hast been a constant preacher, yet thou has abhorred both tithes and hire;

---

58. Hill, *The World Turned Upside Down*, p. 271.

59. *A Fiery Flying Roll*, *II* (London, 1649), ch. 5, reprinted in Norman Cohn, *The Pursuit of the Millennium* (New York: Harper, 1957), p. 376.

60. *Preface to Richard Coppin's Divine Teachings*, quoted in *The World Turned Upside Down*, p. 268.

thou knowest not aforehand who will give thee the worth of a penny. Have a care of the main chance.[61]

Contemptuous of an ethic that could dismiss so coldly the suffering of others, Coppe and the Ranters, on the other hand, saw no harm, only praise of their maker, in sexual pleasure:

Kisses are numbered among transgressors—base things—well! by base hellish swearing and cursing (as I have accounted it in my time of fleshly holiness) and by base impudent kisses . . . my plaguey holiness hath been confounded . . . and external kisses have been my fiery chariot to mount me into the bosom of . . . the King of Glory. . . . I can . . . kiss and hug ladies, and love my neighbor's wife as myself, without sin.[62]

These Ranters, in proclaiming the right of natural man to behave naturally, "gave ideological form and coherent expression to practices which had long been common among vagabonds, squatters and the in-between category of migratory craftsmen."[63]

This counterculture, rooted as it is in the lifestyle of the lower classes, survives, although groups like the Ranters and Diggers disappear with the Restoration's re-establishment of law and order after the turmoil of the civil war. Eighteenth-century England remains a class society where each group retains its own distinctive values. The middle classes control their workers through force; they have not "reformed" them. If Milton can be understood to have embodied the experience of the rising bourgeoisie, so Blake's criticism of that world-view must be understood in the context of his links with the lower class. It is this larger historical connection that makes him, as Hill and A. L. Morton have pointed out, the heir of those lower-class sects, to the left of Milton, who provided the context for Milton's politics.[64]

Like the Ranters and the Diggers, Blake condemns the bourgeois family both for its repression of the individual and for its destruction of the community. The Eternals envision the family as a fall into selfishness; its closed community is the lowest limit that

61. *Fiery Flying Roll, II*, ch. 3, quoted in Cohn, *The Pursuit of the Millennium*, pp. 371–73.

62. Ibid., ch. 5, in Cohn, pp. 376–77.

63. Hill, *The World Turned Upside Down*, p. 259.

64. Ibid., pp. 320–27, for Milton's similarities to the leftist sects; see Don M. Wolfe, *Milton in the Puritan Revolution* (New York: Nelson, 1941), for his differences; see also A. L. Morton, *The Everlasting Gospel* (New York: Haskell, 1966).

bourgeois individualism can be allowed to reach short of complete anarchy:

> Man is a Worm wearied with joy he seeks the caves of sleep
> Among the Flowers of Beulah in his Selfish cold repose
> Forsaking Brotherhood & Universal love in selfish clay . . .
>
> With windows from the inclement sky we cover him & with walls
> And hearths protect the Selfish terror till divided all
> In families we see our shadows born. & thence we know
> That Man subsists by Brotherhood & Universal Love
> We fall on one anothers necks more closely we embrace
> Not for ourselves but for the Eternal family we live
> Man liveth not by Self alone . . .
>
> (133:11–13, 19–25)

In *Songs of Innocence and of Experience* Blake had already identified Puritanism as a class ethos justifying the joyless labor of the working class. The "wise guardians of the poor" ("Holy Thursday," p. 13) forced the children of the lower class into the slavery of the workhouses where they were "Fed with cold and usurous hand" ("Holy Thursday," p. 19)—and glorified this capitalist greed as holy Christian asceticism. Blake saw the direct relationship between the accumulation of misery and the accumulation of capital, which grew from the hard labor and restricted consumption of the working class. He also saw the hypocrisy of middle-class morality, which built the chastity of the bourgeois wife upon the degradation of an army of working-class prostitutes. For the middle class there was domesticity; for their employees, child labor, infanticide, and sexual dissoluteness. From reading Dickens alone we get the sense that a stable working-class family is a rarity; London is overrun with orphans, abandoned by their indigent parents, children bringing each other up in the streets of the city. Engels gives a similar picture:

Family life for the worker is almost impossible under the existing social system. All he has is a dirty and comfortless hovel which is barely adequate as sleeping quarters. . . . The various members of the family only see each other in the mornings and evenings. . . . [65]

---

65. *The Conditions of the Working Class in England,* tr. and ed. W. O. Henderson and W. H. Chaloner (Stanford: Stanford Univ. Press, 1958), p. 145.

Engels also points out that child and female labor "has led to a complete reversal of normal social relationships. If a woman works for twelve or thirteen hours a day in a factory and her husband is employed . . . what is the fate of the children? They lack parental care and control. . . . It is not difficult to imagine that they are left to run wild."[66] Moreover, says Engels, these conditions are not the sort that produce a strict sexual morality. With people crowded together in close quarters, young children supporting themselves in lodging houses, young women the prey of their bosses, a monogamous sexual morality is uncommon in the working class. Rather, its conditions lead to high illegitimacy rates, the abuse of women and children, incestuous family relations, disease, and a "catch-as-catch-can" attitude towards enjoyment of any sort. This, of course, enabled the Gradgrinds and Bounderbys to blame the misery of the working masses on their morals. Blake heard Malthus proclaim laissez faire for the bourgeoisie and abstinence for the masses, attributing all the ills of capitalism to the procreation of the poor. When Blake drew his portrait of Urizen, he put into his mouth the hypocritical moral platitudes of the middle class:

> Listen O Daughters to my voice Listen to the Words of Wisdom
> So Shall [you] govern over all let Moral Duty tune your tongue
> But be your hearts harder than the nether millstone . . .
>
> Compell the poor to live upon a Crust of bread by soft mild arts
> Smile when they frown frown when they smile & when a man looks pale
> With labour and abstinence say he looks healthy & happy
> And when his children sicken let them die there are enough
> Born even too many & our Earth will be overrun . . .
>
> Preach temperance say he is overgorgd & drowns his wit
> In strong drink tho you know that bread & water are all
> He can afford . . .
>   (80:2–4, 9–13, 18–20)

Blake's class stance, then, partly explains his critique of bourgeois culture; but the answer also lies in his particular historical moment. We have said that in the eighteenth century the landed, the moneyed, and the working classes each had their own lifestyle

66. Ibid., p. 160.

and their own world-view, and that middle-class sobriety had little influence on those above or below them. G. Rattray Taylor argues that in the years 1790–1810, when Blake did most of his writing, all that changed. Suddenly the pall of bourgeois morality seems to fall over the entire culture, and we pass from "merrie olde England" to a culture characterized for the first time by the notorious British reserve. Taylor points to a growth in public adherence to religion, an increase of verbal prudery, and, in general, a chilling of the atmosphere.[67] E. P. Thompson tells the same tale—of Hannah More's tracts and Wilberforce's Society for the Suppression of Vice; arrests for "lewd" behavior; legislation against the amusements of the poor, against two-penny hops, gingerbread fairs, obscene pictures; of penalties imposed upon Sabbath breakers, stage dancers, ballad singers, and nude sea bathers.[68] Dickens's "hard times" have come upon England. What these developments represent, according to Taylor, is the achievement of cultural hegemony by the bourgeoisie, who now attempt to impose their ethos on the whole society. Their growth in numbers, wealth, and education now makes them the arbiters of literary taste and manners. They control local government, education, and welfare. With this power they are able to force the upper classes, increasingly dependent on their wealth, to "shape up," and, through the Methodist campaign, to try finally to impose godliness on their workers.

Blake witnessed this conjunction of cultures, the first inroads of bourgeois attitudes into the working class. Like Marx, he watches capitalism as it transforms an entire society and its people. Methodism may not entirely succeed in inculcating its repressive morality in the working class, but it turns a number of chimney sweepers against themselves and creates a dominant social atmosphere against which the working class must fight for its own sense of reality. What Blake sees and captures in his "intellectual War" (139:9) is the extension of the class struggle into culture, and into the psyche itself.

The bourgeoisie never entirely eradicates a working-class counterculture. In the case of the patriarchal family, it was a matter of

67. *Angel-Makers*, ch. 1.
68. *The Making of the English Working Class* (New York: Random House, 1962), ch. 12.

adaptation to pragmatic circumstances. Without birth control, and with no communal provision for child care, the working class is forced to rely on the monogamous family for some semblance of security. In the latter part of the nineteenth century, as child and female labor were restricted, women and children became once again dependent upon the father's wage, and with this inequality, patriarchal ideology often took root.

Nevertheless, Blake could turn to the working class for the source of an alternative vision. For all its misery, the working class clung to a healthy materialism and an affirmation of pleasure. Households in which all the members cooperated in providing support presented a democratic contrast to the patriarchal tyranny of the bourgeois home. And, linked to each other in the social ties of production, the men and women of the working class in their friendly societies and trade unions provided Blake with a vision of cooperation and class solidarity, a vision of a world beyond the selfish bourgeois family, in which humanity would be joined in the Universal Family Divine.

Finally, from the perspective of workers who knew that human beings build their world, Blake is able to see beyond Milton's dichotomy of a static, infantile paradise in nature and the fallen history of civilization. Blake rejects the relationship of child to mother as the model for human bliss and posits instead the mutual interdependency of equals in the fraternal community. Milton never entirely got beyond the bourgeois split of pleasure and work, so his paradise reflects the passivity of infancy, the only moment in which the bourgeois individual could remember enjoyment or security. Blake appends to *The Four Zoas* an epigraph, "Rest Before Labour," putting the passive delights of Beulah in their proper place. Then, generalizing the warmth of maternal love to the universal community, he envisions an Eden in which people neither marry nor are given in marriage, but in which erotic energy overflows into satisfying work. A Divine Humanity, eliminating all divisions of sex and class, is united in the joys of creativity and love.

Blake's vision is a development and a criticism of Milton's. Compared to both, poetry in the years from 1660 to the 1790s seems to lose a certain dimension, and it does. In the eighteenth century the voice of the masses is unheard and the realm of culture left to infighting between landed and moneyed wealth. Even between them the main issues have been settled; the grand compromise of 1688 has only to be embodied in complacently universalized and classicized verse. In a period like Milton's, on the other hand, all norms are challenged and the contradictions of the culture revealed as opposing groups seek to reject it or appropriate it for their particular needs. The accepted language itself, biblical symbolism, becomes a battlefield; ethics and ideas become swords of the spirit indeed, and of material forces as well. Blake realized that this living reality was at the heart of *Paradise Lost.* By writing his epic as also a drama, Milton was able, in the conflicts between Satan and God, Eve and Adam, to give voice to those social disputes, be they over political power or the nature of the family. Blake may alternately praise his radicalism or chastise its limitations; the important thing is that in a period in which the masses are reemerging as a political force, intensifying their struggle again, Blake can appropriate Milton's drama as the social drama that it always was. So doing, he constructs not just *The Four Zoas* but *Milton* and *Jerusalem* out of a rereading of existing traditions, legends, and mythologies that are woven through the Bible and that in Milton's poetry are sharply focused for him. Blake, of course, attempts to replace Milton's theological interpretation of many of these traditions with his own historical version; and in that effort, we can see the essence of Blake's quarrel with Milton. We must, however, exclude Blake from the Romantic company in which Harold Bloom has sought to locate him, Bloom believing that the artist, suffering under "the anxiety of influence," struggles with a poetic ancestor for the guerdon of originality.[69] Blake was really outside, beyond, this "tradition of the new" that has dominated artistic endeavor since the Romantic era: his goal was not to transcend tradition but to understand it.

Poets other than Blake reflect Milton's influence, but the relationship too often involves only a borrowing of his materials, or a deeper historical legacy that the poet himself may not have understood. (Wordsworth, for example, will inherit the interiority of Milton's epic and deepen it, psychologizing Milton's theology in *The Prelude.* However, because he does not understand the histori-

---

69. See *The Anxiety of Influence,* esp. pp. 5–45.

cal basis of this psychological individualism, he will helplessly reflect the transformation of an interiority, revolutionary in the Puritans, into the escapism and self-involvement of the nineteenth century, turning Milton into his opposite, into "fugitive and cloister'd virtue.")

Blake's encounter with Milton is, on the other hand, always historically self-conscious. The very goal of Blake's epics is a revelation of the historical and political basis of cultural symbols and cultural influence. His relationship to Milton's poetry is all the more important because it is incidental to his relationship to the historical forces underlying the poetry. History, Marx wrote, is the history of class struggle; and it is always written by the winners. Blake found in Milton the conflict itself, and, in rewriting his epic from the perspective of the losers, took up the battle anew.

Wordsworth Unalarm'd

JAMES RIEGER

In the Prospectus to *The Recluse,* William Wordsworth walks right
by the big guns of Milton's epic machine:

> All strength, all terror, single, or in bands
> That ever was put forth in personal Form
> Jehovah with his thunder, and the choir
> Of shouting Angels, and th'empyreal thrones
> I pass them unalarm'd.
>
> (31–35)[1]

Read out of context, which I shall restore presently, these lines
may sound too casual a note of independence; their jaunty speaker
may look like a Quixote in reverse, trying to convince himself that
the giant is really a windmill. A reader will especially incline to
take the passage that way if he brings to it a preconception
about poets generally from Blake through Keats, namely, that
they were all to some extent lamed by the achievement of their
mighty predecessors, particularly Milton and Shakespeare in the
major genres. The more loudly they declare their freedom, the
more clearly they reveal their oppression by the past or their
neurotic enslavement to influence, an astral disease.[2] Distinct

---

1. All quotations from the Prospectus are taken from MS 1, conjecturally dated
1798, as printed in M. H. Abrams, *Natural Supernaturalism: Tradition and Revolution in
Romantic Literature* (New York: Norton, 1971), pp. 472–74. The date is much in doubt
and may prove to be as late as 1804.

2. I refer, of course, to Walter Jackson Bate, *The Burden of the Past and the English
Poet* (Cambridge, Mass.: Harvard Univ. Press, 1970), and to Harold Bloom, *The Anxiety
of Influence: A Theory of Poetry* (New York: Oxford Univ. Press, 1973). Readers
familiar with these studies will recognize my indebtedness to both, although I shall deal
directly with neither in the course of this essay. First, I agree entirely with the little that

from those of his contemporaries who did in fact wrestle like
Jacob for their very names, Wordsworth never worried seriously
that everything had been "done" in English. And I hope to show
in the first part of this essay that the oedipal Wordsworth, battling
a wing- and testicle-clipping Nobodaddy for the favors of a maternal Muse, simply never was. Later I shall suggest that such a
Wordsworth might have been if he had read his Milton with a
difference.

Critics have their burdens too, especially when they come late
in the day to a crucial but shopworn topic. The earliest avatar in
the present case is Raymond Dexter Havens, who, near the end of a
prosecutory chapter on Wordsworth, remarks that the later poet
"regarded Milton's authority as supreme, at least in diction, and
accordingly may have thought that borrowing from him was like
taking words from the dictionary."[3] Ignoring the hint of plagia-
rism, I shall also be exploring the implications of Havens' simile.
Certain key terms in Wordsworth's vocabulary achieve their full
meaning only when the totality of *Paradise Lost* is brought to bear
as their defining context, their lexicon. Much more is involved
than what we usually mean by "allusion," "quotation," "borrowing," or, for that matter, "theft."

plagarism?

I

In 1846 an imaginary Walter Savage Landor told an imaginary
Robert Southey that the latter must now smile to see the cleverest

---

Bate says about Wordsworth. Second, I choose not to debate with Bloom, whose book is
far less a work of critical discourse than it is a poem of individuation, like those to which
it alludes, and to that extent "unanswerable." Bloom's sequel, *A Map of Misreading*
(New York: Oxford Univ. Press, 1975), appeared when this essay was already in the
press. See also Leslie Brisman, *Milton's Poetry of Choice and Its Romantic Heirs* (Ithaca:
Cornell Univ. Press, 1973). Brisman's argument is complicated and frequently elusive, but I
agree that, in general (if not in the *Ode to Duty*, which Brisman is discussing at this point),
"Wordsworth shows his relationship with Milton to be a matter of conscious choice, not
unconscious influence with its attendant anxieties about discovery and inadequacy" (pp.
235–36).

    3. Raymond Dexter Havens, *The Influence of Milton on English Poetry* (Cambridge,
Mass.: Harvard Univ. Press, 1922), p. 200. It will be objected that I have set up Havens as

of Wordsworth's admirers "standing on his low joint-stool with a piece of wavering tape in his hand, measuring him with Milton back to back. There is as much difference between them as there is between a celandine and an ilex. The one lies at full length and full breadth along the ground; the other rises up, stiff, strong, lofty, beautiful in the play of its slenderer branches, overshadowing with the infinitude of its grandeur."[4] The comparison disparages the parvenu poet, of course, but more importantly it conjures up those critical tailor's-apprentices who, for several decades, had tried to fit one coat to two grotesquely incommensurable physiques—or, to pursue Landor's shift of metaphor, to apply a single botanical category to plants of different classes.

Coleridge was the first to say that the poets were comparable in ways yet undefined. One week before Wordsworth's thirtieth birthday he communicated to Thomas Poole his sense of the miraculous in his friendship with a poet who might turn out to be greater "than any since Milton. . . .What if you had known Milton at the age of thirty, and believed all you now know of him?—What if you should meet in the letters of any then living man, expressions concerning the young Milton *totidem verbis* the same as mine of Wordsworth, would it not convey to you a most delicious sensation?"[5] Four years later, however, he warned Richard Sharp not to mistake an equal magnitude of promised achievement for any other similarity: "Wordsworth is a Poet, a most original Poet—he no more resembles Milton than Milton resembles Shakespere—no more resembles Shakespere than Shakespere resembles Milton—he is himself: and I dare affirm that he will hereafter be admitted as the first & greatest philosophical Poet."[6] By the time

a straw man, that he cannot answer back, and that far sillier things have been said about Miltonized poetry by more recent critics. My excuse for picking on this solitary predecessor is that it is his simile, not his thesis, that interests me in this essay.

4. Walter Savage Landor, *Southey and Landor: Second Conversation* (1846), as quoted in Joseph Anthony Wittreich, Jr., *The Romantics on Milton: Formal Essays and Critical Asides* (Cleveland and London: Press of Case Western Reserve Univ., 1970), p. 321.

5. Coleridge to Poole, 31 March 1800, in *Collected Letters of Samuel Taylor Coleridge*, ed. Earl Leslie Griggs, 4 vols. (Oxford: Clarendon Press, 1956–59), I, 584; see Wittreich, *Romantics on Milton*, p. 163.

6. Coleridge to Sharp, 15 January 1804, in Griggs, *Letters of Coleridge*, II, 1034; and see Wittreich, *Romantics on Milton*, p. 169.

Coleridge wrote the second letter, Wordsworth had composed the finest of his Miltonic sonnets and was moving rapidly toward what he thought would be the end of the poem that eventually became *The Prelude*. The question of stylistic and thematic indebtedness was already evident to his first and sharpest critic, whose assertion of his friend's originality should not be dismissed as partisanship. The poet's own absolute, even arrogant, self-confidence echoes the claim his "usher" makes for him.

Wordsworth anticipated Keats's hope that "I shall be among the English Poets after my death,"[7] but not his fear that he might not be. Schooled early at home to memorize portions of the standard authors, he consciously and strenuously competed with them all—and with four in particular. "When I began to give myself over to the profession of a poet for life," he told Crabb Robinson (who told Christopher Wordsworth), "I was impressed with a conviction, that there were four English poets whom I must have continually before me as examples—Chaucer, Shakspeare, Spenser, and Milton. These I must study, and equal *if I could*; and I need not think of the rest."[8] Hazlitt complained that Wordsworth "sometimes dares to compare himself with Milton,"[9] and Alaric Watts was astonished that he ranked his own *Laodamia* with *Lycidas* as "twin Immortals" of the elegiac mode.[10] Although these reported remarks do not give us Wordsworth in his own voice, he emerges from them as a more self-reliant figure than the famously sturdy Keats, at least in emulative gusto.

When we speak of "the two generations of Romantic poets," we usually mean that it is pedagogically convenient to schedule Blake-Wordsworth-Coleridge and Byron-Shelley-Keats on either side of a midterm examination. Nevertheless, there *was* a second genera-

7. Keats to the George Keatses, 14 October 1818, in *The Letters of John Keats*, ed. Hyder Edward Rollins, 2 vols. (Cambridge, Mass.: Harvard Univ. Press, 1958), I, 394.

8. Christopher Wordsworth, *Memoirs of William Wordsworth, Poet-Laureate, D.C.L.*, 2 vols. (London: Edward Moxon, 1851), II, 470; misleadingly attributed (from Grosart) in Wittreich, *Romantics on Milton*, p. 135.

9. *The Complete Works of William Hazlitt*, ed. P. P. Howe, 21 vols. (London and Toronto: J. M. Dent, 1930–34), XI, 92; quoted in Wittreich, *Romantics on Milton*, p. 119.

10. *Alaric Watts, A Narrative of His Life*, by his son Alaric Alfred Watts, 2 vols. (London: R. Bentley, 1884), I, 240; and see in Wittreich, *Romantics on Milton*, p. 135.

tion (if not a first) insofar as three tough, emergent poets regarded themselves as offspring of a parent they had not chosen, or, as Byron seems to have seen it, of a dysenteric trinity seated among the waters of the North, like the dragon Pharaoh in the midst of his rivers. Byron and Shelley both passed beyond adolescence as artists in poems that allow Wordsworth his moment of ventriloquism. Childe Harold's apostrophes (in the third canto) to Alps that hear and absorb him sound forced and *were* forced, we know, by Shelley's insistence that Byron compete with the loudest modern voice in its own idiom. The late Earl Wasserman suggested that the speaker of *Alastor* and its problematic Preface is a Wordsworthian puppet who quotes *Tintern Abbey* and the great *Ode* in order to disqualify himself, and that the poem implicitly parodies *The Excursion*, published the previous year.[11] The voices of both poets deepen, strengthen, and become themselves (as we now hear them) through these exercises in mimicry and reaction.

One reason why the literary father is so formidable an opponent is that he has inherited the weaponry of the grandfather. It is not surprising, then, that Byron and Keats tried to analyze the compound avatar, Milton-Wordsworth, into constituent elements which might then be dealt with one at a time. "Thou shalt believe in Milton . . . ; / Thou shalt not set up Wordsworth," Byron thunders in *Don Juan*'s familiar parody of the Decalogue. When Byron invokes Milton and the Augustan satirists in order to chastise his contemporaries, the "Lakers" in particular, he is ostensibly trying to reform his readers. His assaults were also dictated by political partisanship, envy, anti-intellectualism (Wordsworth cannot be "understood" and is "crazed beyond all hope"), snobbery toward anyone who writes for a living, and a delight in bitchiness for its own sake. The aggressive good taste and moralizing tone distract the reader from the real object of concern, Milton. "My poem's epic," Byron announces, and therefore liable to be weighed in the balance with "A drowsy frowzy poem, call'd the 'Excursion' " and the inevitable "epic from Bob Southey every Spring." The arbiter of weights and measures is, of course, Milton, "the prince of poets—so we say." One way of

11. Earl R. Wasserman, *Shelley: A Critical Reading* (Baltimore and London: Johns Hopkins Press, 1971), pp. 11–21.

forestalling judgment is to befriend the judge, and this Byron does in the Dedication to *Don Juan*. A Miltonic disgust with the Laureates and other intellectual eunuchs who serve monarchs becomes a scourge in the hand of a composite figure, grandfather-grandson. Differences between Christian epic and mock-epic become moot, as do dreaded comparisons between the talents of the generations. To paraphrase the Dedication, the poet's strategy makes the word "Byronic" mean "sublime."

Keats's celebrated metaphor of life as a "Mansion of Many Apartments" occurs in the midst of a lengthy discussion of the relative strengths of Milton and Wordsworth. Because his assessment so closely approximates Wordsworth's own view of the matter, it will more appropriately be examined later in this essay. What needs to be noticed now is that whenever Keats wrote individually of Wordsworth and Milton, he, like Byron, was of two minds about the former and revered the latter. *The Excursion* may be one of "three things to rejoice at in this Age,"[12] but its author is an egotist and no philosopher. Milton, however, is a poet to "feast upon,"[13] and Keats found that day by day "the Paradise Lost becomes a greater wonder."[14] Although that poem must finally be regarded as "a curruption [*sic*] of our language," it remains "a beautiful and grand Curiosity. The most remarkable Production of the world."[15] But it does spell death to any later poet who tries to mine its "vein of art," as Keats had tried in *Hyperion*, now abandoned a second time with resolves for a fresh start.

Wordsworth worshiped Milton this side of idolatry, and not always this side. The Prospectus originally called him "Holiest of Men" (25), and in the late poem *At Vallombrosa* (1837–42) he is "that holiest of Bards."[16] The 1849–50 *Poetical Works* substi-

12. Keats to B. R. Haydon, 10 January 1818, in Rollins, *Letters of Keats*, I, 203.

13. Keats to J. H. Reynolds, 27 April 1818, ibid., I, 274; and see Wittreich, *Romantics on Milton*, p. 550.

14. Keats to J. H. Reynolds, 24 August 1819, in Rollins, *Letters of Keats*, II, 146; and see Wittreich, *Romantics on Milton*, p. 561.

15. Keats to the George Keatses, 24 September 1819, in Rollins, *Letters of Keats*, II, 212; and see Wittreich, *Romantics on Milton*, p. 561.

16. *The Poetical Works of William Wordsworth*, ed. Ernest de Selincourt, rev. Helen Darbishire, 5 vols. (Oxford: Clarendon Press, 1952–59), III, 224; and see Wittreich, *Romantics on Milton*, p. 141.

tutes "In holiest mood" for the first phrase, presumably out of the same septuagenarian reluctance to give "pain to some good and pious persons" that led him to protest to Isabella Fenwick that the great *Ode* does not preach the pre-existence of the soul.[17] Book Fifth of *The Prelude,* devoted to "Books," calls Shakespeare and Milton "Labourers divine!"[18] and ranks the latter with Homer and the Hebrew poets,

> as Powers
> For ever to be hallowed; only less,
> For what we may become, and what we need,
> Than Nature's self, which is the breath of God.
>
> (219–22)

The 1850 text adds the qualifying line, "Or His pure Word by miracle revealed," but this time the afterthought amplifies the metaphor rather than blurring it. Throughout his career, even in decline, Wordsworth found vatic strength in Milton and ranked his works with those of the Psalmodist and the Prophets, one step removed from the Logos itself. The 1815 Preface says it best: "The grand store-house of enthusiastic and meditative Imagination, of poetical, as contradistinguished from human and dramatic Imagination, is the prophetic and lyrical parts of the holy Scriptures, and the works of Milton, to which I cannot forbear to add those of Spenser."[19]

The Hebrews were a river, "the voice/ Which roars along the bed of Jewish Song" (*Prelude* V.203–4), and Milton had "a voice whose sound was like the sea."[20] The running and tidal waters sing in Wordsworth, and always of origins: the remembered and revisited Wye rolling with "a soft inland murmur," the "mighty waters rolling evermore" on the shore where unborn children play, the crooning Derwent that "lov'd/ To blend his murmurs with my Nurse's song" and meanders, checked and baffled, like a figured

17. *Poetical Works,* IV, 464.

18. Line 165 in the 1805 text, which will be followed throughout except where otherwise noted, *Wordsworth's Prelude,* ed. Ernest de Selincourt, rev. Helen Darbishire (Oxford: Clarendon Press, 1959); and see Wittreich, *Romantics on Milton,* p. 113.

19. *Literary Criticism of William Wordsworth,* ed. Paul M. Zall (Lincoln: Univ. of Nebraska Press, 1966), p. 150. Hereafter cited as *Criticism.* See Wittreich, *Romantics on Milton,* p. 130.

20. "London, 1802," *Poetical Works,* III, 116.

bass throughout *The Prelude*. The *continuo* of the waters, never idle or ornamental in Wordsworth, links human song with the divine poetry of "Nature's self" or the "pure Word." An implicit and serious pun transforms Milton and the prophets into sources whose mouth is *The Recluse*.

Wordsworth's reverence for his great original contrasts sharply with Byron's enlistment of Milton as a Whig crony and with Keats's characteristically gluttonous metaphor of feasting upon him. Admiration so intense would ordinarily forestall criticism and cripple emulation. For Wordsworth it did neither. The marginalia in his own copy of *Paradise Lost* employ such adjectives as "injudicious," "inconsistent," and "not consonant." Milton is twice "guilty of an oversight" and elsewhere "entangled in difficulties." The murder of Abel "is inelegant and reminds one too strongly of a Butcher's stall."[21] These comments seem to belong to the years in which *The Prelude* was begun, just as Wordsworth's strictures on Milton's sonnets coincide with his attempt to reproduce their force in the English of a later day. In November 1802, he told an unknown correspondent that he thought them "manly and dignified compositions" and musically successful on the whole. Nevertheless, they are "in several places incorrect, and sometimes uncouth in language, and perhaps, in some, inharmonious."[22]

Pugnacious as a practical critic, Wordsworth was likewise unconvinced that the great epic subjects had been exhausted. It is easy to misread his search for a topic early in *The Prelude*:

> Sometimes, mistaking vainly, as I fear,
> Proud spring-tide swellings for a regular sea,
> I settle on some British theme, some old
> Romantic tale, by Milton left unsung . . .
>
> (I.177–80)

The unsung tale is the "Brittonicum" proposed as music for a changed and shrill pastoral pipe ("fistula . . . mutata . . . strides") in *Epitaphium Damonis* (167–71). In *Manso* as well Milton had

21. "Annotations to *Paradise Lost*," as printed in Wittreich, *Romantics on Milton*, pp. 103–9.

22. *The Letters of William and Dorothy Wordsworth: The Early Years*, ed. Ernest de Selincourt, rev. Chester L. Shaver (Oxford: Clarendon Press, 1967), p. 379; and see Wittreich, *Romantics on Milton*, p. 110. The editors conjecture that the correspondent may have been Lamb or Coleridge.

hoped to call back in English song such native kings as Arthur, still battling beneath the earth, and the great-hearted heroes of the unconquered Table.[23] When Wordsworth toys with the possibility of settling on what Milton has "left," the scraps, as it were, of the Arthurian "invictae mensae," he does not mean that every other option has been closed to the heroic poet. He does not see himself as a tardy dinner guest in Eden, like the speaker of *The Fall of Hyperion*, who has to make do with "refuse of a meal/ By angel tasted or our Mother Eve." Rather, as the context shows, the legends of the ancient Britons head a list that includes such lesser stories as those of Mithridates-Odin, Dominique de Gourges, Gustavus, and Wallace, and concludes with a yearning towards "some philosophic Song/ Of Truth that cherishes our daily life" (I.230–31). This "last and favourite aspiration" (229) is dramatically ironic, a literal *aspiratio* or "breathing upon" the Aeolian harp defrauded of its harmony some one hundred and twenty lines earlier, when present-tense "vernal promises" that a "long-continued frost" is breaking up yield to the revisionary preterite, " 'Twas Autumn" (I.49–50, 74). It is also ironic insofar as the shilly-shallying and consequent writer's block recorded here are obviously being exorcised right now, in the therapeutic re-enactment that will introduce the "philosophic Song" itself. There, in lines leading up to those that would be extracted and printed separately as the Prospectus, Wordsworth will echo Othello as he gives up forever all traditionally epic occupations:

> Then farewell to the Warrior's schemes . . .
> . . . and farewell
> That other hope, long mine, the hope to fill
> The heroic trumpet with the Muse's breath!
>
> (*Home at Grasmere*, 745, 748–50)[24]

Henceforth he will muse "On Man on Nature and on Human life" (754) in Milton's vocabulary and, as we shall see, in apparent ignorance that Milton has already done so.

---

23. "Si quando indigenas revocabo in carmina reges,/ Arturumque etiam sub terris bella moventem,/ Aut dicam invictae sociali foedere mensae/ Magnanimos Heroas . . ." (*Manso*, 80–83).

24. *Poetical Works*, V(Appendix A), 337. These lines bear an obvious relationship to Milton's claim in the invocation to Book IX that his own "argument" is "Not less but more Heroic than the wrath/Of stern *Achilles* . . ." (13–15).

II

If, as Keats put it, modern poets are electors of Hanover, whereas
"the antients were Emperors of vast Provinces,"[25] Wordsworth
may look like an up-to-date imperialist, content to seize the
mineral rights. He did indeed loot Milton's vocabulary as if he
were taking words from the dictionary, but despite Havens' indig-
nation, the practice is as ancient and honored as "secondary epic"
itself.[26] Let us begin with some lines in which Wordsworth "bor-
rows" from his two major storehouses of "enthusiastic and meditative Imagination," Milton and Scripture:

> Nor perchance,
> If I were not thus taught, should I the more
> Suffer my *genial spirits* to decay:
> *For thou art with me* here upon the banks
> Of this fair river . . .
> (*Tintern Abbey*, 111–15; my italics)

The second italicized phrase leaps out immediately as David's
address to his Shepherd in Psalm 23. The moment is remarkable in
many ways: here, at the opening of the fourth and final verse
paragraph, the monologue unexpectedly becomes dramatic. (So
does the Psalm, as it switches from the third- to the second-person
pronoun, from speaking of to speaking to the Lord.) Earlier there
has been "some uncertain notice" of humanity in the landscape—
vagrants, perhaps, or a hermit sending up a doubtful smoke-signal
from his cave in the houseless woods. There has also been a
moment of direct address to the "sylvan Wye" (56). Now it is
revealed that "my dearest Friend" (115) has accompanied the
speaker from the beginning and that she would have been his
nurse, guide, and guardian if nature had failed him.

If Psalm 23 may be taken in its entirety as the lexical context
here, the dear Sister emerges not as a tutelary genius of classical
idyll, but rather as the pastor of the fallen Hebrew pastoralist in an
image that begins with David and culminates in the Agnus Dei who
is simultaneously the Good Shepherd. The adjective itself, "pas-

25. Keats to J. H. Reynolds, 3 February 1818, in Rollins, *Letters of Keats*, I, 224.
26. The term originates with C. S. Lewis in *A Preface to* Paradise Lost (Oxford and
New York: Oxford Univ. Press, 1942).

toral," slipped in unobtrusively and symmetrically in the sixteenth and the next-to-last lines of the poem, becomes generic and prefigures *Michael: A Pastoral Poem,* which two years later will move backwards from "the prophetic and lyrical parts of the holy Scriptures" to terrible Genesis, with its herdsman patriarchs who agree to bleed their sons in order to appease the parched God of the desert pasture. Finally, the Psalm suggests "still waters" beneath the rolling of the Wye, just as the landscape seen again with dimmed vision after five long years evokes David's walk through the valley of the shadow.

The first phrase, "genial spirits," comes from *Samson Agonistes:*

> All otherwise to me my thoughts portend,
> That these dark orbs no more shall treat with light,
> Nor th'other light of life continue long,
> But yield to double darkness nigh at hand:
> So much I feel my *genial spirits* droop,
> My hopes all flat, nature within me seems
> In all her functions weary of her self . . .
>
> (590–96; my italics)

Samson's fear that the darkness of death will soon follow that of blindness provides insight into Wordsworth's denial that the light will fade twice for him too. The mighty world of eye and ear is already at one remove, as is "my former heart" (117), when he returns to the Wye. The Sister's saving presence assures him that neither will retreat further: he reads his "former pleasures in the shooting lights/ Of thy wild eyes" and beholds in her "what I was once." Coleridge uses Milton's phrase in much the same way in *Dejection: An Ode.* The verbs "to gaze" and "to see" dominate the second strophe, and both are morbidly disjunct from "to feel." The third strophe opens with a confession to the "Dear Lady" who, in this case, cannot rescue the poet: "My genial spirits fail."

One does not have to consult the mint in which phrases like these were coined in order to know their weight in common currency. It will, in fact, be a mistake to do so, unless one can resist the temptation to turn overtone into allegory (Wordsworth= David, Coleridge=Samson). When does one profitably apply the lexical definition, and when not? For instance, to what extent should the "celestial light" whose loss is mourned in the great *Ode* recall Milton's prayer: "So much the rather thou Celestial light/ Shine inward" (*PL* III.51–52)? Something like "a Universal blanc" appears to both poets, each opaque in his way to "sight of vernal bloom, or Summer's Rose," and each hopes to "tell/ Of things invisible to mortal sight" (*PL* III.48, 43, 54–55). But it would be manifestly absurd to issue Wordsworth's light a birth certificate as "ofspring of Heav'n first-born,/ Or of th' Eternal Coeternal beam" (*PL* III.1–2), or as kin to anything of good family in theological optics. Where does one cross the line? The problem in critical tact cannot be solved until one knows what thing tact is, other than the rule-of-thumb one trusts in oneself and deplores in one's students and colleagues.

One final example of practical difficulty: the Wordsworthian verb "to brood" comes right out of the Miltonic lexicon, from the Holy Spirit that "Dove-like satst brooding on the vast Abyss/ And mad'st it pregnant" (*PL* I.21–22). Because Wordsworth habitually turned Milton's pantheon into faculties, we know where we are when he says that the poet's "meditative mind" is "best pleased, perhaps,/ While she, as duteous as the Mother Dove,/ Sits brooding" (*Prelude* I.150–52). The same definition extends to the *Ode*, where Immortality, a principle of spiritual origin, continuity, and fecundity, "Broods" over the child like the light of day, or like "a Master o'er a Slave" (120). But what may be done with the fifth line of *Resolution and Independence:* "Over his own sweet voice the Stock-dove broods"? Shall we call it bird, wandering voice, or what? The poem deals with the self-deification and inevitable suicide of the poet's "spirits" (with perhaps a punning glance at Burns), a downward spiral of self-intoxication that pirns from "gladness" to "madness" (47–49). To brood over one's own voice may, then, constitute surrender to redundant and anxious inactivity, the artist's fecklessness squared and cubed and raised to an overwhelming power. Again, psychology implies theology: the poem praises Milton's latter-day coreligionists, "grave Livers . . . in Scotland" (97), and ends with an imperative appeal to God as help and stay. But hope throughout has been minimal, and the poet has toyed so roughly with the callow, younger self who is the protagonist that the Stock-dove may mean everything or nothing: perhaps the Paraclete, and perhaps a bundle of feathers and appetite, no more to be chosen as a companionable form than are the chattering magpie, the warbling skylark, the playful hare, or those blind mouths, the leeches.[27]

Such puzzles are rare. Normally, Wordsworth's language explodes when original contexts are superimposed, like photographic transparencies, on later ones. This is not to say that Wordsworth means what Milton means, but rather that Wordsworth's meaning emerges only when the phrase is *read through* Milton's meaning. A few examples are in order. Near the end of Book VI of *The Prelude,* the mountains appear "more by *darkness visible/* And their own size, than any outward light" (645–46; my italics). Because the adjective does not modify the noun, the italicized phrase is not grammatically parallel to Milton's use of it:

> . . . yet from those flames
> No light, but rather *darkness visible*
> Serv'd only to discover sights of woe,
> Regions of sorrow, doleful shades, where peace
> And rest can never dwell . . .
>
> (*PL* I.62–66; my italics)[28]

When lit by the luridness of hell, the situation of the touring student and his companion becomes far more fearsome. The second night of their journey into Italy, they got "lost, bewilder'd among woods immense." Tormented by "the stings/ Of insects . . . the cry of unknown birds . . ./ And sometimes rustling motions nigh at hand," they "wish'd to sleep but could not" (VI.642–50). The adumbrations of Dante's "selva oscura" and Milton's "doleful shades" of everlasting insomnia appear in retrospect after one has followed the clue of the repeated phrase. The only *positive* light imagery in the passage even suggests Satan weltering on the burning lake: on the "sullen water" of Como "a

27. See Wordsworth's remarks, in the 1815 Preface, on this use of the verb: "The Stock-dove is said to *coo,* a sound well imitating the note of the bird; but, by the intervention of the metaphor *broods,* the affections are called in by the imagination to assist in marking the manner in which the Bird reiterates and prolongs her soft note, as if herself delighting to listen to it, and participating of a still and quiet satisfaction, like that which may be supposed inseparable from the continuous process of incubation" (*Criticism,* p. 147). It will be noticed that the sex of the Stock-dove has changed between 1802 and 1815.

28. This and numerous other parallel passages are listed by Havens, *Influence of Milton,* Appendix A, pp. 607–20.

dull red image of the moon/ Lay bedded, changing oftentimes its form/ Like an uneasy snake" (635–38). The danger for the reader confronted with allusions of this kind is that he may forget that they are necessarily ironic, similes rather than metaphors, comparisons rather than equations. The poet shows us how alike things are in order to prove a saving difference. In the present case, the narrow gap between a similarity and an identity is that through which two bewildered boys escape. Satan's black flames stand for perpetual ignorance and torture; Wordsworth and Jones are in a state of *agnosia*, of indeterminacy or "not-knowing," rather than one of mis-knowing. The mountains visible by darkness are the Alps they have just hiked through, whose ontological status has been the target of a skepticism that climaxed at the physical summit, when the light of sense went out with a flash that revealed "the invisible world" (VI.536). All that is behind them now—the dawn will rise in a hour or two, and the holiday will continue.

Later in *The Prelude*, the same passage from *Paradise Lost* colors Wordsworth's "reverie" of Druid sacrifice at Stonehenge:

> I called upon the darkness; and it took,
> A midnight darkness seem'd to come and take
> All objects from my sight; and lo! again
> The desart visible by dismal flames!
> It is the sacrificial Altar, fed
> With living men . . .
>
> (*Prelude* XII.327–32)

Once we recognize the Miltonic dimension of this vision of "the past" (320; the 1850 text reads "Our dim ancestral Past"), we can see an epic descent in these lines, with the poet himself as Odysseus or Aeneas or Dante. The excursion to hell also moves the poet-hero backward into the abyss of time. He cannot progress until he has stood up to his origins, personal and racial, and made his peace with them. This historical spot of time helps to initiate him in the same way that his recollections of childhood do; the wizardry of words conjures and then masters memory, the ghost of buried time and mother of all the muses. Her "demonic" realm of below and before is not the precise place Milton and Virgil intended,[29] but without their dark fires Wordsworth would have lacked one element in his iconography of that chiaroscuro and amoral world (the foundry of Blake's Energy) whose ancestral and life-giving voice is sometimes a nurse's song and sometimes the groans of British captives flaming on the night in wicker cages.

Water seals this world from the sober observer who floats "Incumbent o'er the surface of past time" as if it were a lake, and mistakes refractions and reflections for what is really down there (*Prelude* IV.263). Whatever pokes up through the soup of the forgotten and the possible does so as volcanic islands burst suddenly from the sea. The climactic vision from Mount Snowdon, Wordsworth's strongest analogy from natural to mental forces of individuation and integration, turns on yet another "loan" from Milton:

> . . . on the shore
> I found myself of a *huge* sea of mist,
> Which, meek and silent, rested at my feet:
> A hundred hills their dusky *backs upheaved*
> All over this still Ocean . . .
> (*Prelude* XIII.42–46; my italics)

The source is nothing less than God's gathering of the waters on the third day:

> Be gather'd now ye Waters under Heav'n
> Into one place, and let dry Land appear.
> Immediately the Mountains *huge* appear
> Emergent, and thir broad bare *backs upheave*
> Into the Clouds, thir tops ascend the Sky . . .
> (*PL* VII.283–87; my italics)[30]

Once again, the echo does not merely enrich the meaning but supplies it. Here, as succinctly and unobtrusively as anywhere in Wordsworth, the nascent human personality repeats Coleridge's "eternal act of creation in the infinite I AM." As man crawled and

---

29. The oxymoron of "darkness visible" recalls Virgilian chiaroscuro, which is especially prominent as the controlling metaphor of Book VI of the *Aeneid*.

30. W. J. B. Owen, who first pointed out this parallel in 1957, discusses it and the suggestion of Coleridge's Primary Imagination in "Literary Echoes in *The Prelude*," *The Wordsworth Circle*, 3 (1972), 10–11.

his earth erupted from the sea, and as God learned to name himself by making something "other," so the infant differentiates his conscious self as an exile in a "dry Land" where the amniotic fluid no longer cradles him to rest, the breast has ceased to flow, universal personality has shattered into first-, second-, and third-person pronouns, and the repeated terminal verb, "appear," is all that one can trust. Lionel Trilling's classic essay on "oceanic" feelings demonstrates that Wordsworth understood these processes long before Freud dissected them.[31] But Milton saw them first, in the imagery of gestation that dominates the lines preceding the speech last quoted:

> The earth was form'd, but in the Womb as yet
> Of Waters, Embryon immature involv'd,
> Appear'd not: over all the face of Earth
> Main Ocean flow'd, not idle, but with warm
> Prolific humor soft'ning all her Globe,
> Fermented the great Mother to conceive,
> Satiate with genial moisture, when God said . . .
>
> (*PL* VII.276–82)

Milton does not provide a "context" for Wordsworth's tags so much as *they* condense *him*. That is why the tags explode whenever we recognize them as such and add water.

Let us look last at the most familiar of instances,[32] which needs to be examined one more time if we are to relate Wordsworth to contemporary and ancestral epic "borrowers":

> The earth is *all before* me: with a heart
> Joyous, nor scared at its own liberty,
> I look about, and should the *guide* I *chuse*
> Be nothing better than a *wandering* cloud,
> I cannot miss my *way*. I breathe again . . .
> (*Prelude* I.15–19; my italics)

> The World was *all before* them, where to *choose*
> Thir place of rest, and Providence thir *guide:*

31. Lionel Trilling, "The Immortality Ode," in *The English Institute Annual, 1941* (New York: Columbia Univ. Press, 1942), reprinted in *The Liberal Imagination* (New York: Viking Press, 1950), pp. 125–54.

32. See, for instance, Owen's excellent discussion, "Literary Echoes in *The Prelude*," pp. 11–12. This parallel, like several others looked at in this essay, has been noticed so many times that further documentation would be superfluous.

> They hand in hand with *wand'ring* steps and slow,
> Through Eden took thir solitary *way*.
>
> (*PL* XII.646–49; my italics)

To wander is to err, as the devils, the foster-fathers or debating coaches of all future heretics, discovered when they split hairs about "Providence, Foreknowledge, Will, and Fate . . ./ And found no end, in wand'ring mazes lost" (I.559–61). Eve too, according to Adam, was misled by her "strange/ Desire of wand'ring this unhappy Morn" (IX.1136). Milton's diction draws strength from his awareness that in languages like Greek and Latin (and German still), cognate mental and bodily activities often rely on a single verb, such as Πλαvâv, or *errare*, or *irren*. In a language like English, with its imported, class-belligerent vocabularies for abstractions and stones, pork roasts and pig-meat, such tautologies as Milton's "Erroneous there to wander" (*PL* VII.20) remind the Christian reader that flesh is a metaphor for spirit and warn metaphysicians that their mind/matter problem may simply be the litigation that follows a linguistic accident.

The freed prisoner at the opening of *The Prelude* wanders as Adam and Eve do at the end of their poem, and his error, like theirs, is directed by a higher agency. Providence becomes the benediction of "this gentle breeze," a "sweet breath of Heaven" that stirs up within the poet a "corresponding mild creative breeze,/ A vital breeze," and drives the cloud (I.1, 41, 43–44). The same spirit makes the daffodils flutter and dance in a very great poem about wandering and clouds that should be retired forever from the high-school curriculum. Although he seems foot-loose, the poet is walking homeward through the subjected plain. After forty years of marching in circles through such another desert, Joshua led Israel into the Promised Land; after forty days of temptation in the wilderness, Joshua's namesake, the second Adam and hero of *Paradise Regained*, "Home to his Mothers house private return'd" (IV.639). The journey that is *The Prelude* ends where *The Recluse* begins, "Home at Grasmere" with a matronly virgin. Whatever restlessness remains will find its voice in the character of the Wanderer in *The Excursion*. But for the moment the poet and his sister resemble Adam and Eve domiciled again, or the pair of "milk-white Swans" that once nested on the lake:

> From afar
> They came, to sojourn here in *solitude,*
> *Chusing* this Valley, they who had the *choice*
> Of the whole *world.*
>
> (*Home at Grasmere,* 239–43; my italics)

Milton read Scripture typologically, and Wordsworth regarded them both that way, as a combined "grand store-house" that could be raided at will by anyone daring enough to think he could get away with it. A cursory search among writers whose lives overlapped Wordsworth's turns up a number of desperadoes who plundered the Milton dictionary. The great lexicographer himself, as well as Mary Shelley and Dickens, are among those who expropriated the passage we have been looking at, the last four lines of *Paradise Lost.*[3] Rasselas in Cairo protests to Imlac that, as a prince, he can make a choice of life: " 'My birth has given me at least one advantage over others, by enabling me to determine for myself. I have here the world before me; I will review it at leisure: surely happiness is somewhere to be found.' " Frankenstein's Monster, who has read the poem in French translation, burns the adopted home that has rejected him and sets forth to find his creator: " 'And now, with the world before me, whither should I bend my steps?' " The "first stage of Pip's expectations" ends with a homesick boy on the high road to London: "It was now too late and too far to go back, and I went on. And the mists had all solemnly risen now, and the world lay spread before me."

In each of these three cases, the Miltonic tag works as a structural principle, a narrative finger-post pointing to the end of innocence, or the beginning of the end. The Monster insists, explicitly and often, that his auditor and maker understand him in epic terms, as Adam or Satan. In *Rasselas,* however, a single, buried allusion hints that a re-reading "through" *Paradise Lost* will show why the

---

33. Byron, on the eve of his first departure from England, also thought of the expulsion from Paradise as he anticipated the grand tour that would become the first two cantos of *Childe Harold's Pilgrimage:* "As to money matters I am ruined, at least till Rochdale is sold, & if that does not turn out well I shall enter the Austrian or Russian service, perhaps the Turkish, if I like their manners, the world is all before me, and I leave England without regret, and without a wish to revisit any thing it contains, except *yourself,* and your present residence," Byron to Mrs. Catherine Gordon Byron, 22 June 1809, in *Byron's Letters and Journals,* ed. Leslie A. Marchand, 5 vols. (London: John Murray, 1973–), I, 206. The phrase appears several times in Byron's poetry.

travelers can "return to Abissinia" (the book's last words), but not to the Happy Valley, why that literally postdiluvian return must follow "the inundation of the Nile," and why Johnson situated the Valley at the source of "the Father of waters," where fabulists still placed Eden and the Royal Geographical Society would explore for it in the nineteenth century.

Similarly, Pip's fall looks like a bourgeois parody of Adam's, for he is "fondly overcome with Female charm" *and* "deceiv'd" (*PL* IX.998–99) in a world where sexual relationships, as well as social and economic ones, have degenerated into a game of beggar-my-neighbor. The novel ends as its first volume did, with a caricature of Milton's parting tableau of the chastened lovers: "I took her hand in mine, and we went out of the ruined place; and, as the morning mists had risen long ago when I first left the forge, so, the evening mists were rising now. . . . " Pip and Estella re-enact Adam and Eve, who held hands as they took their first, halting steps into diminished possibility while the destroying Cherubim, God's love changed to fire, glided along the ground "meteorous, as Ev'ning Mist/ Ris'n from a River o'er the marish glides" (XII.629–30). *Great Expectations* originally concluded with an embarrassed handshake in Piccadilly. The later, "happy" ending in Miss Havisham's wrecked garden is in fact stern and multivalent, artistically happy insofar as the covering myth, once recognized, defines the joining of hands as an impulsive, tentative contract for fruitless labor, the banker's sweat and the barrenness of menopause. In Dickens' final version, the "tranquil light" of a misty evening near the Thames shows Pip "no shadow of another parting from her." The intermediate text published in *All the Year Round* casts "the shadow of no parting from her" and reconfirms his bondage.

I have widened the scope of this discussion in order to suggest that Wordsworth was typical of his time, rather than the reverse, in his freedom from anxiety over his relationship to the mighty dead. It is impossible *not* to find such concern in *The Fall of Hyperion* and Blake's major prophecies; it is difficult to find it in *The Prelude*. The poem is therapeutic, as I have said, but the writer's block it analyzes and thus cures was not caused by frowning, bearded avatars in the epic genre. The failure of the French Revolution, for instance, was traumatic for Wordsworth.

But there simply was no "Milton problem." Like Johnson, Mary Shelley, Dickens, and many others, Wordsworth saw that the Christian scheme of Creation → Fall → Redemption conforms to the structure of secular experience. Because Milton's poem definitively expresses that pattern, allusion to it in Milton's own words reminds the reader that any significant human life resonates in myth. Keats put it best: "A Man's life of any worth is a continual allegory—and very few eyes can see the Mystery of his life—a life like the scriptures, figurative—which such people can no more make out than they can the hebrew Bible."[34] The "history" may move from the Happy Valley to Cairo to Abyssinia, or from Windermere to Cambridge-London-Paris to Grasmere, but the anagogy progresses from Paradise to the wilderness to "A paradise within thee, happier far" (*PL* XII.587).

If Wordsworth's practice is typical, it is also traditional, descending from Virgil in a direct genealogical line. A brief look at how each of two avatars met his own Laius at the crossroads should show conclusively why Wordsworth was unalarmed.

III

The first six books of the *Aeneid* mean more when they are read through the *Odyssey*, just as the last six require the *Iliad*. A single example will suffice. When Aeneas lands in Sicily, he meets a marooned Ithacan who recounts the horror-story of the Cyclops' cave. The details of gore and vomit are as harrowing as those in Homer. When Polyphemus himself appears the next moment, the mood shifts to one of pathos. The monster moans and gnashes his teeth as he stumbles into the waves and washes the oozing blood from his eye-socket. Aeneas notices his flock of sheep and thinks of them as Polyphemus' only joy and the only solace of his misery:

> lanigerae comitantur oves; ea sola voluptas
> solamenque mali.

34. Keats to the George Keatses, 19 February 1819, in Rollins, *Letters of Keats*, II, 67.

The metrical deficiency of the two-foot second line calls attention to this spontaneous act of sympathy, or "feeling with," which is not at all the same thing as "feeling sorry for" the cannibal giant. Recalling from Homer how the escaping Odysseus mocked and baited the blinded Cyclops, we see in miniature Virgil's rationale of history. Compassion is not simply an aspect of Trojan-ness as opposed to Achaean ruthlessness and guile. It is Roman-ness itself, that ability to spare the defeated which is one of a civilized conqueror's three chief arts and which gives the Augustan *imperium* the moral right to rule the world. This is what Anchises will tell Aeneas in the underworld, at the precise moment in which he gives his son a new name: "tu, Romane!"

Dante's use of Virgil depends heavily on verbal echoes and games. Because Virgil's word for fate (*fatum*) is the past participle of his verb for speech (*for, farier*), and because human destiny is filled with the tears of things, his characters weep as they "recreate fate" in speaking of those past actions that have predicated their present situation. One's lifetime determines one's eternity in the *Inferno* also, where damnation consists in the remembrance of sin. Thus Francesca da Rimini tells her story like one who weeps and speaks together ("come colui che piange e dice"), and so does Ugolino ("parlare e lacrimar inseme"). Blood rather than tears flows with the words of the Suicides ("usciva inseme/ parole e sangue"); the tears of the Traitors freeze at once and grow backwards as icicles into the brain.[35]

One final example: Virgilian *pietas,* the untranslatable quality that defines heroic virtue, becomes both "pity" and "duty" in Tuscan *pietà.* Dante plays the two meanings against each other and shows that the latter must drive out the former if the soul is to live. When Dante, the sinful central character, swoons for pity ("di pietade") of Paolo and Francesca, he falls down as a dead body falls. No simile is idle in the *Commedia,* and this one defines pity as a morbid sentiment that questions the infinite goodness of God. The whole duty of man is to acquiesce in the will of the father, human or divine; it is precisely this "pieta del . . . padre" that

35. Coleridge may have been playing on the Virgilian connection between weeping and speech when he rephrased "Thoughts that do often lie too deep for tears," the last line of the *Immortality Ode,* as "Thoughts all too deep for words!–" (*To William Wordsworth,* 11).

Dante's Ulysses neglects when he sets out on his presumptuous voyage to the sunset.

Dante's treatment of Virgil as a character in the poem provides the key to Wordsworth's attitude toward Milton. The disciple always addresses his master with the respectful "voi" and is called by the familiar "tu" in return. Nevertheless, Dante the author must at last condescend to his teacher, who had the misfortune to die nineteen years before the Christian revelation and therefore, as a type of unaided human reason, can accompany his pupil no farther than to the top of Purgatory. Virgil, by which I mean here the ethos of the *Aeneid*, clearly feels the same way about Homer, whose heroes, from an Augustan viewpoint, are a pack of murderous farmers out on a vendetta. For each poet a single decisive historic event, the founding of the City or the Church, distinguishes his time from that of his predecessor. Armed with a belief in spiritual progress, one may raid the dictionary with a clear conscience, confident that the lexicographer did not know what his words really meant.

The lines quoted from the Prospectus at the beginning of this essay continue as follows:

> The darkest pit
> Of the profoundest hell, night, chaos, death
> Nor aught of blinder vacancy scoop'd out
> By help of dreams, can breed such fear and awe
> As fall upon me often when I look
> Into my soul, into the soul of man
> My haunt, and the main region of my song.

(35–41)

The passage suggests that the latter-day poet, freed from gross fundamentalism, can, like a demythologizing theologian, see the true, human import of Christian symbolism. Does it also implicitly endorse the notion of a *universal* awakening, an Enlightenment separating his age from Milton's? Keats had no doubts whatever on the subject: Milton "did not think into the human heart, as Wordsworth has done—Yet Milton as a Philosopher, had sure as great powers as Wordsworth—What is then to be inferr'd? O many things—It proves there is really a grand march of intellect—, It proves that a mighty providence subdues the mightiest Minds to the service of the time being, whether it be in human Knowledge or Religion—"[36] Insofar as Wordsworth agreed, and it seems more likely than not that he did, our major problem solves itself: the ancestor is not only not a threat, he may be patronized. But another problem arises in its place. Both later poets have apparently failed to notice what any modern reader sees at once, that Milton does indeed haunt the heart and soul, that chaos and the pit are the mind's own places of conflict and despair.

Our modernity may be precisely the point. More than fifty years ago T. S. Eliot observed that later works alter the significance of earlier ones, and that the reason why we know so much more than the dead writers did is that "they are that which we know."[37] Coleridge made much the same point when he told Wordsworth "that every Author, as far as he is great and at the same time *original*, has had the task of *creating* the taste by which he is to be enjoyed."[38] It is also the taste by which his predecessors will henceforth be enjoyed. The invocations to Books III and VII of *Paradise Lost* confess that the Stygian pool and Aleian field are regions within the poet as well, but it is doubtful that we would attribute a consistent psychological dimension to Milton's figurative geography if we did not look back at it through our experience of such works as *The Four Zoas, Prometheus Unbound, The Fall of Hyperion,* and of course, *The Prelude.* If Wordsworth and Keats could not recognize that dimension, that may be because the ability to do so did not exist until they created it.

Two poems related to each other as *Paradise Lost* and *The Prelude* are have only that relational existence, world without end. So it must also have been in the beginning that seemed a latter

36. Keats to J. H. Reynolds, 3 May 1818, in Rollins, *Letters of Keats,* I, 282; see Wittreich, *Romantics on Milton,* p. 552.

37. "Tradition and the Individual Talent" (1919), reprinted in *Selected Essays,* 2d ed. (New York: Harcourt and Brace, 1950), p. 6. After several generational removes, we may find ourselves caught up in a family romance of our own, in which the junior critic's problem reproduces the critical problem: what can we add to this essay's remarks on interplay, simultaneity, and legitimate succession among writers in the "tradition"? The inevitably quoted Eliot seems our Aristotle on this subject (if not our Aristides), as perdurable as he is narrow in charting a main stream. The analogy may prove encouraging. Just as the *Poetics* remains the first and last word on Sophocles, but works not at all as a paradigm of the dark farces of Euripides, so Eliot's model (in his total critique) persuades by excluding "heretical" poets who were not, like those considered here, too bold and self-assured to be nervous about their ephebic stature.

38. "Essay, Supplementary to the Preface" (1815), in *Criticism,* p. 182.

day, when we were literally grounded on the dirt floor of the *oikos*, aware that Demodokos was earning his supper by distorting the Matter of Troy, but unaware that his songs were pre-Homeric. If the meaning of an apparent redaction does not emerge until it is deliberately read through an apparent original, the converse activity, which psychologizes Milton, or finds Christian elements in Virgil's Stoicism, or pacifistic second thoughts in Homer, is involuntary and historically inevitable. Debtor becomes creditor in infinite regression.

One could wish that all such debits and credits might be forgiven in the Great Society, as envisioned by William Wordsworth. "There is," he tells Coleridge in *The Prelude,* "one great Society alone on earth,/ The noble Living and the noble Dead" (X.968–70). The context establishes him as a post-Revolutionary man, like Milton, compassed round by encroaching darkness. It also shows that a commonwealth or freemasonry of epic poets is not at all what this supremely arrogant young writer had in mind.

The Siege of Hateful Contraries:
Shelley, Mary Shelley, Byron,
and Paradise Lost

STUART CURRAN

I dreamed that Milton's spirit rose, and took
  From life's green tree his Uranian lute;
And from his touch sweet thunder flowed, and shook
All human things built in contempt of man . . .

—Shelley

Few can pretend to the cheek of C. S. Lewis, who first told
Milton's readers that none of them knew what *Paradise Lost* was
about and then, with the primness of a Tory vicar confident of
taking tea with royalty in heaven, informed his auditors that the
lesson for the day was obedience.[1] But without his *hauteur,* one
can feel as adamant in one's convictions and press a thesis somewhat less primary, if equally less erroneous. Simple and negative, it
is likewise easier to substantiate. Romantic Satanism, the pervasive
heresy supposedly celebrated by the younger Romantics, does not
exist, but, like the chimeras of Eve's dream, continues to dis-
temper the mind. On that occasion Milton assured us that "Evil
into the mind of God or man/ May come or go" (V.117–18); but
we may also assume that it ought not to remain unquestioned for
a century and a half.

1. *A Preface to* Paradise Lost (London and New York: Oxford Univ. Press, 1942), p.
70.

To lift this burden from shoulders wearily accustomed to bear it is not to deny that there are those who deserve to have it to themselves. A succession of Milton's critics, with a sophistical blindness to the text, placed a self-indulgent and idiosyncratic taste above sober judgment and determined Milton to be Satan's apologist. For obscure reasons of cultural dynamics this line of argument seems to have reached its most vociferous pitch around the time of the Second World War, and the subsequent development of criticism on *Paradise Lost* appears to have taken impetus from the perceived necessity of refuting the Satanic view. With professional standards of courtesy governing so much of academic life, critics may be pardoned for displacing E. M. W. Tillyard or A. J. A. Waldock in favor of Shelley and Byron, long dead and immured within their scandalous reputations. A curious gentility it is, however, that would make the younger Romantics scapegoats and distort their views to accord with those of later commentators. One finds Merritt Y. Hughes, whose scholarly judgment was otherwise finely balanced, claiming that "Milton's Satan deceives himself so well that he deceived Shelley into thinking him a Promethean apostle of human regeneration, and Byron into thinking him an inspiring symbol of revolt against political tyranny."[2] Shelley, suggests John S. Diekhoff, conceived of Satan "as a thoroughly admirable moral agent," and Diekhoff dismisses the famous remarks on *Paradise Lost* in *A Defense of Poetry* with blistering scorn: "If this is eloquent, it is eloquent nonsense."[3] The moral archness of these comments serves to remind us that Romantic Satanism has an exact source in literary history, a source that might surprise later critics who lightly inherit the term:

Men of diseased hearts and depraved imaginations, who, forming a system of opinions to suit their own unhappy course of conduct, have rebelled against the holiest ordinances of human society, and hating that revealed religion which, with all their efforts and bravadoes, they are unable entirely to disbelieve, labour to make others as miserable as themselves, by infecting them with a moral virus that eats into the soul! The school which they have

2. *John Milton: Complete Poems and Major Prose* (New York: Odyssey Press, 1957), p. 179.

3. *Milton's* Paradise Lost: *A Commentary on the Argument* (London: Routledge and Kegan Paul, 1946), pp. 29, 30.

set up may properly be called the Satanic school; for though their productions breathe the spirit of Belial in their lascivious parts, and the spirit of Moloch in those loathsome images of atrocities and horrors which they delight to represent, they are more especially characterized by a Satanic spirit of pride and audacious impiety, which still betrays the wretched feeling of hopelessness wherewith it is allied.[4]

Robert Southey began this diatribe in the third section of his preface to *A Vision of Judgement* by suggesting that the laws be strengthened to prohibit the publication and distribution of "those monstrous combinations of horrors and mockery, lewdness and impiety," by which he characterized the mature works of Byron and Shelley.[5] Of course, it is unjust to taint later attacks on Romantic Satanism with guilt by association; but Southey's combination of humorless orthodoxy and censorious repression must give one pause. His correct assessment of the Satanic mentality is expressed within a context utterly abhorrent to Milton. Had Milton been alive when his conceptions were first invoked against the Satanists, one would confidently predict him to have joined the devil's party posthaste.

The moral of Southey's position should thus be observed. In rejecting the simplistic tendencies of the Satanist critics, readers of Milton have at times followed C. S. Lewis into the equally simplistic pieties of Anglo-Catholicism. The contemporary view of *Paradise Lost*, buttressed by extensive theological scholarship and a close reading of textual patterns, is more orthodox, one might submit, than ever before in the history of the poem's reception. If the Satanists commonly treated Milton as if he did not know how to express his deep allegiances, the orthodox critics also tend to separate the artist from the artifact, as if *Paradise Lost* were another, sublime example of God's creation. But the Satanic impulse did not leap forth as a fully formed perversion, like Sin from the head of her creator, when the Bastille gates fell and the ancient hierarchies toppled: it surfaces throughout the poem itself, as Milton obviously intended it to do. If the greatest artist of English verse wished to create a masterpiece that never probed or questioned orthodox conceptions, he had the certain capacity.

---

4. Robert Southey, *A Vision of Judgement* (London: Longman, 1821), pp. xix–xxi.
5. Ibid., p. xvii.

Instead of avoiding problems or tacitly ignoring them, Milton goes out of his way to emphasize them. And the central issue, claiming our attention from the first, may be summarized in Sir Herbert Grierson's sardonic observation: "If the third part of a school or college or nation broke into rebellion we should be driven, or strongly disposed, to suspect some mismanagement by the supreme powers."[6] Such suspicions Milton actively encourages, shrewdly understanding that the surest means of creating epic dynamism out of a myth where all the answers are known is to call those answers into question, one by one. It is noteworthy that so many of the commentaries on the poem set as their aim the gentle guiding of the reader back to orthodoxy. If the untutored reader has been seduced, it is not by Shelley and Byron, but by Milton. As Shelley affirms in the Preface to *Prometheus Unbound,* "the sacred Milton was, let it ever be remembered, a republican, and a bold inquirer into morals and religion."[7] Thus conceived, he became the exemplar for the skeptical endeavors of Shelley and Byron, and a classic antagonist to the hired sanctimoniousness of poets laureate.

The bold inquiry of *Paradise Lost,* as Shelley reads the poem, stems from distinctive ramifications of its largeness of vision, which he analyzes in the famous passage in *A Defense of Poetry* and re-creates in several of his major poems. In the *Defense* he celebrates Dante and Milton together:

The Divina Commedia and Paradise Lost have conferred upon modern mythology a systematic form; and when change and time shall have added one more superstition to the mass of those which have arisen and decayed upon the earth, commentators will be learnedly employed in elucidating the religion of ancestral Europe, only not utterly forgotten because it will have been stamped with the eternity of genius.

(Prose, VII, 130)

That comment has an authentically Shelleyan ring to it, but it is no mere reiteration of his pervasive irreligion. Rather, it represents

---

6. *Milton and Wordsworth* (Cambridge: Univ. Press, 1937), p. 116.

7. My text for the poems is *Shelley: Poetical Words,* ed. Thomas Hutchinson (Oxford Univ. Press, 1905). For the prose (cited in the text as *Prose*), I have used the appropriate volumes of the Julian edition of Shelley, ed. Roger Ingpen and Walter E. Peck, 10 vols. (London: Ernest Benn; New York: Charles Scribner, 1926–30). I have used the original edition of *Frankenstein,* as edited by James Rieger (Indianapolis: Bobbs-Merrill, 1974).

the considered perspective from which he reads Milton's epic: as comparable to the Homeric or Virgilian epics, a mythic structure independent of the religious principles that inform it. To Shelley *Paradise Lost* represents Christianity but it does not inculcate it. If anything, Milton's objective rendering of Christian myth draws attention to its inadequacies, especially for a reader predisposed to emphasize them:

> ... Milton's poem contains within itself a philosophical refutation of that system, of which, by a strange and natural antithesis, it has been a chief popular support. Nothing can exceed the energy and magnificence of the character of Satan as expressed in "Paradise Lost." It is a mistake to suppose that he could ever have been intended for the popular personification of evil. Implacable hate, patient cunning, and a sleepless refinement of device to inflict the extremest anguish on an enemy, these things are evil; and, although venial in a slave, are not to be forgiven in a tyrant; although redeemed by much that ennobles his defeat in one subdued, are marked by all that dishonours his conquest in the victor. Milton's Devil as a moral being is as far superior to his God, as One who perseveres in some purpose which he has conceived to be excellent in spite of adversity and torture, is to One who in the cold security of undoubted triumph inflicts the most horrible revenge upon his enemy, not from any mistaken notion of inducing him to repent of a perseverance in enmity, but with the alleged design of exasperating him to deserve new torments. Milton has so far violated the popular creed (if this shall be judged to be a violation) as to have alleged no superiority of moral virtue to his God over his Devil. And this bold neglect of a direct moral purpose is the most decisive proof of the supremacy of Milton's genius.
>
> *(Prose*, VII, 129–30)

To assert that this passage "presents Satan as the great moral agent" of *Paradise Lost,* or to remind us sarcastically that "the purpose which he has conceived to be excellent" is merely the destruction of the human race, is wholly to distort Shelley's statement.[8] Miltonist commentary on this passage has invariably

---

And for Byron's *Cain* I have used the standard text of Ernest Hartley Coleridge, ed., *The Works of Lord Byron:Poetry,* 7 vols. (London: John Murray, 1898–1904).

8. Diekhoff, *Milton's* Paradise Lost, p. 31. It is true enough that in the Preface to *Prometheus Unbound* Shelley refers to Satan as "the Hero of *Paradise Lost.*" That, of course, is the term Dryden popularized and a commonplace even among those who, unlike Shelley, are unaware that Satan is, indeed, heroic in a classical sense, and thus the representative of a false moral code. Reactionaries of Shelley's time use exactly the same expression: the *Quarterly Review,* for instance, favorably compares Southey's portrait of the Emperor Kehama to Satan, "the hero of Paradise Lost" (9 [1811], 57).

seized upon isolated subordinate clauses (for example, "although redeemed by much that ennobles his defeat"), converting them into declarative and unmodified assertions, or has rewritten two sharply circumscribed, sequential constructions—"as far superior to . . . as One who perseveres"—"has so far violated the popular creed . . . as to have alleged"—so that they appear to be direct affirmations. In the main body of the passage there is a single unconditional declaration around which all else revolves: "*these things are evil*" (my italics). The enveloping clauses seek to discriminate the fine gradations of this evil, not to exonerate it. If a reader seeks a moral representative, Shelley suggests, it is obvious that he will not find one in Satan; and, less apparent but equally clear, since God acts as Satan's antagonist with superior hatred, cunning, and plotting, he self-evidently suffers from the same defects. The only extenuation of Satan's evil is that accorded a victim of greater evil. No moral superiority can be claimed, however, because the antagonism of Satan and God is itself not moral.[9]

Shelley would have welcomed the clarity of Lewis's memorable utterance: "Many of those who say they dislike Milton's God only mean that they dislike God."[10] He would have assented without feeling any need to follow Lewis into apologetics. For Shelley, the Christian vision of *Paradise Lost* is a mythic structure conceptually removed from questions of faith or belief, a dynamic model whose universal tensions have been accentuated by Milton. In his brief analysis Shelley ignores the psychological validity of Milton's rendering of evil, though it is clear from many of his writings—and in particular the direct confrontation of Christ and Satan in the rejected choral prelude to *Hellas*—that the poet was indebted to Milton for his own comprehension of a reductive, self-consumed, and self-consuming evil. The account focuses on *Paradise Lost* as macrocosm, a mythological paradigm, as befits the emphasis of

9. Though generally I am in agreement with the most balanced statement on this subject, that by Joseph Wittreich ("The Satanism of Blake and Shelley Reconsidered," *Studies in Philology*, 65 [1968], 816–33), I would go farther than his claim: "Satan *in the poem* is morally superior to God *in the poem*. It does not follow, however, that Satan is morally admirable" (p. 827). The paradox of Shelley's series of comparative clauses is that they effectively eradicate any moral premise that distinguishes between God and Satan.

10. *Preface to* Paradise Lost, p. 126.

Shelley's original context, the unfinished essay "On the Devil, and Devils," dating from a year and a half before the *Defense,* the autumn of 1819. And in turn, the context for that essay, flippant as it generally is, was Shelley's serious, indeed obsessive, concern with the nature of evil in the poems of this year.[11] Shelley's conception of *Paradise Lost* as mythological paradigm is scarcely sketched in his critical paragraph. His principal statements on Milton's model are not discursive but recreative. Although *Prometheus Unbound* and *The Cenci* revert, respectively, to classical and Renaissance literary patterns, their essential dramatic conflict derives immediately from the view of *Paradise Lost* contained in these remarks. In *The Cenci* Shelley transposes the model into human society, elaborating its necessarily tragic consequences. In *Prometheus Unbound* he recreates it from an independent mythological stance, balancing cosmic and microcosmic, historical and psychological, perspectives, in order to expose, explode, and replace the inherited model.

Count Cenci ends his extraordinary curse of his daughter and his presence on the stage with an intimation of his largest purposes:

> O, multitudinous Hell, the fiends will shake
> Thine arches with the laughter of their joy!
> There shall be lamentation heard in Heaven
> As o'er an angel fallen.
>
> (*The Cenci* IV.i.183–86)

Cenci, conceiving himself a "scourge" (IV.i.63) wielded by God, with characteristic megalomania identifies the divine purposes as his own. His daughter's independence thus becomes a Satanic revolt. "A rebel to her father and her God" (IV.i.90), Beatrice is to be forced not merely to concede her will to Cenci, but simultaneously to convict herself of irredeemable evil, to "Die in despair, blaspheming" (IV.i.50), and thereby ensure her damnation. Cenci the theologian is as ingenious as he is insane, for he effectively leaves Beatrice without options. To concede or not to concede her will to her father as representative of God alike would

11. I have interpreted the poems of this year as a skeptical revision of the Christian theodicies of Dante and Milton in *Shelley's Annus Mirabilis: The Maturing of an Epic Vision* (San Marino: Huntington Library, 1975).

damn her. Beatrice's view of her situation is the mirror-image of
her father's in its assumption that salvation can be secured only
through becoming God's representative. Thus her father's murder
becomes the fulfillment of providence. In confronting the agents
of society's justice, which in this play consistently echoes Cenci's
justice, she affirms that heaven has intervened because they have
"Bar[red] all access to retribution first" (IV.iv.118). Later, in
accepting the court's conviction, Beatrice transposes the guilt to
the logical and theological center from which emanates the pattern
she has been forced to retrace:

> Or wilt thou rather tax high-judging God
> That He permitted such an act as that
> Which I have suffered, and which He beheld;
> Made it unutterable, and took from it
> All refuge, all revenge, all consequence,
> But that which thou hast called my father's death?

(V.iii.78–83)

To question the source is to question the reality of all her and
society's values. The passage ends significantly:

> Which is or is not what men call a crime,
> Which either I have done, or have not done;
> Say what ye will.

(V.iii.84–86)

Expelled from the center of her beliefs, the center of society's
ideals, Beatrice cannot return. Her fate is Satanic, as judged by her
father, by her culture, by herself.

Shelley's lengthy disquisition on the nature of Italian Catholi-
cism in the play's preface—as "interwoven with the whole fabric of
life . . . not a rule for moral conduct"—deliberately propounds a
cohesive religious structure like the one he saw in *Paradise Lost*. It
abrogates, rather than enforces, morality. Both Cenci and Beatrice
see themselves allied with God's purposes; both also momentarily
discover an identity with Satan. What Shelley poses is not a riddle
in which his audience is to sort out the proper identifications,
assigning Cenci and Beatrice to their respective categories, but a
single dynamic model of which God and Satan are the polarities.
Defiant opposition is the motive force of the personal relationship
between father and daughter, and of the society that encompasses

them. And yet, ironically, it results from the compulsive assertion of power throughout the social frame in order to compel unity to a single source of power. Cenci conceives of his daughter as a "particle of my divided being" (IV.i.117), and his incestuous attack is an outrage of syllogistic precision designed to "confound both night and day" (II.i.183) by reassimilating his daughter to himself. Beatrice, in turn, comprehends her body as an Eden now violated by Satanic corruption, and in destroying the source— which, paradoxically, is also an assimilation of her father—she will extirpate the evil within. Cenci, however, holds the ironic trump, a parody of God's capacity to frustrate Satan eternally by transmuting his evil into good. Nothing Beatrice does can free her from the consequences of her father's act. She is effectively denied free will, as all acts become sins against God, and non-action becomes the greatest sin of all. There is only one means of liberation, in an agnostic rejection of this model which enforces the whole society, but that is only possible once Beatrice has accepted the inevitability of her death and, beyond hope, draws her fellow-victims with her into the dual intensities of suffering and compassion.

The conceptual labyrinth of *The Cenci*, winding through increasingly oxymoronic frustrations, like so many of Shelley's complex structures, elaborates a simple truth: a model that is fundamentally amoral cannot encompass and invest a moral society. The pretensions of *Prometheus Unbound* are far larger, for its theater is the cosmos and its purpose, like Milton's, is justification. The scene opens upon "A Ravine of Icy Rocks" (I.s.d.) high above the earth, the barren setting for a deadlocked antagonism that has endured for three thousand years, the span of documented human history. "No change, no pause, no hope! Yet I endure" (I.24). Shelley has conflated the Dantean and Miltonic visions of hell: "Black, wintry, dead, unmeasured" (I.21), replicating in an exact sense Milton's prescription: "A Universe of death, which God by curse/ Created evil" (*PL* II.622–23). The source of human misery has been a curse, a curse suddenly recalled by Prometheus as he discovers the ethics realized by Beatrice at the end of her tragic agony: "I wish no living thing to suffer pain" (I.305), he asserts, as the Phantasm of Jupiter retreats into subterranean darkness and dawn begins to glow on the horizon. The curse repeated by the Phantasm has no basis in Aeschylus or in the

Promethean myth, but from first phrase—"Fiend, I defy thee!"
(I.262)—to last—"Scorn track thy lagging fall through boundless
space and time" (I.301)—derives from *Paradise Lost:*

> All that thou canst inflict I bid thee do;
> Foul Tyrant both of Gods and Human-kind,
> One only being shalt thou not subdue.
>
> . . . .
>
> O'er all things but thyself I gave thee power,
> And my own will.
>
> . . . .
>
> On me and mine I imprecate
> The utmost torture of thy hate;
>
> . . . .
>
> Heap on thy soul, by virtue of this Curse,
> Ill deeds, then be thou damned, beholding good.
>   (I.263–65, 272–73, 278–79, 292–93)

That Prometheus is cast in the role of Satan cursing Jupiter in the
role of Jehovah does not negate the relationship of Shelley's poem
to Milton's, but rather intensifies it. For the curse repeated to
Prometheus by the Phantasm of Jupiter—who reproduces the
"gestures proud and cold/ And looks of firm defiance, and calm
hate,/ And . . . despair" (I.258–60) with which it was originally
uttered—is the equal product of both, the seal of their identity
even as it establishes their antagonism. In negating Satan for
eternity God becomes a Satanic negation himself. Self-justifying
and self-righteous, the polarized terms of the model are interchangeable.

Shelley's conceptual preoccupations seldom stand in isolation:
at least during his lifetime even the most obscure are delineated
more extensively and more openly in the writings of his wife.
Frankenstein; or the Modern Prometheus, published six months
before Shelley undertook *Prometheus Unbound,* is the most pro-
nounced imaginative recreation of *Paradise Lost* in the Romantic
period. Mary's derivations are congruous with Shelley's later ones
and would seem, like his additions to the holograph, to indicate
his marked influence on her symbolic allegory.[12] Although the

12. Rieger assembles the evidence in the preface to his edition.

fiction is ostensibly concerned with the creation of a new Adam, the issues recoil continually toward the primal antagonism of God and Satan; and, as in Shelley's dramas, the imagery is mutually implicative. The initial allusion to the Miltonic context is an unexpected inversion, as the narrator Walton observes that Victor Frankenstein "must have been a noble creature in his better days" (p. 22). The analogy of Frankenstein, the creator, with Satan grows insistent, punctuated on the last page of each of the first two volumes, which remark the mental inferno he bears with him (pp. 84, 145). But, of course, the deformed monster who begins his existence, like Michelangelo's Adam, by stretching out his hand to his creator, is immediately transformed into "a thing such as even Dante could not have conceived" (p. 53), and after repeated rejection isolates his cold rage amid the icy Alps, descending with superhuman power to walk by night and revenge himself upon his maker. Frankenstein's pursuer through much of his career, he becomes at last the pursued, even as, originally Frankenstein's dependent creation, he later assumes divinity, uttering the imperative verb that resounds through Milton's epic: "You are my creator, but I am your master;—obey!" (p. 165) Likewise, Frankenstein, having created a monster, transforms himself into a monster: "My abhorrence of this fiend cannot be conceived. When I thought of him, I gnashed my teeth, my eyes became inflamed, and I ardently wished to extinguish that life which I had so thoughtlessly bestowed" (p. 87).

A relationship conceived without love becomes predicated on the intensity of hate. "I, too, can create desolation" (p. 139), the monster exults; and revenge becomes the "devouring and only passion" (p. 198) for both. Unprotected in the arctic wastes, Frankenstein testifies that "revenge kept me alive" (p. 199), and when he discerns the dog-sled of his adversary before him, he experiences the ecstasies of a lover: "Oh! with what a burning gush did hope revisit my heart! warm tears filled my eyes, which I hastily wiped away, that they might not intercept the view I had of the dæmon" (p. 205). Each denying the other a spouse, they commit themselves wholly to the suicidal consummation of their relationship. It is the monster who points to the frustration his creator cannot articulate: "Whilst I destroyed his hopes, I did not satisfy my own desires" (p. 219). The murderous mirror-images are like those of Francesco and Beatrice Cenci; and the monster's plan for his suicide, a spectacular immolation atop the north pole—"I shall ascend my funeral pile triumphantly, and exult in the agony of the torturing flames" (p. 221)—not only climaxes the inverted image patterns of this work but becomes the prototype for Cenci's plan, once he has destroyed his family, to make a pyre from his belongings, mount it, and "resign" his soul "Into the hand of him who wielded it" (IV.i.63–64). The self-destructive nature of Satanic revenge both Shelley and Mary saw in Milton. What they also conceived was that God's revenge was equal in effect, as it was superior in design, and that the creation resulting from such antipathy must be reductive.

The paradigm that the Shelleys abstract from Milton's epic is, it hardly need be acknowledged, not the Christian vision one expects Milton to propound. The tendencies of the model are radically heretical. It fell to the least systematic or philosophically learned of the three members of Southey's "Satanic school" openly to avow the heretical implications, as he redesigned the amoral antagonism of the model within the Gnostic trappings of *Cain*. Although Byron was sensitive enough to the laws on blasphemous libel to render his heretical notions within a dramatic framework—and, indeed, to have them stated by the most traditionally unreliable of narrators, Lucifer—there are no events in the play to contradict the cosmic scheme in which he instructs Cain. God exists in the isolation of his ennui, tinkering with the universe, sitting

> . . . in his vast and solitary throne—
> Creating worlds, to make eternity
> Less burthensome to his immense existence
> And unparticipated solitude.
>
> (*Cain* I.148–51)

He is "the Destroyer . . . The Maker—Call him/ Which name thou wilt: he makes but to destroy" (I.266–67). Omnipotent over the material universe, God is nonetheless baffled by his inability to reconcile the claims of spirit with those of matter. Lucifer, admitting their incompatibility, indulges in the luxury of aristocratic disdain for the god who must work, shielded through his incessant garrulousness from confronting his own state as an equally "unparticipated solitude," with nothing to do except frustrate Jehovah's aspirations to create the perfect machine. Cain, inheritor of that knowledge which is self-consciousness, is the incidental victim of the irreconcilable polarities. Jehovah and Lucifer are brothers who have separated, a pattern soon to be repeated by Cain and Abel, and now contend for a single purpose: "To reign" (II.ii.388). The power struggle is pointless; but then in this ironic universe Jehovah's creation is also pointless, a mere ego-extension, and Lucifer's vaunted liberty of thought reduces to the spoiler's art.

The universal order is petty, if massive in its consequences for man. Cain, the familiar Byronic hero caught between antitheses he cannot control, in accepting his exile paradoxically commits himself to a human destiny. "That which I am, I am" (III.i.509), he maintains to the angel who marks his brow, thus acknowledging himself and his progeny a third identity in the cosmos. Unlike Jehovah and Lucifer, Cain is resigned to his limitations; unlike them he is susceptible to the values of beauty and love, which cannot redeem him but are distinctively human realities. As a fugitive, Cain turns his back upon the struggles of Jehovah and Lucifer, to which the Adamic family is still committed, and sets forth to create a moral order. His is the solution of Beatrice, of Prometheus, and of Robert Walton, the narrator who mediates the nightmare vision of *Frankenstein* and returns from the ice-locked arctic to the values of a civilized and social life. The educational process of these works is alike in its insistence on the inextricable unity of human faculties and the absoluteness of human moral responsibility.

There are, of course, essential distinctions, ideological as well as temperamental, among these authors and their works. Byron never denies that man's nature is, like Napoleon's, "antithetically mixed" (*Childe Harold's Pilgrimage* III.317), or, as Manfred would have it, "half dust, half deity" (*Manfred* II.i.40). His solution is existential, an acceptance of the absurdity inherent in a consistent inconsistency, a compound so pure as to be itself elemental. Shelley, at least in *Prometheus Unbound,* denies that the duality is intrinsic to human nature, discovering the source of evil not in society, but, beyond it, in the structural models by which the mind organizes reality, the patterns it imposes. Mary's romance stands somewhere between these positions, its ambiguities largely unresolved, emphasizing human accountability and the reductive nature of hatred. The most sympathetic treatment of the Satanic character is that of *The Cenci;* but, notwithstanding Shelley's effort to expunge from his heroine the ugly concomitants of Satan's revenge, Beatrice's condition is unremittingly tragic. The "restless and anatomizing casuistry" (Preface) by which one defends her actions cannot alter the mode in which one is forced to view her life. To bring the same attitude to Milton's Satan, however, is to engage in a "pernicious casuistry," as Shelley defines it in his Preface to *Prometheus Unbound,* one that undermines the moral basis for judgment it seeks to discover. Such casuistry demands that one accept the context for Satan's rebellion, and it is that context which each of these authors sees as pernicious. Paradise is incompatible with a universe created through antagonism. Deadlocks issue in death.

There is no little irony in the fact that the younger Romantics went out of their way to show that the position with which they are commonly associated, the Satanist view of *Paradise Lost,* was indefensible. But a single paragraph of abstracted principles, and a series of recreated works, cannot be called a reasoned and systematic criticism of Milton's epic; and it remains to be seen to what extent their view is a defensible reading of the poem. Where so many erroneous opinions have been attributed to the Romantics, one naturally hesitates to speak for Shelley yet once again. But if we are sure of his premises, or of his view of Milton's premises, our margin of error is considerably reduced. At basis, Shelley would have vehemently opposed any notion that only an orthodox Christian could rightly appreciate *Paradise Lost.* Milton, like Dante, did not write as a Christian, but as an epic poet.

He mingled as it were the elements of human nature as colours upon a single pallet and arranged them in the composition of his great picture according to the laws of epic truth; that is, according to the laws of that principle by which a series of actions of the external universe and of intelligent and ethical beings is calculated to excite the sympathy of succeeding generations of mankind.

(Prose, VII, 130)

The Christian mythology was, for Milton as for Dante, "merely the mask and mantle in which these great poets walk through eternity enveloped and disguised" (*Prose*, VII, 129). In turn, it clothes a conceptual drama whose principles pertain to a human reality that will be judged by succeeding generations independent of the vestment. This premise rejects as specious any scheme that resolves the dramatic conflicts of the poem by a circular reference to its enveloping mythology. God, being "All in All" (*PL*, III.341; VI.732), cannot be wrong as emanating center of a mythology; but the system then begs the questions raised by his actions. Shelley, who was too masterful a craftsman himself ever to propound that there were unconscious impulses warring against the conscious intent of *Paradise Lost*, suggests instead, and characteristically, that the poem "contains within itself a philosophical refutation of that system" of mythology it recreates.

A "philosophical refutation" implies a syllogistic series, the terms of which Shelley would first find stressed in the second book. "High on a Throne of Royal State" (II.1), Satan begins his eternal parody of God and the persons of God: like the Son, he is "by merit rais'd" (II.5). His legions surround him, performing their automatic ritual: "Towards him they bend/ With awful reverence prone; and as a God/ Extoll him equal to the highest in Heav'n" (II.477–79). With "fixt mind/ And high disdain" (I.97–98), Satan establishes the politics of hell "As being the contrary to his high will/ Whom we resist" (I.161–62), a reactionary politics to the core. But then, an antithesis, even a parodic one, reflects its thesis. The divine emblem that dominates the heavens at the close of the epic's first third, the scale of justice, may represent the Father's primal value, but in its very bifurcation distinguishes a closed system of contraries. The primal syllogism— the spurned son turning upon his father—engenders its dependents. Sin leaps from the head of Satan, but returns as mistress to her author. Death tears through Sin's womb, but returns to gnaw her bowels as a grotesque extension of Satan's revolt against the Father. And Sin recognizes the prescribed limitations to Death's voracity as fulfilling the repeated pattern: Death,

> . . . me his Parent would full soon devour
> For want of other prey, but that he knows
> His end with mine involvd.

(II.805–7)

Similarly, to turn God's creation against its author becomes the
Satanic program, again conceived as a negation incestuously
wedded to its contrary:

> This would surpass
> Common revenge, and interrupt his joy
> In our Confusion, and our Joy upraise
> In his disturbance.
>
> (II.370–73)

Satan purposes "To wreck on innocent frail man his loss/ Of that
first Battel, and his flight to Hell" (IV.11–12); and in return man
is promised *his* revenge. Eve, contemplating suicide or abstinence,
is forestalled by Adam's persistent memory of God's promise,
imaged not as a liberating hope but as a vengeful conclusion to the
cycle:

> that thy Seed shall bruise
> The Serpents head; piteous amends, unless
> Be meant, whom I conjecture, our grand Foe
> *Satan*, who in the Serpent hath contriv'd
> Against us this deceit: to crush his head
> Would be revenge indeed; which will be lost
> By death brought on our selves, or childless days . . .
>
> (X.1031–37)

That perspective, one might argue, is irreparably fallen even as it
struggles to rise; but when Adam's prayer is answered with effulgent grace, it produces only a more serene contemplation of his
just deserts:

> Methought I saw him placable and mild,
> Bending his eare; perswasion in me grew
> That I was heard with favour, peace returnd
> Home to my Brest, and to my memorie
> His promise, that thy Seed shall bruise our Foe.
>
> (XI.151–55)

The rhythms of a fragmented eternity become the cyles of
history in time, as Michael unveils the future of the race. Cain kills
Abel; Enoch is persecuted by his tribesmen; Noah alienates himself
to perfect his mountain labors; and providence deluges the earth.
Adam anticipates a peaceful aftermath, but the postdiluvian
tranquility is soon rent by the dispersal, and at the beginning of

the twelfth book another Satanic manifestation, in symmetrical balance with the first, arises "as in despite of Heav'n" (XII.34), the Hunter Nimrod who installs political tyranny on earth as Satan has in Hell:

> And from Rebellion shall derive his name,
> Though of Rebellion others he accuse.
>
> (XII.36–37)

From Nimrod to Charles I it is but a short step, as Michael admits:

> So shall the World goe on,
> To good malignant, to bad men benigne,
> Under her own waight groaning till the day
> Appeer of respiration to the just,
> And vengeance to the wicked, at return
> Of him so lately promis'd to thy aid. . .
>
> (XII. 537–42)

History cannot be redeemed except by being halted. Free will cannot be justified except through its dislocation. The primal syllogism contains all others: the initial separation into sheep and goats presupposes the last judgment. This is what the younger Romantics stress: the justice of God to Adam and Eve is secondary to the question of his justice to Satan. "The character of Satan engenders in the mind a pernicious casuistry, which leads us to weigh his faults with his wrongs and to excuse the former because the latter exceed all measure." Lewis scoffed at this assertion, countering with an Oxonian sniff that Satan's wrong was that he did not know his betters.[13] Oxford, after consulting God's high purposes, taught Shelley much of what he knew about expulsion: it included no means of redress except forfeiture of one's will. The impulse to expel is the flaw in God's scheme: it is the psychological premise for the ensuing cycles of fragmentation and can only end as it began, with an eternal bifurcation that abrogates free will. Although one can presume to read in Satan's soliloquy on Mount Niphates the possibility of a reconciliation (IV.79–81), no utterance of the Father's supports it.

> [Satan] breaks union, and that day
> Cast out from God and blessed vision, falls

---

13. The quotation is the full statement in the Preface to *Prometheus Unbound*. See Lewis, *Preface to* Paradise Lost, p. 94.

> Into utter darkness, deep ingulft, his place
> Ordain'd without redemption, without end.
>
> (V.612–15)
>
> Man therefore shall find grace.
> The other none.
>
> (III.131–32)

For God to have sat down for a chat with Satan, of course, would presuppose a very different poem from the epic Milton wrote. It also, from Shelley's point of view, would have produced a very different universe from that depicted in the poem, one compatible, as the antagonistic model is not, with Michael's enunciation of a democratic politics and a humanist ethics at the end:

>   onely add
> Deeds to thy knowledge answerable, add Faith,
> Add vertue, Patience, Temperance, add Love,
> By name to come call'd Charitie, the soul
> Of all the rest . . .
>
> (XII.581–85)

It is no more accidental that Demogorgon's closing benediction is so strongly reminiscent of Michael's than it is that Prometheus's curse echoes Jehovah's. The two points of similarity cast in a strong light the "philosophical refutation" Shelley saw in *Paradise Lost*. There is no logical progression that can unite that curse with that benediction. The polar opposition of God and Satan is a Platonic model for myriad extensions of the primary syllogism, but a locked antagonism is amoral and incapable of progression. Creation is set in motion, but no true dialectic can issue from a circular prototype. As Satan reacts to God, God reacts to Satan. Within that sealed context, free will is a conceptual sophistry. As the political liberation Milton stresses throughout the twelfth book is denied by the cycles of history Michael anticipates, Milton's commitment to a Christian *eschaton* suppresses his faith, and the equal faith of the younger Romantics, in one that is human. In the largest sense a humanist *eschaton* can be realized only through the Charity that is the soul of all, which refuses to countenance that Woe and Foe are the end rhymes of a closed couplet polished by a divine hand. Love disintegrates oppositions, negations, otherness. Hatred perpetuates a polarized universe and frustrates the will to regeneration.

Shelley's celebration of Dante and Milton in *A Defense of Poetry* culminates in one of his most memorable utterances:

A great poem is a fountain for ever overflowing with the waters of wisdom and delight; and after one person and one age has exhausted all its divine effluence which their peculiar relations enable them to share, another and yet another succeeds, and new relations are ever developed, the source of an unforeseen and an unconceived delight.

(*Prose*, VII. 131)

One can never ignore the "peculiar relations" the younger generation of Romantics established with the literature and culture of the past. They survived the intellectual terrors of a quarter-century of war that devastated and impoverished Europe within a pervasive metaphorical assumption. Napoleon pitting himself against that amalgam known as the Holy Alliance was the Satanic rebel defying the upholders of orthodoxy. The Napoleonic Wars appeared to the sensitive minds of the age as a reality whose imperatives were no less categorical for being fruitless, but more so, enforced with historical urgency. To these writers—and to the finest minds throughout Europe—there was no public position that was not reactionary, as the interchangeable empires committed their citizenry to the ruthless mechanism of an inherited paradigm. The deliberated refusals of Prometheus and Cain are characteristic of a sober optimism that will no longer abide by the standards of antagonism informing western culture. Milton's genius for their creators was to have discerned that model at the center of Christian thought, the conceptual framework for modern culture. A man unable to sustain his commitment to a corrupt church, a corrupt monarchy, or a corrupt Commonwealth, Milton exemplified his own refusal in the libertarian rhetoric of Book XII of *Paradise Lost*. If the New Model Army of Cromwell was only the old model refurbished, predicating its existence on opposition, it was doomed to reenact the warfare of God and Satan to no avail. The epic written by this spiritual fifth columnist severely questions the order it reproduces, nowhere more than in those examples of human charity and divine mercy that transcend the rigorous claims of eternal justice. To the younger Romantics, at least, *Paradise Lost* is neither a poem that justifies God nor a poem out of joint and internally at odds, but rather an epic large enough in scope and in intellect to stand beyond its culture and religion, sustaining their philosophical tensions with honesty.

"Back to Shelley," William Empson adopted as his slogan, and, returning with some ingenuousness and an exhilarating passion to the vehement polemics of *Queen Mab*, he roundly denounced the immoral who wrapped themselves in Milton's respectability.[14] "Back to Shelley," deliberately echoes Harold Bloom in his *Anxiety of Influence*, though he evidently means something else. After an opening acknowledgment that Shelley conceived of all poets as contributing to a single great poem, his back is ironically turned on Shelley and on what Bloom agrees with Yeats is "the most profound discourse upon poetry in the language," *A Defense of Poetry*.[15] The sad determinism and the distortions to which Bloom's theory leads need not be rehearsed or battled with, but his model deserves recognition. Milton rules over English poetry with the omnipresence of his own conception of God, and subsequent poets are forced into the Satanic role, recoiling from the dominating paternity of his heritage. It is the same primal syllogism, producing the same hopeless, circular *angst* that the younger Romantics saw in Milton's depiction of Christianity.

Back to Shelley. To the post-Enlightenment libertarianism of that "most profound discourse upon poetry in the language." To a conception of the artist as not one further, cynical extension of the thrust of American competitive capitalism—the manipulator of a craft, beggared by the past, playing beggar-thy-neighbor on the present, and threatening the future with utter exhaustion of resources—but as legislator of the vision by which civilization frees itself from local obsessions and selfish interests in order to forge a

14. *Milton's God* (London: Chatto and Windus, 1961). Although ostensibly a Shelleyan reading of *Paradise Lost*, Empson's arguments tend to exculpate Satan, and to some extent he resurrects the view that the poem is schizophrenic. Still, to lump him with Wal9ock, John Peter, and other such critics whom Stanley E. Fish calls the anti-Miltonians (*Surprised by Sin: The Reader in* Paradise Lost [London and Melbourne: Macmillan; New York: St. Martin's Press, 1967], p. 2) is a gross distortion.

15. *The Anxiety of Influence: A Theory of Poetry* (New York: Oxford Univ. Press, 1973), pp. 23, 19, 39.

community. To the affirmation that art can liberate and that artists, rather than being overwhelmed by the past, can be "the mirrors of the gigantic shadows which futurity casts upon the present" (*Prose*, VII, 140). To a joyful celebration of one's mentors, honoring their independent integrity in the vigorous assertion of one's own. To "that great poem, which all poets, like the co-operating thoughts of one great mind, have built up since the beginning of the world" (*Prose*, VII, 124).

The co-operating thoughts of one great mind. . . . Back to Shelley.

A Defense of Poetry is an enduring testament to the healthy, vital, and continual influence of Milton on the future course of English poetry. It is written by a working poet, who, after Blake, was probably the most strongly touched by the art and exemplary life of John Milton.[16] Although Shelley's skeptical interpretation of *Paradise Lost* may not today gain a great many scholarly adherents, it is important to emphasize that it is not a compulsive misinterpretation of the poem. His view of *Paradise Lost* can be supported from the text: it can also be supported to some extent from what we know of the development of Milton's political and theological positions.

What is most significant in Shelley's conception of *Paradise Lost*, however, is not the precise view of the relationship of God and Satan, but rather the attitude to the poem embodied in that view. Modern emphasis on structural and rhetorical repetitions has built up a work of art that is a monument of form. There is something almost abstract and nonideological in the purity of this multifaceted, enormous jewel, and it is powerfully dazzling. Interpretations of *Paradise Lost* written from such an aesthetic perspective have been among the most influential and satisfying of those produced under the impetus of the current Milton renascence. One thinks, for instance, of Isabel Gamble MacCaffrey's examination of *Paradise Lost as "Myth"* (1959), where the idea of myth

---

16. Bloom distorts the entire Shelleyan canon in order to see him as floundering in the wake of Wordsworth. One might note, incidentally, that Shelley knew Bloom's essential view of poetry, as well as his ideology, though without modern psychological trappings. Indeed, as expressed by Peacock in his deteriorationist *Four Ages of Poetry*, the position is that against which Shelley wrote his discourse.

appears as a pure distillate from the work of Jung, and the poem attains a crystalline stasis of aesthetic clarity. *Paradise Lost* asks for such a conception; so, one must add, does *Prometheus Unbound*.

But *A Defense of Poetry* records an encounter, a myth that is invigorating, unsettling, morally ambiguous. The cold jewel of aesthetic perfection is for Shelley an enormous dynamo, engaging the reader in moral casuistry, nagging questions, complex and shifting balances. That, of course, is what Stanley Fish has seen in *Paradise Lost*—though with a vital difference. Shelley is not surprised by his sin—not even, one would suppose, by his *hamartia*. The active engagement of the reader with this massive work of art does not resolve itself in orthodoxy. The epic does not restrict vision or slap down with an authoritarian hand the very impulses it encourages. Rather, it demands from its reader a maturity of moral response within the large and open structure of its vision. Its implicit assumption is that of the *Areopagitica*, that men are educable within a free environment of ideas. As God has forced responsibility upon Satan, and upon Adam and Eve, so Milton makes his readers responsible to and for the entire Christian vision he has remolded.

It is this free, dynamic relationship with his reader that has made Milton so bountifully influential upon later poets and upon generations of readers. *Paradise Lost* is, as Shelley suggests, "a fountain for ever overflowing," casting its vision not as a closed and finished record of the Christian cosmos, but as a challenge of intellect and commitment. Shelley accepted that challenge as the distinctive, indeed supreme, gift of a Christian heritage he intellectually rejected; and if a later generation disagrees with the ideological implications he draws from *Paradise Lost,* it can only profit from his contemplation of the dynamic tensions of the epic. In *Adonais* Shelley places Milton, after Homer and Dante, "third among the sons of light" (36). He is so honored as a celebration of his art and influence, for as a poet, not as a Christian, Milton extracted from the reigning mythology an imaginative drama whose grand accents, though uttered on a cosmic stage, are human and humane.

Walking on Water: Milton, Stevens, and Contemporary American Poetry

JOAN WEBBER

X Mr. Griswold justly and wisely observes: "Milton is more emphatically American than any author who has lived in the United States." He is so because in
him is expressed so much of the primitive vitality of that thought from which
America is born, though at present disposed to forswear her lineage in so
many ways. He is the purity of Puritanism. He understood the nature of liberty, of justice—what is required for the unimpeded action of conscience—
what constitutes true marriage, and the scope of a manly education. He is one
of the Fathers of the Age, of that new Idea which agitates the sleep of
Europe, and of which America, if awake to the design of Heaven and her own
duty, would become the principal exponent. But the Father is still far beyond
the understanding of his child.

—Margaret Fuller, 1846[1]

There is no secret to poetry, but undoubtedly you are right in saying that the
influence of a work depends largely on this: that it must create what it seeks.
There is no reason whatever why a poet, in the sense that I have in mind,
should not exist now, notwithstanding the complexity of contemporary life
and so on. Have you ever stopped to think of the extraordinary existence of
Milton, in his time and under the circumstances of the world as it was then?
Milton would be just as proper, so to speak, today as he was in his actual day,
and perhaps today, instead of going off on a myth, he would stick to the
facts.

—Wallace Stevens, 1935[2]

1. S. Margaret Fuller, in "The Prose Works of Milton," *Papers on Literature and Art*
(New York: Wiley and Putnam, 1846), pp. 38–39.
2. *Letters of Wallace Stevens*, ed. Holly Stevens (New York: Knopf, 1966), p. 299.

There is of course no way or need to prove that Milton has directly affected American poetry. But the influence which turned the seventeenth-century poet from grandly traditional epic planning toward a more individual, subjective poetry is the same that has distinguished or plagued our own Puritan-based history. In the course of Milton's lifetime, as in the whole span of American literature, an intense national and religious idealism encounters a hostile reality, and the poets are thrown back hard upon their own resources. Margaret Fuller regards Milton as an exemplar for American culture, and it is through their cultural situations that American poets might begin to make use of him. Stevens indicates that "the extraordinary existence of Milton, in his time," would be just as extraordinary and just as "proper" in 1935. Much more extensively, in the 1970s, a landscape of disillusionment and indifference both demands and makes more brilliant any personal affirmation.

Milton provides a remarkable precedent for the poet's power to accept the loss of all that once sustained him, and to create anew. After an idealistic early period of learning and writing, he spent twenty years trying to bring into being a political state that was never realized; he was increasingly, sharply dissatisfied with all existing political and religious models.[3] In his poetry and prose we find a movement away from older forms and beliefs, away from public assumptions, to an emphasis on the subjective struggle of the individual. While one can never quite say that a Miltonic character is cast upon his own resources, it is true that the God without increasingly gives way to a God within, and that the poetry often seems to have little in common with the more nearly orthodox *De Doctrina Christiana*.[4] From the time of his *Nativity Ode* onward, Milton is remaking myth.

In a somewhat analogous larger movement, almost the whole history of American literature can be seen as an effort to express

3. For Milton's life, see William Riley Parker, *Milton: A Biography*, 2 vols. (Oxford: Clarendon Press, 1968). For his theological views, see my essays, "The Son of God and Power of Life in Three Poems by Milton," *ELH*, 37 (1970), 175–94; and "Milton's God," *ELH*, 40 (1973), 514–31.

4. This is a point of some significance. For opposite viewpoints, see Maurice Kelley, *This Great Argument: A Study of Milton's* De Doctrina *as a Gloss upon* Paradise Lost, Princeton Studies in English, 22 (Princeton: Princeton Univ. Press, 1941), and C. A. Patrides, *Milton and the Christian Tradition* (Oxford: Clarendon Press, 1966).

the energy of a new people creating a new land. Up until the time of T. S. Eliot and the Second World War, the "main" tradition of American poetry, which Roy Harvey Pearce and many others have called Adamic,[5] was still strong. Yet there was always danger in its innocent tendency to suggest that America might be or become a prelapsarian world. The gradual loss of religious and nationalistic fervor, together with retention of a fierce antinomian insistence on the sacredness of the individual, has led both to cosmic self-celebration and to sterile self-confession. Characteristically, the American poet tries to make meaning and myth out of personal experience.

By establishing an impersonal conservative tradition, T. S. Eliot and others tried to escape from that set of alternatives, but a backward-looking vision could not remain attractive for long. Eliot had an enormous, exciting effect on American letters, but that effect was also perverse and temporary compared to the more fertile (and Miltonic) influence that Wallace Stevens now exercises over our contemporaries. The hope to be found in contemporary poetry must be in its own self-regard: what is so often, and rightly, called its weakness is also its most tenacious characteristic and strength. The poet has the power to create (in the sense of "become") himself,[6] and to anchor that power philosophically, as Milton and Stevens did. The hope to be fostered resides in that self as poem, not an antihero descended from Prufrock, but a person capable of discovering his own myths, and in them the present and the future:

> He who would not be frustrate of his hope to write well hereafter in laudable things, ought him selfe to bee a true Poem, that is, a composition and patterne of the best and honourablest things; not presuming to sing high praises of heroick men, or famous Cities, unlesse he have in himselfe the experience and the practice of all that which is praise-worthy.
>
> (*Apology against a Pamphlet, CM*, III, i, 303–4).

The joyous self-dependence of this achievement, in a seemingly desolate human landscape, is like walking on water, letting the

---

5. Roy Harvey Pearce, *The Continuity of American Poetry* (Princeton: Princeton Univ. Press, 1961), p. 187.

6. Roy Harvey Pearce uses the word "make" (see p. 187), and that may have been the intention of some poets, but the unqualified words "make" and "create" are misleading and sometimes vainglorious, as Milton and Stevens knew.

destructive element bear one up. Milton knew about that; it is one of the most striking parallels between him and our contemporaries.

Obviously there is a close connection between culture and epic. Milton has often been accused of ending the epic tradition, and Americans have a notorious history of great desire—mingled with great inability—to succeed in this form. It will be useful, then, to begin by looking at Milton's treatment of epic, and particularly at those self-regarding characteristics, of poet, hero, and poem, which foreshadow American poetry.

Beginning with Milton's glorification of Cromwell in *Defensio Secunda,* one can easily follow his progress from glorification of epic action in a particular nation, to a cosmic narrative that is simultaneously metaphysical statement in *Paradise Lost,* to a subjective analysis of the maturing of a man's soul in *Paradise Regained.* The universality of the form is never abandoned, but Milton discovers the limitations of nationalism (both religious and political), epic warfare, and historical idealism, and gives his attention increasingly to the spiritual warfaring of one man who can represent all men.

In *Paradise Regained,* the ideal everyman is Christ, second Adam. His task is to realize himself as man-god by denying all dehumanizing or Satanic aspirations and needs, to speak alone in the wilderness in response to each separate demand of Satan upon him. Here, as in *Paradise Lost,* the protagonist (like the poet) depends upon his own resources, which of course include faith. Institutional religion is denied or absent; God never intervenes in personal struggle; the character's battle is his own, and his victory is his identification with God's image in his soul. All men are God's sons, and Milton emphasizes Christ's humanity. His poetry is in transition between the old idea of transcendence and the more modern notion of an immanent God. It has been argued that Satan and Christ are two parts of the self, and that, for the denial of the ego, the Satanic part has to be expelled.[7]

7. See Albert W. Fields, "Milton and Self-Knowledge," *PMLA,* 83 (1968), 398; and Stuart Curran, "The Mental Pinnacle: *Paradise Regained* and the Romantic Four-Book Epic," in *Calm of Mind: Tercentenary Essays on* Paradise Regained *and* Samson Agonistes *in honor of John S. Diekhoff,* ed. Joseph Anthony Wittreich, Jr. (Cleveland: Press of Case Western Reserve Univ., 1971), pp. 133–62.

At the same time that the epic narrator and the subjective or psychological struggle of hero or narrator are becoming stronger or more explicit than in most classical epic, Milton carries to an extreme the traditional paradoxical epic undermining of the culture that it glorifies.[8] He nearly abandons nationalism as a concern. The culture which he celebrates is that of Protestant Christianity, represented by the God of *Paradise Lost*, Book III; but the true God of *Paradise Lost* is a creative force that by choosing to share the power with created intelligence, beginning with the Son, will eventually bring about a universe wholly good, in which God is all in all.[9]

Cultural undermining of the tradition goes side by side with the epic's unyielding and seemingly paradoxical assumption that life is worthwhile. The epic hero has stature not because of his warlike prowess (since this genre never glorifies warfare), but because of his ability to confront and accept his own mortality.[10] This hero at some stage in his development wants either to die or to retreat significantly from the life he has been given, and he finally chooses to live. Thus Adam's choice after the fall gives him heroism without any of the traditional epic paraphernalia: he is but a naked man affirming existence. And, like human history, the way each epic so purposefully takes apart and remakes its predecessors—as Virgil rewrote Homer, and Dante Virgil—demonstrates that death and destruction are necessary to life and to creation alike. This is perhaps the most profound way in which poetry, then and now, is and should be about itself. This is how Milton justifies the ways of God to men. Death and destruction are inevitable; chaos is the good-evil material from which the world was made.[11]

8. See my "Milton's God," and see also Joseph Anthony Wittreich, Jr., " 'Sublime Allegory': Blake's Epic Manifesto and the Milton Tradition," *Blake Studies*, 4 (1972), 15–44. Also useful are recent books on particular epics, such as Michael C. J. Putnam's *The Poetry of the* Aeneid (Cambridge: Harvard Univ. Press, 1965).

9. See my "Milton's God." See also Irene Samuel, *"Paradise Lost as Mimesis,"* in *Approaches to* Paradise Lost, ed. C. A. Patrides (Toronto: Univ. of Toronto Press, 1968), p. 19.

10. Thomas M. Greene, *The Descent from Heaven* (New Haven: Yale Univ. Press, 1963), p. 15.

11. See A. B. Chambers, "Chaos in *Paradise Lost*," *Journal of the History of Ideas*, 24 (1963), 55–84.

Finally, Milton very sharply underlines the fragility of human accomplishment. It can scarcely be called accomplishment, even, this ability man has to face himself and his mortality, to create out of destruction what must itself be destroyed, and to trust that this process has meaning. Yet the trust and the affirmation are stupendous, perhaps just because of the fragility of it all. That affirmation in the face of death, the use of death to justify itself, is characteristic of the epic and of Milton, and it is a quality that American poetry at its best, in its own terms, also possesses.

One other, closely related, phenomenon is the way in which, as the public subject matter of the poem becomes less significant, the poem's narrator greatly increases in importance. The English seventeenth century, from which the American Puritans came, was a period in which many writers were learning to use the personal first person singular, re-creating themselves in art, and Milton characterizes this tendency at its best.[12] No one at this time isolates himself from his context, as will happen later, in the nineteenth century; rather, the individual defines himself in relation to family, church, state, king, or God. But both in his poetry and in his prose, Milton uses himself to support his own arguments, binding together public and private, personal and universal.

Of course, the epic poet in particular is supposed to express inspired truths and must therefore have more credibility than the writer of lyrics. For Milton, this trustworthiness was crucial because as a radical Puritan, or simply as a man significantly involved in civil warfare, he was subject to *ad hominem* attacks; his whole being was to be tested in everything he wrote. He repeatedly says so, and defends himself, in his prose tracts, and the famous prologues of *Paradise Lost* are of a piece with those earlier passages.

William Riggs has recently shown[13] how Milton constantly tests himself in the fiercest way, comparing himself with Satan to test his egoism and with Christ to test his humility. The narrator thus undergoes the whole experience of the poem; Satan is so vivid to us partly because the poet wonders whether his own poetic ambi-

12. Joan Webber, *The Eloquent "I": Style and Self in Seventeenth-Century Prose* (Madison: Univ. of Wisconsin Press, 1968).

13. William Riggs, *The Christian Hero in* Paradise Lost (Berkeley: Univ. of California Press, 1972).

tion may be Satanic, and he can respond only by consistently submitting his will to God's, by letting the epic depend upon the nightly inspiration of the sacred Muse. Riggs believes that in this way the poet undergoes experiences that every Christian man ought to endure, and so becomes an everyman.

The fact that in this struggle humility and egoism are so close together, that so much depends upon the spirit of the affirmation of the isolated individual, repeats itself in American poetry and in some ways has been its bane. The myth-accepting faculty that keeps men humble is severely weakened by the secularization of myth made possible by Milton's undermining of traditional Christianity and by his outright rejection of national destiny as an epic theme. In any case, America's rejection of a national religion would have made that kind of epic celebration untenable. And the idea of national destiny that might have served for epic did not at the right moment (unless perhaps in Melville in a different medium) encounter a poetic sensibility that could both celebrate and deplore. Yet the main tradition of American poetry is bardic and Adamic, in the sense given by Roy Harvey Pearce, in his brilliant book, *The Continuity of American Poetry:*

The Adamic poem—to define it as a basic style, a kind of ideal type—is one which portrays the simple, separating inwardness of man as that which at once forms and is formed by the vision of the world in which it has its being. Expressively, this poem is one which makes us aware of the operation of the creative imagination as an act of self-definition—thus, whether the poet wills it or not, of self-limitation. The poem may nominally argue for many things, may have many subjects, may be descriptive of the world at large; but always it will implicitly argue for one thing—the vital necessity of its own existence and of the ego which creates and informs it. Its essential argument, its basic subject, is the life of poetry itself, as this life makes viable a conception of man as in the end, whatever commitments he has had to make on the way, radically free to know, be, and make himself.[14]

Of course Milton's vocabulary—his way of defining—is different from that of later, and secular, poets. But the poet of *Paradise Lost* who compares himself with Christ, and the Christ of *Paradise Regained* who says to Satan, "Tempt not the Lord thy God," are progenitors of that same radical freedom, which they call obedi-

14. Pearce, *Continuity of American Poetry*, p. 187.

ence to self. Milton speaks in his prose of the self-honoring that
makes men free, where giving in to any of the world's idols would
bring bondage. The obvious identity of self-honoring with God-
honoring helps to create in some readers a sense that Milton is
egotistical just where to others he seems most humble. When, in
American literature, sacred myth is increasingly denied, while
Milton's bardic zeal is retained, the problem of the first-person
singular is greatly intensified. Whitman fits Pearce's definition of
the Adamic poet, and he is one of the few Americans who can lay
any sort of claim to the title of epic poet as well. His "I" is a
cosmic personality; his obedience is to mankind, and he earns the
right to say, as an epic poet might, "I am the man, I suffered, I
was there."[15] He is Adamic and epic in his penchant for naming,
and epic in his effort to create a communal myth of America. He
is related to Milton in his recognition that the poet helps to make
his world, literally enables and justifies life, by being a conductor
of the "afflatus," "the origin of all poems," "original energy":

> I bequeath myself to the dirt to grow from the grass I love,
> If you want me again look for me under your boot-soles.[16]

Walt Whitman, whose poetic personality is cosmic, and Emily
Dickinson, whom Pearce considers the greatest of our forebears
because she so fully knows and fulfills her private self, exemplify
two different ways in which the persona alone, devoid of, even
hostile to, traditional myth, can make itself into poetry. Roy
Harvey Pearce argues that the self-singing and the mythmaking
poet are never one in America, and that the dominant strain is that
of the self-singer, the Adam who makes his world by naming or
recognizing it. Yet I think that Pearce's categories are too nearly
arbitrary, like Wallace Stevens' assumption that Milton, if living
now, "would stick to the facts." The great tradition of American
poets, from Whitman to Stevens, is one of mythmakers: Whitman's vision of American community differs from Milton's idea of
God as all in all only in its utter secularity. The American Adamic
poet was once nearly as optimistic as the first Adam in his garden,
and perhaps as Milton himself before the revolution, when he

15. Walt Whitman, *Song of Myself*, in *Leaves of Grass*, ed. Harold W. Blodgett and
Sculley Bradley (New York: New York Univ. Press, 1965), p. 66.
    16. Ibid., pp. 52, 30, 29, 89.

thought all things could be made new. The self-singing energy that makes great poetry must often be generated by a mythmaking—that is to say, a visionary—capacity that makes the bard worthy of his name.

It is hard to justify secular myth because one has to believe that it can actually be realized in this world. And a focus on the individual poet is risky too. The self-reliance of antinomianism—a Puritan and Miltonic strain—begins as heresy, but has become a defining characteristic of American poetry. Because it tends toward inwardness (as in Dickinson) as well as self-reliance, and because it is freer of universal assumptions and especially of belief in the transcendental, American poetry is more vulnerable than Milton's to egotism and solipsism. Often it appears to be dead-ending in its own subjectivity. For this reason, Whitman's influence has seemed so ambiguous. *Song of Myself* has influenced poems which are really no more than that, and his open bardic style has helped lead some poets, like Allen Ginsberg, to a literary self-indulgence that often accompanies visionary power. In imitators of Dickinson, loss of communal myth and increasing dependence on self-reference have sometimes stiflingly narrowed the scope of the verse: because of this and because of its vulnerability to exhibitionism, "confessional poetry" today is belittled as much as it is admired.

For these reasons, among others, in the early twentieth century, the effort was made, by T. S. Eliot and others, to submerge modern poetry in a traditionalism whose lines they themselves chose. Nowhere other than here could the parallelism between Milton and the mainstream of American poetry be clearer; for in this movement, which Pearce calls "counter-current," Milton's poetry was rejected. Eliot called for the submergence of the poet in tradition: Milton's strong personality and his contempt for tradition became the enemy. In need of a style violently different from the prevailing mode, a style that would satisfy their need for an impersonal, conservative viewpoint set forth in "strong lines," poets influenced by Eliot began to learn their craft from Donne, Herbert, Marvell, and others of that school. Readers with nearly opposite viewpoints could in fact find what they wanted here, since Donne's poetry flouted sexual conventions and probed the psychology of human relationships, while metaphysical poetry in general stood for political and religious orthodoxy. Donne seemed impersonal in his willingness to adopt almost any dramatic pose: the real Andrew Marvell is nowhere to be found. At the same time, Milton with his radical politics and theology, his directly personal voice, and his formal, ritualistic style, seemed both inimical and superfluous.

T. S. Eliot's two essays on Milton are of course well-known, and personal incompatibility between the two men is apparent in both.[17] But Eliot's argument about the poetics changes. The first essay attacks Milton as outside the mainstream of English poetry, and detrimental to it because he is inimitable and unavoidable. By 1947, however, Eliot decided that the time has passed when Milton could endanger poetry. He then believed that the poetry of our time had found a voice so distinct that the past could no longer threaten.

He was wrong, at least in the way he formulated his conclusions. The idea of the past as threat is uncommon in contemporary literature, and poets draw what help they can from any useful source, without reference to traditions. Eliot's influence has vanished almost completely: his conservatism, his obscurity, and his authoritarianism make an uncomfortable mix, and his poetry, as well as that of his contemporaries, has itself begun to seem more formal and ritualistic than Milton's. Contrary to Eliot's expectations, the voice of poetry had been settled, but not by him. Roy Harvey Pearce was exactly right in calling Eliot's movement a "counter-current." The mainstream of American poetry is committed to the personal, affirmative, social, and forward thrust of the best of its Puritan history. American poets naturally think directly in terms of their own ancestral experience. The Puritan diarist, checking the events of the day to find evidence of his salvation or damnation; the prophets for whom social justice is a personal concern; the poet who wrote for revolution and justified God's ways by justifying his blindness, by celebrating creation, and by writing epic poetry—these are our spiritual and aesthetic forebears.

Robert Lowell and others working in a new climate of feeling pioneered, not a new kind of verse, but a vigorous and original

17. T. S. Eliot, *On Poetry and Poets* (New York: Farrar, Straus and Cudahy, 1957).

return to the confessional antinomian mode. At the same time,
two related phenomena occurred. Milton recovered all of his lost
status and more. And poets rejecting Eliot's authority emphatically claimed a connection with Wallace Stevens, who all during
Eliot's heyday had been impressively maintaining what now seems
the authentic American tradition. "Brother, he's our father!" [18]
says Roethke, who himself is a father to many. And Adrienne
Rich writes, in a poem dedicated to Stevens, "Sinner of the
Florida keys,/ You were our poet of revolution all along."[19] With
both Milton and Stevens, one may first have a feeling of remote-
ness, abstraction, formality: they should, one thinks, be the last
poets to appeal to our age. Yet the order so important to both has
nothing in common with Eliot's version of historical tradition,
which they would find life-denying. Their order is self-generated
and self-sustaining. To compare these two poets is to demonstrate,
backward and forward, the affinity between Milton and American
poetry.

At a time when most poets had given over that function, Milton
assumed that the poet's role was to teach and prophesy. He has
the prophet's rejection of the way things are, his insistence that
change, even revolutionary change, must move men toward the
unknowable end when God will be all in all. He rejects wholesale
what can be categorized as "external things," imposed patterns of
behavior or belief, static reliance on tradition. His God is a force
composed of good and evil, a direction toward good requiring
man's participation. When the Christ of *Paradise Regained*, conceived of as a man, stands on the pinnacle of the temple (before all
earthly temples) and says, "Tempt not the Lord thy God"
(IV.561), the ambiguity of his statement enables a humanistic
interpretation: by rejecting all Satanic temptations, Christ fully
possesses himself of the godlike humanity that Adam was meant
to have.

The idea of poet as prophet is wholly congenial to Americans,
and Stevens, like his predecessors, chooses this role, calling himself
a rabbi. He also is a prophet of change: for him there is no validity

18. Theodore Roethke, "A Rouse for Wallace Stevens," in *Collected Poems* (Garden
City: Doubleday, 1966), p. 266.
19. Adrienne Rich, "The Blue Ghazals," in *The Will to Change* (New York: W. W.
Norton, 1971), p. 21.

in the static or traditonal. "It must change" is the second require-
ment for the supreme fiction;[20] yet the supreme fiction, perhaps
never to be arrived at, may be a meeting place of imagination with
reality, the equivalent of the time when God will be all in all.
Acceptance of reality is acceptance of it as good-and-evil; the
death of Satan, who made possible a formal grasping of the idea of
evil, throws this responsibility too on man. In *Chocorua to Its
Neighbor* (pp. 296–302), Stevens conceives of Christ as major
man, "an image of man projecting himself imaginatively into the
furthest reaches of his humanity, and no more."[21]

Milton believed that God created the world out of chaos—an
unusual belief in a time when the world was supposed to have
been made from nothing.[22] Since his chaos is made of warring
elements—good and evil, light and dark, and so forth—reality at
least risks imperfection. The antitheses of chaos are necessary to
creation; yet the intention of creation is finally to overcome them.
For Stevens, what is created is the fiction by which man orders
reality; and in the spaces between such fictions, when one is
passing and the other not yet born, there is chaos, which is part of
the principle of change.

For Milton, the fall of Adam was the source of "all our woe";
yet Adam is able to call the fall fortunate (XII.470ff.) when he
foresees the coming of Christ. Indeed, even before that, Michael
tells Adam, he can possess within him a paradise "happier far"
than Eden (XII.586). Stevens has also a sense of the *felix culpa*,
which involves man's recognition of his own condition, outside of
Eden. Stevens' concept of Eden is different from Milton's since he
thinks of it as static and therefore unacceptable to men. But he
does, like Milton, accept the necessity—and the desirability—of
change and death as essential to creation.

Looking at the history which Michael shows him, Adam feels
renewed despair until he is taught to accept the paradoxes of the

20. Wallace Stevens, *Notes toward a Supreme Fiction*, in *The Collected Poems of
Wallace Stevens* (New York: Knopf, 1961), p. 389. Future references to poems by
Stevens will be to this edition and will be given in the text.

21. Pearce, *Continuity of American Poetry*, p. 393.

22. In addition to my "Milton's God," and Chambers's "Chaos in *Paradise Lost*," see
Walter Clyde Curry, *Milton's Ontology, Cosmogony and Physics* (Lexington: Univ. of
Kentucky Press, 1957); and Michael Lieb, *The Dialectics of Creation: Patterns of Birth
and Regeneration in* Paradise Lost (Amherst: Univ. of Massachusetts Press, 1970).

happier paradise and the fortunate fall. He accepts mortality for all humanity, beginning with the fratricide of his own son. This acceptance, as pointed out earlier, is the major task of the epic hero. It is echoed in the morality of Stevens' major man, whose task is to endure without despair a reality imaginatively known, and to learn wholly to accept the necessity of pain and death:

> Pain is human.
> There were roses in the cool café. His book
> Made sure of the most correct catastrophe.
> Except for us, Vesuvius might consume
> In solid fire the utmost earth and know
> No pain (ignoring the cocks that crow us up
> To die). This is a part of the sublime
> From which we shrink. And yet, except for us,
> The total past felt nothing when destroyed.
>
> (*Esthétique du Mal*, p. 314)

Adam is already all men, containing within himself all the possibilities of the race. Christ becomes all men by creating (or perhaps decreating—a word of Stevens')[23] himself in the wilderness, rejecting and dehumanizing temptations. In a sense, Christ is created by himself and Satan, and could not be free in his power unless Satan offered him the chance. Stevens' major man is the Christ who "rose because men wanted him to be" (*Chocorua to Its Neighbor*, p. 299), an amalgamation of particular men who have so given themselves to that abstraction that although they can be seen partially as their old selves, rabbi or chieftain, they have grown beyond that:

> What rabbi, grown furious with human wish,
> What chieftain, walking by himself, crying
> Most miserable, most victorious,
>
> Does not see these separate figures one by one,
> And yet see only one, in his old coat,
> His slouching pantaloons, beyond the town . . .
>
> (*Supreme Fiction*, p. 389)

---

23. Wallace Stevens, "The Relation between Poetry and Painting," *The Necessary Angel* (New York: Random House, 1951), pp. 174–75. The word "decreation" was adopted by Stevens to describe the way in which poetry must cleanse the world of its old myths.

The major man is not comprehensible to worldly people, who see him as foolish because he has rejected the static elements of their kind of elegance in order to achieve his own. Similarly, Satan, running out of temptations, loses patience with Christ:

> Since neither wealth, nor honour, arms nor arts,
> Kingdom nor Empire pleases thee, nor aught
> By me propos'd in life contemplative,
> Or active, tended on by glory, or fame,
> What dost thou in this World? The Wilderness
> For thee is fittest place . . .
>
> (*PR* IV.368–373)

That is the triumph of Christ, whose task is to begin in the waste wilderness which is the world rightly seen, for only there can Eden be raised; for the major man, only there is reality to be met:

> For the listener, who listens in the snow,
> And, nothing himself, beholds
> Nothing that is not there and the nothing that is.
>
> ("The Snow Man," p. 10)

It is important for Christ to have said no to almost everything supposedly human before he can make that tremendous final affirmation, itself couched in the negative: "Tempt not the Lord thy God." The first Adam voiced another kind of no, the no of despair, the hatred of his own existence, before he could achieve his own affirmation simply of existence, refusing suicide. Stevens' hero is also the one who affirms after that thoroughgoing rejection:

> After the final no there comes a yes
> And on that yes the future world depends.
> No was the night. Yes is this present sun.
>
> ("The Well Dressed Man with a Beard," p. 247)

I stress this affirmation again because it seems to me so particularly American in the major Adamic tradition,[24] and so essentially

---

24. For the American everlasting no, see Melville writing on Hawthorne, as quoted in *The Melville Log*, ed. Jay Leyda, 2 vols. (New York: Harcourt and Brace, 1969), I, 410: "We think that into no recorded mind has the intense feeling of the visible truth ever entered more deeply than into this man's. By visible truth, we mean the apprehension of

like the affirmation in Milton. T. S. Eliot's gradual acceptance of orthodox Christianity is a submersion of self in tradition completely different from this discovery of myth and meaning in the self.

For both Milton and Stevens, the necessity of change requires the rejection of old idioms. Milton begins his career in imitation, and then from stage to stage quite explicitly turns his back on whole categories, styles, and modes of literature. In the elegy, *Epitaphium Damonis,* he gives up Latin poetry and pastoralism. In the transition from his early poetry to his prose tracts, he obviously gives up verse, and will never come back, except in occasional poems, to set verse structure or regular rhyming. Before *Paradise Lost,* he rejected the idea of writing a national epic, which had informed his poetic planning, as well as the writing of *Defensio Secunda.* And in *Paradise Regained* he strips the epic of almost all its traditional language and machinery.

Stevens' idiom is formed by rejection of the old. "The dump is full/ Of images," and the poet sits on the dump, surrounded by words he can no longer use because they have lost their relation to reality. "One feels the purifying change. One rejects/ The trash" ("The Man on the Dump," pp. 201–2). Metaphors are banned

---

the absolute condition of present things as they strike the eye of the man who fears them not, though they do their worst to him . . .

There is the grand truth about Nathaniel Hawthorne. He says NO! in thunder; but the Devil himself cannot make him say *yes.* For all men who say *yes,* lie; and all men who say *no,*—why, they are in the happy condition of judicious, unincumbered travellers in Europe; they cross the frontiers into Eternity with nothing but a carpet-bag,—that is to say, the Ego."

Pearce's comment on Stevens's "Yes" is useful: "The tragedy is that to say yes, Stevens had in the end to say no to so much—to jettison the creative for the decreative, the actual for the possible, men for man, the world for the Rock. Yet he did so to save himself and them for the creative, the actual, the men, and the world to which, once they know themselves as and when they were, they might triumphantly return. More than any other American poet, Stevens saw that Melville's celebrated thunderous No! called forth, inevitably, a Yes!—the Yes! of the kind of "realist" which indeed Melville himself was at the height of his power" (*Continuity of American Poetry,* p. 416).

Some of the kind of jettisoning to which Pearce refers is the flattening of poetry to statement that occurs in the quotation from *Esthétique de Mal* on p. 243 of this essay, and which Milton also does to some extent in *Paradise Regained.* That is only a symptom of what Pearce is talking about; yet I see nothing tragic in the direction taken by either poet. Stevens himself regarded his work as the opposite of tragic, and Milton too passed by tragedy into a higher affirmation. The ability to jettison is the ability to stay alive.

because they distort vision. Stevens once said that if he could he would throw all his belongings out each year and make a fresh start.[25] Pearce comments that as he gropes toward the ultimate fiction, Stevens' language necessarily becomes less and less poetic.[26] I would say, at any rate, that it is less poetic in the accepted sense, just as *Paradise Regained* seems unpoetic because Milton is abandoning all he can of external help.

Yet, despite their insistence on traveling light, forging their own tools as they go, both poets have a formality of expression that is unique in its own time and that inevitably, in Stevens, reminds us of the earlier poet. Their language is philosophical because their thought is; both are expressing a system of belief. Their vocabularies are, as William Haller once said of Milton's prose, "not quite English":[27] Milton draws heavily on Latin language and syntax; Stevens tends to borrow European, especially French, vocabulary, as well as to use extensive archaisms. Consciously or unconsciously Stevens also imitates Milton's ritualistic bardic tone, achieved through repetition, archaisms, foreign words, formal syntax, and extensive verbal music. More successfully, perhaps, than any other English poet, he is at home in the high style of Miltonic blank verse.

The similarity is partly accounted for by the religious seriousness with which both poets regard their work of re-creating. While the poet remakes the past he uses it; jettisoning much, he also transforms much, indicating a continuity of life and life-worship that subsumes and feeds on all change. This is the epic spirit of renewal through destruction. Milton's God is a force for life and for creation that works through and beyond man. Stevens' God is what man himself is, makes, and is made by. Both are to be celebrated, and the style of both poets is intended to convey that sense of celebration. Stevens denies mythmaking and scolds Milton for "going off on a myth"; yet unless mythology has to be transcendental, I cannot see that the idea of man inventing himself is very different from the self-honoring that for Milton promotes

25. *Letters of Wallace Stevens*, p. 659.
26. Pearce, *Continuity of American Poetry*, p. 405.
27. William Haller, *Liberty and Reformation in the Puritan Revolution* (New York: Columbia Univ. Press, 1963), p. 50.

life, or from the process of self-realization that men must share with Milton's God.

Stevens' "Sunday Morning" is familiar partly because of its simplicity, but also because it so availably expresses important aspects of his style and thought. It compares well with Milton's *Nativity Ode*, since both poems reject tradition without rejecting man's religious impulse. They are early poems, not to be taken as their authors' final statements on life, yet they suggest much of what is to come.

Both poems try to relocate the Word as immanent rather than wholly transcendent. Milton's poem is more explicitly revolutionary, its subject the invasion of time by eternity, the world by the Word.[28] Not so much a baby in a cradle as a cataclysmic and imminent force, the Word drives out the established false gods who possess the lands, temples, and power; despite (or because of) their seductiveness, their tyranny is dangerous. Milton imitates the coming of the Word in his poem by silencing all such human activity as warfare, then allowing sound to be born again with the simple conversation of the shepherds, or poets, sitting on the lawn. And he makes the poem immediate by putting himself into it: this song of praise will be his gift to the Christ child.

Milton dispenses, too, with the idols of institutional Christianity. He is a transitional poet, and, as with all his work, it is possible superficially to read the *Nativity Ode* in a traditional way. But that is only barely possible, and only because he uses the stereotypes to emphasize the vitality of the real thing. The usual nativity scene is briefly allowed at beginning and end, but the main events of the poem are the music of the spheres that unites all time and space, and the silencing and blinding of the pagan gods by the speechless, powerful Child. Although that power is necessary and wondrous, there is certainly regret in the dismissal of the pagan past, even in the naming of the banished gods, and in the descriptions of their emptied places:

> The lonely mountains o're,
> And the resounding shore,

28. Webber, "The Son of God and Power of Life in Three Poems by Milton," pp. 175–94. For contemporary mention of the Nativity as revolutionary, see Rich, *Will to Change*, p. 23.

> A voice of weeping heard, and loud lament;
> From haunted spring, and dale
> Edg'd with poplar pale,
>   The parting Genius is with sighing sent,
> With Flowre-inwov'n tresses torn
> The Nimphs in twilight shade of tangled thickets mourn.
>
> (181–88)

Like the stereotype of the Child, the nymphs, too, cling to the imagination, but unequivocally these are false gods, blinding men to reality, and they have to go.

Stevens intentionally archaizes his poem, reminding us in language and theme of that earlier exorcism:

> "But when the birds are gone, and their warm fields
> Return no more, where, then, is paradise?"
> There is not any haunt of prophecy,
> Nor any old chimera of the grave,
> Neither the golden underground, nor isle
> Melodious, where spirits gat them home,
> Nor visionary south, nor cloudy palm
> Remote on heaven's hill, that has endured
> As April's green endures . . .
>
> (p. 68)

Both poems attempt to free the language and men's minds of myths that prevent an accurate and unfrightened encounter with reality. Death and destruction inevitably become liberating forces. Thus, for Stevens, "Death is the mother of beauty" (p. 68): unlike Milton he sees the Christian paradise as changeless and invidious. His earthly paradise owns, because of death, the same kinds of variety that Milton envisaged as existing in a prelapsarian world. Time and death, in the *Nativity Ode,* will bring again the golden age.

For both poets a kind of deep, spontaneous harmony replaces the tyranny of imposed religion. For Milton, that harmony is represented by a recovery of the music of the spheres. Hearing that music, the poet experiences the world almost as God would; time ceases to become relevant just at the point when it is most important; both the creation of the world and the last judgment are evoked by the Nativity, and the golden world is here, yet not

here. Time must be lived out, yet the Revolution—the coming of
the Word—has made each moment eternal.

For Stevens, redemption is a human "chant of paradise," the
binding together of mortal men in love of their mortal world.
Milton's minor-key regret for the oracles' passing is paralleled in
Stevens' evocation of the ambiguous joys of earth's beauty:

> And, in the isolation of the sky,
> At evening, casual flocks of pigeons make
> Ambiguous undulations as they sink,
> Downward to darkness, on extended wings.
>
> (p. 70)

This too is the loneliness of Adam and Eve leaving paradise and
immediate communion with God, knowing that what they have—
earth and each other—is in some way better.

Obviously both poets exalt the Word, whether or not identified,
as in Milton, with the Word of God. In *Sunday Morning*, Stevens'
vision of the chanting men creates the beauty of the world, as he
says poetry ought to do. As the *Sunday Morning* poet creates this
idea of humanity, the poet in the *Nativity Ode* presents his poem
to Christ, thus giving credence to or in some sense even creating
Christ as timeless Idea. Both poets believe in poetry as a vehicle of
reality, and Milton's God is justifiable only if creation, as we
understand it, is good.

I have already considered the need felt, by Stevens and Milton,
to face and absorb into their philosophies the fact of evil. At the
other extreme the two stand out in their times, not only as
"Puritan" poets, but also as poets unusually alive to the desirable
sensuousness of the material world. The rigorousness of their own
requirements for art and life, and the sternness with which materialism is rejected, point up in a uniquely effective way their stress
on the goodness of the sensory world. Their techniques are identical. There is frequent, explicit advocacy, for example, in Milton's
account of Creation itself, in his descriptions of Eden, particularly
in the discussions of food and sex in the Garden; in Stevens, earth
is often praised, as in *Sunday Morning* or *Esthétique du Mal.* In
support, there is lush poetic evocation of all the senses:

> for drink the Grape
> She crushes, inoffensive must, and meaths

From many a berry, and from sweet kernels prest
She tempers dulcet creams, nor these to hold
Wants her fit vessels pure, then strews the ground
With Rose and Odours from the shrub unfum'd.
(*PL* V.334–48)

Why set the pear upon those river-banks
Or spice the shores with odors of the plum?
Alas, that they should wear our colors there,
The silken weavings of our afternoons,
And pick the strings of our insipid lutes!
(*Sunday Morning*, p. 69)

It is important for us to keep in mind this aspect of their affirmation of life, an affirmation which may otherwise seem too well characterized by Stevens' word "abstract." Man creates, or fulfills, himself in his poetry, or else he allows the process of creation to take place in his poetry: whether secular or sacred, poetry is literally a vital force. For these poets, that is, art and life are one because poetry is life's heart and blood in all of its sensuousness as well as its pain. This is just the reason why so much poetry in our time is about writing. The impulse is metaphysical, not precious. We study the creative force, just as Milton did in *Paradise Lost,* in order to find out what life means. For Milton and Stevens (as for us at our worthiest), metaphysical rigorousness has to be combined with sensuous play because their understanding of life is so fully affirmative. Stevens has been accused of dilettantism because of the names of such poems as "Connoisseur of Chaos"; this is no different from Milton's "unwieldy Elephant," who, to please Adam and Eve, "us'd all his might, and wreath'd/ His Lithe Proboscis" (V.345–47). It may be that the very complexity of the endeavor of both poets, the philosophical intensity that affirms life by taking full account of the creative inevitability of real agony and real joy, requires the poetic rigorousness that makes them difficult for some readers.

This is the core of the heritage, to contemporary poetry, of Milton, Stevens, and the main American tradition. No poet writing today, perhaps no American poet other than Stevens, has so consciously elaborated his aesthetic theory. Like Milton, he seems almost to have ended a tradition by his rigorous purification of it. In contrast, critics writing of contemporary art speak of its uncertainty of direction, as well as of a variety of characteristics less philosophical than at least some of those which identify Stevens.[29] Yet it is easy enough to trace the essential kinship, as well as to find, in the different context of our poetry, a different kind of affinity with Milton.

The first, or most encompassing, likeness is the poets' need to put themselves on the line. It is his overwhelming personal presence in his poetry and prose that has so strongly divided critical attitudes toward Milton; no one is ever neutral about him. That insistence on personal presence has dominated American poetry as well, except during the brief period when Eliot tried to make us objectify ourselves. Milton is present as poet, as prophet, as individual involved in the world. When he says that the poet "ought him selfe to be a true Poem" (*Apology against a Pamphlet, CM*, III,i,303–4), he does mean the poet himself. So does our contemporary Gregory Corso: "The times demand that the poet— that is, man—be as true as a poem."[30] It is an impossibly brave position, almost calculated to draw attack from people who must see this stand as hypocritical or egotistical, or who simply take him at his word and therefore require him to be a great deal better than human. Yet it is, just to begin with, a valuable defense against alienation, against the use of art as analyzable object. The effort to banish the poet's life and beliefs from his poetry fails when it comes to Milton, as it would do if attempted with most of our contemporaries.

The poet then inevitably becomes a hero (if not the hero) in his own poem; in fact, he may well loom larger than the poem itself in the eyes of his readers, since he does not cease when the particular poem does. Milton's insistence that his own private self is his "I" coincides in his time as in ours with a strong political, even revolutionary, pressure on human consciousness. Because he has accepted the vocation of prophet, he is vulnerable to the belief that he cannot write his poetry properly unless he has been actively involved in the world. Milton wrote, in *The Reason of*

29. For example, Paul Carroll, in *The Poem in Its Skin* (Chicago: Follett, 1968), lists as characteristic of the poets of the sixties, celebration of the city; testimony to another and possibly supernatural reality; political activism; humor; sex; mingling of poetry with what is usually considered prosaic.

30. Gregory Corso, in *Poets on Poetry*, ed. Howard Nemerov (New York: Basic Books, 1966), p. 176.

Church-Government, that, whether or not his cause was successful, if he had failed to take part in England's struggle, he would feel unworthy:

> But now by this little diligence, mark what a privilege I have gain'd; with good men and Saints to clame my right of lamenting the tribulations of the Church, if she should suffer, when others that have ventur'd nothing for her sake, have not the honour to be admitted mourners. But if she lift up her drooping head and prosper, among those that have something more than wisht her welfare, I have my charter and freehold of rejoycing to me and my heires.
>
> > (*CM*, III, i, 233)

The loss of capacity to write traditional formal poetry seems commonly to characterize revolutionary art: that was more of a problem for Milton than it is for us. During the 1640s and 50s, he wrote, aside from sonnets, a lot of political prose that oscillates rapidly between the savage violence of street diction and prose-poetry so exalted that some critics have thought it too poetic to be considered prose at all. Even in *Reason of Church Government,* where he speaks of writing with his left hand, he does the opposite of what he implies; this *is* poetry:

> For although a Poet soaring in the high region of his fancies with his garland and singing robes about him might without apology speak more of himself than I mean to do, yet for me sitting here below in the cool element of prose, a mortal thing among my readers of no Empyreall conceit, to venture and divulge unusual things of my selfe, I shall petition to the gentler sort, it may not be envy to me.
>
> > (*CM*, III, i, 235)

In many of these revolutionary tracts, Milton moves back and forth between public and private, topical and universal, prose and poetry, so that they all seem bound together as one thing. The prose has been thought bad because it follows no recognized rules. It has been thought egotistical because all the issues Milton raises are of immediate concern to him. Similarly, the personal or political parts of *Lycidas* have been called digressions, even though the poem could hardly hold together without them. The personal drive in the great prologues of *Paradise Lost* gives them far more weight than their formal status suggests. Milton treats nothing objectively in the sense that it thereby becomes impersonal; but he has no personal mission that is not a universal cause.

In our time, too, to be a prophet has meant that poets take personal responsibility to attack injustice. Allen Ginsberg adopts the most obviously prophetic stance, but the majority of our contemporaries feel the necessity to write political poetry, and to the extent that their involvement is evident in their lives and in their art they too have been accused of egotism and of bad writing. Since decorum is much more relaxed at this time than it was in Milton's, freedom of expression comes easier—the poets keep writing poetry; but they often incorporate into their art chunks of what would once have been thought unpoetic—"found" poems in the speech of other people, street placards in Denise Levertov's account of a Berkeley demonstration. Her book, *To Stay Alive,* is a collage of poems and prose poems about revolution, and about the poet finding her place, meshing the rhythms of revolution with those of poetry, so that the singing can begin.[31]

Adrienne Rich is typical of many contemporary poets, though more conscious and more successful than most, in creating a poetic mode meant "to tell what she experiences on the front lines of a life made political by the world in which she lives."[32] Poems like "The Burning of Paper Instead of Children" and "The Blue Ghazals" range between prose and poetry, private and public, in order to force a reawakening of the deadened senses, an acknowledgment of the connection between one's whole life and the whole of things. In "The Burning of Paper," she describes the inadequacy of verbiage which has been used to ward off sensation, and uses prose to restore meaning to "the oppressor's language." Written in five sections, its first and third parts are public, the second and fourth primarily private. Here are selections from 3 and 4:

> 3. "People suffer highly in poverty and it takes
> dignity and intelligence to overcome this

---

31. Denise Levertov, *To Stay Alive* (New York: New Directions, 1971), pp. 73–74.

32. This quotation is taken from the back cover of *The Will to Change* (New York: Norton, 1971). In a review of Robin Morgan's *Monster*, in *Ms.*, 2 (August, 1973), 42, Rich criticizes Morgan for her "implied assumption that the 'subjective' or personal poem has less collective force than the 'political' poem, or that the 'political' poem must strip itself of the mystery and density of the individual inward life—and language. Such assumptions arise from deep schisms in our culture."

suffering. Some of the suffering are: a child
did not had dinner last night: a child steal
because he did not have money to buy it: to
hear a mother say she do not have money to
buy food for her children and to see a child
without cloth it will make tears in your eyes."

(the fracture of order
the repair of speech
to overcome this suffering)

4. We lie under the sheet
after making love, speaking
of loneliness
relieved in a book
relived in a book
so on that page
the clot and fissure
of it appears
words of a man
in pain
a naked word
entering the clot
a hand grasping
through bars . . .

The fifth section combines both modes in a very rapid shifting
that hammers at the identification of public and private, thought
and feeling, and seeks out a new kind of prose-poetry that can be a
fit vehicle for this:

Some of the suffering are: it is hard to tell the truth; this is America; I cannot
touch you now. In America we have only the present tense. I am in danger.
You are in danger. The burning of a book arouses no sensation in me. I know
it hurts to burn. There are flames of napalm in Catonsville, Maryland. I know
it hurts to burn. The typewriter is overheated, my mouth is burning. I cannot
touch you and this is the oppressor's language.[33]

The need is to reshape the language to make readers know that in
a ruined society a lover's touch can burn like napalm. The fusion
of literary with peasant language and the incorporation of herself

33. Rich, *Will to Change*, pp. 15–18.

into her poem as lover and politician forces a closing of the gap that will burn in order to make whole.

Thus, while political literature may defy conventional standards of word usage and organization, its indecorous juxtapositions and gaucheries are responsive to its society and to the poet's need to express herself as a whole person. There is continual acknowledgment that our sense of the poetic must be inadequate to our needs unless our idiom changes, and clashes, almost as rapidly as it is used. Milton wants and needs to be more violent and extreme than Rich in his attacks on the sources of power and his subversions of generic forms associated with tradition. Both reject conventional syntax and argument in search of a more physical language directly used as experience.

I do not mean to suggest that the art is chaotic. Rather, this poetry shows remarkable control over its unique and unequal idioms. But the control has been gained by an abandonment of the usual kinds of discipline, a willingness to allow the art not to measure up at all to conventional standards. It dictates its course from within. What is true of all valuable art is true to an extreme degree of this revolutionary literature. Much more sensitively than usual, the medium is made to become its subject, forcing prose out of poetry or poetry out of prose, constantly crossing generic limits, even forcing the language or convention to reject itself, as in *Paradise Lost* and "The Burning of Paper."

Poetry and prose like this can easily become topical, a problem for us because it has been a shibboleth of English poetry (as opposed to European or Romance poetry) that the topical makes bad verse. Political passion, in particular, is supposed to be undignified and out of place in poetry, pushing it toward the shrill and the transient. That may be true, yet insistence on separation of the immediate from the general is another kind of alienation: we can write about what matters if it doesn't come too close to home. And rejection of political passion has the disadvantage of restricting the range of our traditions, forcing us to study poetry, like history, written by winners.

Milton's numerous political sonnets are worth studying if only for the sake of forcing the reader to confront this issue. More than anywhere else, in such poems as *On the Detraction Which Followed, On the Lord General Fairfax, On the New Forcers of*

Conscience, and *On the Late Massacre,* he deals directly with specific political or social events and personalities with now-forgotten names. It is a sort of outrageous triumph in itself to take a form traditionally used for love and inform it with political energy. Beyond this, one can safely argue that the poem *On the Late Massacre* succeeds better than the others because it does not depend upon external knowledge of the event, and because it so clearly deals with the tragedy and ultimate futility of tyranny. One can make similar distinctions among the moderns. Robert Bly's "Hatred of Men with Black Hair,"[34] and Randall Jarrell's "Transient Barracks,"[35] filled with such topical references as those in Milton's "Fairfax" or his divorce-tract poems, will probably depend for their survival on the future reputations of their authors. On the other hand, Jarrell's "Death of the Ball Turret Gunner"[36] and Bly's "Counting Small-Boned Bodies,"[37] powerful unlocalized statements about war and human nature, will help to determine the poets' stature.

Yet to stop here and regard the "problem" of topicality as solved would be a mistake, for there is something about the topicality itself, about the untidiness and undistanced passion of revolutionary art, which is important and appealing. The in-process artist is not only that intensely self-conscious artful variety typified by Donne, but also the revolutionary who is always not just in process of expelling dross, but using what others regard as dross and true metal almost indifferently, understanding that what to other generations has seemed most valid (like the trappings of the epic in *Paradise Lost*) may soon be wholly dispensable. Discounting any intrinsic value in tradition, Milton always has to be able to find both his own principles and his own materials. Thinking all the way through his immediate topic, to find the ultimate source of his rage, is one of Milton's great strengths, and one which contemporary poets have to learn. But that furious process is untidy by the usual standards of English literary criti-

34. Robert Bly, *The Light Around the Body* (New York: Harper and Row, 1967), p. 36.
35. Randall Jarrell, *The Complete Poems* (New York: Farrar, Straus and Giroux, 1969), p. 147.
36. Ibid., p. 144.
37. Bly, *Light Around the Body,* p. 32.

cism: it involves Milton, and our contemporaries, in illogicality, in gutter-language, in passionately associative and *ad hominem* rhetoric. What has to be said about even the least apparently defensible of Milton's prose tracts is that this is a valid and necessary aspect of revolutionary creativity. It has its own kind of identifiable recurrent decorum, which, when we learn to understand it, can help us to understand our own times.[38]

Milton understood his vocation to be prophetic, and he insists that if his muse cannot seriously be believed to dictate his unpremeditated verse, then his poetry is nothing. Contemporary poets describe both possession and desertion by the muse as frightening and formative. Just as they are more willing than their predecessors to identify themselves with their poems, they seem more vulnerable in their dependence on inspiration, as well as in their immediate urgency of mission. Although it is certainly not always true that for our poets, as for Milton, prophecy, didacticism, and a sense of the sacred are linked, it is true often enough to be worthy of comment.

A total rejection of dead institutions often clears the way for a new sense of the sacred. Even, or perhaps especially, poets believing themselves to be clearing away the rubbish of humanism, the plastering of human values over a natural landscape, seem somehow to conclude in the discovery of a landscape to be reverenced. Milton had no use for a wide range of "externalized" styles, institutions, and beliefs—the prelacy, the universities, indissoluble marriages, and the God worshiped by most of his contemporaries. In his writing he "decreates" both institutions and literary genres, discovering an immanent force that he thinks of as God. Writing of postmodernist poetry, Charles Altieri argues that "God for the contemporaries manifests himself as energy, as the intense expression of immanent power."[39] Altieri's characterization of postmodern poetics as radically Protestant seems to me exactly accurate, as opposed to the Anglo-Catholic symbolizing of Eliot's generation. Despite his insistence on secularity, Wallace Stevens is one philosophical father of this later school, whose members

38. See my "Stylistics: A Bridging of Life and Art in Seventeenth-Century Studies," *New Literary History*, 2 (1971), 283–96.

39. Charles Altieri, "From Symbolist Thought to Immanence: The Ground of Postmodern American Poetics," *Boundary 2*, 1 (1973), 610.

include Charles Olson, Denise Levertov, and Robert Duncan. For all these poets, as for Milton I think, the process of self-realization is a recognition of God as the ground of being.

To subscribe to this scheme, as it exists either in Milton or in postmodern poetry, does not require any kind of traditional belief in God. Art and life come from one source. The process of poetry or life is the tapping of a power which most poets experience as real and palpable, a power without which most poetry could not exist. God is not simply all good. Milton locates the forces of destruction and creation so close together that they often become one motion: Satan is different from God because his direction is against life and decreative, whereas God's is for life and creative. But God and Satan both use and include both destruction and creation.[40] The justification of God's ways to Milton is that creation and life are good.

While Wallace Stevens would strip his philosophy of traditional Christian language, the essential likeness of his view of creation to Milton's is obvious, and clear enough in his poetry to be an obvious source for younger poets. Yet despite Stevens' strenuous effort to enable men to rejoice in their changeful, and mortal, paradise, contemporary poetry is haunted by the fear that men have been defeated, the word damaged beyond repair, the unbelieving self found inadequate to the comprehensive meaning it is asked to sustain. So far I have set forth two ways—political and religious—in which the challenge to the individual has been modified so that the poem does not begin and end with the poet alone. These ways coexist in Milton and in many of our contemporaries. But, together or separately, it is obvious that they may fail, since political action does not bring about utopia, and faith, especially today, is hard to come by.

The right use of the single self remains a problem, and poets are criticized either for hiding behind masks, like Robert Bly,[41] or for being too confessional, doing a psychological striptease, as Sylvia Plath purposely does in "Lady Lazarus."[42] Dependent on his own

40. See my "Milton's God."

41. Galway Kinnell, "Poetry, Personality, and Death," *Field*, 4 (1971), 56–75.

42. Sylvia Plath, "Lady Lazarus," in *Ariel* (New York: Harper and Row, 1966), pp. 6–9. The explicitly political striptease of this poem is justified, as some superficially comparable self-revelations are not. The opening line of Robert Lowell's "Man and

ego, the poet either evades or exploits it; in either case he is out of touch with himself and lacks a context. If the problem cannot be met by recourse to something more engrossing than the "I," as in political or religious poetry, then it must be taken head-on. Galway Kinnell argues that ideally the poet should go so deeply into the self as to find that he is everyone. The self dies into rebirth and a wholeness that transcends personality. Such was surely Plath's aim, but she was unable sufficiently to understand her personal dilemmas. Kinnell cites the bardic Whitman and Ginsberg as important precursors and examples of what has to be done.

For many contemporary poets, as for Plath, this effort has been too arduous. The essay in which Kinnell discusses the problem is called "Poetry, Personality, and Death." Adrienne Rich has consistently argued that contemporary poetry, and she particularly means poetry by men, is desperate, obsessed by death.[43] Poets like John Berryman, James Wright, Delmore Schwartz, and Sylvia Plath have given evidence in their poems and in their lives of a hatred of life and of themselves which has caused readers to question the worth, even the morality, of such art. When one must, like James Wright, try to persuade a suicide (whom he calls his muse!) back to life merely to give comfort to a fellow sufferer who would also commit suicide if he dared,[44] or when suicide is extolled as the ultimate art,[45] there seems little, even of comfort, that a reader can gain. It is the negative pole of self-reliance: if you can't walk on water, then you drown.

A third major way of postmodern poetry, bound inextricably in some writers, as it is in Milton, with politics and religion, is sexuality. For him, as for our contemporaries, to desire to unite public with private requires a thorough revision of our understanding of sexual roles, and an acceptance or even merging of male and

Wife," in *Life Studies and For the Union Dead* (New York: Farrar, Straus and Giroux, 1967), p. 87, "Tamed by Miltown, we lie on Mother's bed," seems a good example of undistanced topicality, overinvolving the reader in brand names and case histories. On this, see M. L. Rosenthal, *The New Poets* (New York: Oxford Univ. Press, 1967), pp. 18–19.

43. Adrienne Rich, "Poetry, Personality, and Wholeness: A Response to Galway Kinnell," *Field*, 7 (1972), 11–18.

44. James Wright, "To the Muse," in *Collected Poems* (Middletown, Conn.: Wesleyan Univ. Press, 1971), pp. 168–69.

45. Sylvia Plath, "Edge" and "Lady Lazarus," in *Ariel*, pp. 84 and 6–9.

female principles. Adrienne Rich's response to Kinnell's argument
is that men despair because they reject the feminine in themselves
and, locked in their own partial being, can find no way out of the
grave they have built for mankind:

> A man is asleep in the next room
> He has spent a whole day
> standing, throwing stones into the black pool
> which keeps its blackness . . . [46]

We have looked at things the other way round for so long that it is
easy not to notice, in *Paradise Lost,* that without Eve Adam can
find no reason to want to live. They ruin one another, but it is Eve
who is first able to begin the restorative process. Their recovery
then is only less spectacular than the fact that Milton is able to
make it believable. We seem to accept unquestioningly that total
reaffirmation of one another which, if we thought about it in
real-life terms, would seem entirely miraculous. We see them
respond to their intuitive knowledge of each other, cease to think
of one another as adversaries, believably create a new myth of
oneness, a happier paradise, as they leave paradise hand in hand.
For Rich the renewal of the myth is the creation of the andro-
gyne. The fall was the separation of the sexes:

> This is the place.
> And I am here, the mermaid whose dark hair
> streams black, the merman in his armored body
> We circle silently
> about the wreck
> we dive into the hold.
> I am she: I am he
>
> whose drowned face sleeps with open eyes
> whose breasts still bear the stress
> whose silver, copper, vermeil cargo lies
> obscurely inside barrels
> half-wedged and left to rot
> we are the half-destroyed instruments
> that once held to a course

46. Adrienne Rich, *Diving into the Wreck* (New York: W. W. Norton, 1973), p. 12.

the water-eaten log
the fouled compass[47]

The men who wrote classical epics, perhaps because their work was inspired and mythic, did consistently confront the need for the merging of feminine and masculine in life. As a member of this tradition and as a political radical, Milton emerges with more credit than has generally been assigned him. Unlike anyone else that I am aware of in his time, he suggests not only that hierarchy is arbitrary and that sometimes the wife may be superior and hold authority in marriage, but also that androgyny is a higher state. When Adam asks Raphael about sex in heaven, Raphael says that heavenly sex is superior (VIII.620–29). Elsewhere it has been said that angels can assume either sex or both; they are androgynous (I.423–24). And they can merge totally with one another. Since Adam and Eve were intended to achieve the state of angels, one can assume that the androgynous life is an aspect of that perfect unity toward which the whole creation moves.

Even more interesting, perhaps, is the ambiguous sex of Milton's muse, which some scholars have identified with the Son. In some places called "she," in others "he," identified variously with Urania, the Son, the Spirit, and God, the traditionally feminine source of inspiration is not a woman on a pedestal but a creative drive that incorporates and transcends both sexes. I cannot think of any other answer to the accusation against Milton that he is sexist than to say that as in everything else he is very much in transition. On the most literal level, his poetry is theologically and sexually traditional; but he does not operate only on that level, which is continually undermined by subversive ideas about the nature of God, the world, and people.

To face mortality, then, for Milton, as for contemporary poets, must be to face the whole experience—male and female—of being. Once that is established, the religious spirit is more easily understood as communal. That is, the person, whole in himself, can perceive himself as every person, and his private poetry has a better capacity to express the human race. For some poets, that recovery of wholeness is in itself religious. Knowing who you are is

47. Ibid., p. 24.

knowledge of God and all other people. This is the profession of
Milton, Abdiel, and Christ; it is the epic communal tradition which
is strong in an utterly different but obviously related way in
America's bardic or prophetic poets.

For Milton, politics, religion, and sex are all parts of one
thing—the life of a free human being. Yet even when he demonstrates that, it is clear that the issue of despair does not go away;
understanding one's needs doesn't ensure their gratification. It is
necessary to come round once more to the solitary human being
alone in the wilderness—the poet, Christ, the American Adam—and
to ask again what solace one can find.

If the postmodernist clears away all the rubble of imposed
meanings, he hopes to let the myth that is implicit within the
world respond to the myth of the self, or vice versa: the poet-hero
becomes the device that reveals and makes meaning. That is
different from being the prophet of an imposed or humanly
articulated myth because the prophet himself becomes the gram-
mar of a myth that already exists; in his poetry he is the way of
which it is the ground. But the ground may prove meaningless or
worse. The poet may find nothing but wilderness, destruction,
chaos, death. Discovering himself to be in the business of writing
elegies, he wonders why he should continue. John Berryman
writes of his dead friends:

> Your torment here was brief,
> long falls your exit all repeatingly,
> a poor exemplum, one more suicide
> to stack upon the others
> till stricken Henry with his sisters & brothers
> suddenly gone pauses to wonder why he
> alone breasts the wronging tide.[48]

Figures of swimming or of walking on water are important both
for Milton and for many of our contemporaries because, although
inexact and confused by Christian association, they do suggest
what the arduous task of the poet in times like these must be.
Simple insistence on survival forces the destructive element to

---

48. John Berryman, *The Dream Songs* (New York: Farrar, Straus and Giroux, 1969),
p. 191. Robert Lowell's *History* (New York: Farrar, 1973) is full of elegies for his
contemporaries.

provide grounds for being. The desire to survive well enables him to walk on water, or on air. Milton, like many of our contemporaries, relies from moment to moment on what amounts to a delight in his capacity to achieve the impossible—that is, to live and to live triumphantly with the facts of suffering and death.

The choice of *Lycidas* as illustration is in a way arbitrary, since it is an early poem, and almost anything else of Milton's would work as well. But it is interesting to look at Milton's treatment of the elegiac form, to ensure the explicit comparison between him and our contemporaries when they have to write directly about mortality.

Lycidas appears to be a poem which, in response to the death of an acquaintance, allows Milton to face the fact of death and to conclude that all is well because Edward King is in Heaven. Yet if the joy at the end is only to be ascribed to Christian immortality, it is unlikely that this poem could have such power now, still outranking Shelley's *Adonais* and Arnold's *Thyrsis,* despite their greater secularity. Northrop Frye's analysis helps a good deal.[49] He sees the poem working on four levels—the level of simple brute reality in which death is the bloated corpse; the level of natural regeneration in which suns rise and set; the level of natural mythology in which Lycidas can be the genius of the shore; and that of Christianity, which sends Lycidas to heaven. All of the first three levels are still viable, and there is some way in which the admission of the reality of pain and death, of the fact that corruption cannot be wished away, makes the other interpretations more valid. The level of natural mythology is the most congenial to the contemporary religious spirit. Immortality is simply the living on of the dead person in the midst of his friends, the genius that enables them better to live and work in the world.

Lycidas was unable to walk on water, so he died. Christ walked on water and Peter's example tells us that anyone can follow him. Water imagery in the poem stresses this theme, makes us aware both of the corrupting power of water and of its restorative character. We walk on that which corrupts and that which gives faith; they are one, for in our world good does not exist without

49. Northrop Frye, "Literature as Context: Milton's 'Lycidas'," in *Fables of Identity: Studies in Poetic Mythology* (New York: Harcourt and Brace, 1963), pp. 119–29.

evil. In this sense, the poem is simply didactic, a fact which should make us recognize there is more to it, since Milton's poems are never so simply employed.

There is a sense in which Christianity itself is walking on water, and Milton dares the reader to make a leap of faith. For this reason he purposely causes the poem, at the end, to shift without a break from despair to overwhelming faith, from the nightmare image of bones hurled through the waves to the command not to weep because Lycidas is in heaven. That kind of leap was exciting and possible for Renaissance people, but it is rare among us. For us it is probably more pertinent that the poem encourages us to believe by deviously calling forth the will to faith. Repeatedly, Milton suppresses information that could strengthen our hopes for survival, as when he says that poetry is useless because the Muse couldn't help when Orpheus was torn to pieces. What Milton does not say is that when the head of Orpheus reached the Lesbian shore, its inhabitants were gifted with song—that is, poetry is valuable because it enabled Orpheus in his most important characteristic to survive. Because Milton suppresses all such obvious answers to his complaints, our minds recall them for us, believe them, and prepare us for larger claims.

Survival is from moment to moment, walking on water or over an abyss. *Lycidas* is distinctive in its way of repeatedly using itself up and having to start over from nothing. It contains not digressions but full stops. Why should the poem continue after such impressive closing lines as "As he pronounces lastly on each deed,/ Of so much fame in Heav'n expect thy meed"; or "But that two-handed engine at the door,/ Stands ready to smite once, and smite no more"; or "Look homeward Angel now and melt with ruth,/ And, O ye Dolphins waft the hapless youth"? And there are numerous minor stops, too, less weighty than these, but also risky when forced stopping and starting seem so likely to make the reader lose interest.

Here, though, the thoughtful reader may more likely ask what has happened and why. For what purpose does the poem appear to finish its business at line 84 by announcing that real fame is in heaven, not on earth, and therefore mortality is unimportant? Each time water keeps the poem going. Each time, Milton has to start over by invoking water imagery that calms the excitement and slides us over the impasse as if we ourselves were learning to walk on water, to survive from one perilous moment to the next. These full stops are intentional, and they are here to force us to learn to walk on water, avoiding the temptation to give up, to be stopped by what is out there, but to make the alien element itself carry us along.

This sort of discontinuity is almost characteristic of contemporary poetry. In fact, despite a general yearning for the ability to write epic, what does most frequently emerge is a sequence, like Berryman's Dream Songs, which are not only individually separated from one another, but are also blocked off in groups, the first group of seventy-seven ending *Lycidas*-like with the poet moving on:

> it is a wonder that, with in each hand
> one of his own mad books and all,
> ancient fires for eyes, his head full
> & his heart full, he's making ready to move on.[50]

There is no guarantee for the poet that any one of these poems will lead to another; each is complete, yet not complete in itself. The crossing of each boundary-line from one poem to the next is an act of faith; the poems reside existentially in their own moments and touch another moment only through the poet's capacity to take the next step. In this they resemble the stopping and starting of *Lycidas*.

In such a poem, obviously life is imitated, or reproduced, and whatever the subject of the poem, the poet is the hero. In fact it is an argument of contemporary poetry that in a secular age the capacity to write poetry is a test of our capacity for life, and the affirmation of poetry is proof that life is worthwhile. It is a circular proof, and its genre is exactly the Miltonic one which argues that life is worthwhile because the creation of life is. As Berryman's death unfortunately testifies, the belief is fragile; its triumph is our fragile, moment-to-moment survival.

Denise Levertov's sequence *To Stay Alive* is in some sense an elegy for her sister Olga. It moves on most, perhaps all, of the levels of *Lycidas*, proceeding in the discontinuous style sometimes thought of as collage, through numerous different episodes in

50. Berryman, *Dream Songs*, p. 84.

Levertov's life. More than most contemporary poets, she is aware
not only of the discontinuity of time but also of the way in which
all time and space inhere in any given moment, which nevertheless
cannot be preserved:

> Have you ever,
>   in stream or sea,
>   felt the silver of fish
> pass through your hand-hold? not to stop it,
> block it from going onward, but feel it
> move in its wave-road?
>   To make
>   of song a chalice,
>   of Time,
>   a communion wine.[51]

Olga's own limited life is translated into the revolutionary spirit
continually reborn. And that spirit is made to mesh with music as
it could not do for her.

Of Wallace Stevens' three criteria for the supreme fiction, the
second and third are "It must change" and "It must give pleasure." I would paraphrase the third to read "It must affirm." The
pleasure is in the affirmation. These two criteria in themselves can
distinguish the art of John Donne and T. S. Eliot from that of
Milton and Stevens. For Donne and Eliot, change is not desirable.
The maintenance of the tradition is what matters, and trust in an
unchanging, transcendent reality. For Milton and Stevens, different as they are, such an attitude is unthinkable. For Milton,
perfection and unity are only to be brought about by change,
occurring in the clashing and interdependency of good and evil,
the formation of life and art out of chaos.

There is an intrinsic relationship between the acceptance of evil,
death, and change, and the sense of the necessity of affirmation.
Donne and Eliot needed to rejoice in worship, but there is an
essential difference between that need and the kind of affirmation
required by Milton, Stevens, and many contemporary poets. The
cause for rejoicing is the creation of life. The joy is in the teeth of
change, in the fact of change. It asserts itself, justifying the ways

---

51. Denise Levertov, *To Stay Alive*, p. 39.

of God to men out of sheer love of creation that hardly distinguishes between the creator as God and the creator as human being. It affirms that the fall is fortunate, that death is the mother of beauty, and that when the pulse of revolution beats with the pulse of art, then the singing can begin.

The task of the American Adam has never been prelapsarian, has never been to inherit Eden, but it has been, as fallen man, to raise Eden in the waste wilderness. By confusing this issue, blurring the difference between fallen and unfallen men, Americans, including their poets, have not often seen the extent to which they would mistake Satanic control as a means to Paradise. Disillusionment became inevitable, and the Christ of *Paradise Regained* now seems an impossible ideal. Everything that Satan offers to this self-knowing second Adam is superfluous and entirely tempting. Christ is given a hostile environment in which to prove his humanity by rejecting Satan's imaginary vistas of rule and empire, luxury and artificial wisdom. His capacity to refuse the false vision is incomprehensible to Satan, for whom false dream is the only reality. Having tested Christ with all the world's vanity and failed to move him, Satan cries, "What dost thou in this World? The Wilderness/ For thee is fittest place" (IV.372–73). Satan neglects to realize that Christ is going to be in the wilderness in any case—either that wasteland which man's willfulness allows Satan to make, or the natural wilderness that is the fallen world in process of change. Christ is major man, no more and no less. A realist capable of understanding the limits of mortality, he is thereby able to come as close as man can to transcending limits. At the end of the poem, he has saved himself; he has not yet begun to save mankind.

Disillusioned as they may be, American poets still insist on their paradoxically bardic and antinomian heritage. They constantly risk both self-pity and immersion in transient causes. Generally speaking, it is their vocation, as it was Milton's, to run those risks. The fulfillment of their vocation is the capacity to find in their own experience the universal element and to speak out as prophets even when they know they cannot succeed in changing the world. More capable now perhaps than ever before, both of realistic vision and of despair, they can at least seek their own salvation.

Milton, crying out against the return of tyranny in 1660, when so many of his former allies were running for shelter, stood on the pinnacle of the temple. In *Paradise Lost* and *Paradise Regained,* he reaffirmed the same values for which he had fought and lost. Faith in creation, in life itself, enabled him to maintain his perilous balance. That kind of faith can sustain our poetry now.

Index

Abrams, Meyer H., 142, 185

Adam, 16, 17, 243; fall of, 90, 92. *See also* Milton, *Paradise Lost*

Aeschylus, 102, 217

Albertus Magnus, 74–75

Allegory, 8, 10–11, 12, 21, 25, 28, 47, 68, 114, 195, 218

Allen, Don Cameron, 11, 41

Allusion, xvi, 82, 105, 116–17, 186, 198

Altieri, Charles, 257

Anglicus, Bartholomaeus, 70–71

Apocalypse, The. *See* Bible, Revelation; John of Patmos; Prophecy; Prophets

Apollo, 6, 81

Areopagus, 57

Aries, Phillip, 162

Ariosto, Ludovico, 14, 26, 120, 132

Aristotle, 78, 106, 141, 207

Arnold, Matthew, 263

Arthuriad, 11

Artifacts: self-consuming, 106, 110, 111. *See also* Fish, Stanley E.

Astrology, 70

Auerbach, Erich, 17

Authorial intrusion, 82

Barker, Arthur E., 116

Barrow, Samuel, 48

Bate, Walter Jackson, 185

Berger, Harry, Jr., 40, 53

Berkeley, David Shelley, 107, 117

Bernard, Richard, 127, 130–31

Berryman, John, 259, 262, 265

Bible, 59, 91, 98, 100, 124, 143, 144, 183, 191, 194, 195, 202; King James Version, 73; aesthetics of, 106, 110; its structural intricacy, 134

—Revelation, xv, 32, 39, 101, 116, 122–23, 130–31, 137, 140–41; and the Book of Daniel, xv; ideology of, 100, 101, 108–9; aesthetics of, 100, 101, 109–10, 124–25, 129; style of, 100, 102, 113; commentary on, 100, 107, 114, 119, 121, 123, 124, 127, 132–34, 137; theory of influence in, 101; as a literary form, 101; themes of, 101; strategies of, 101, 116; as a model for prophecy, 102; as a mixed genre, 102, 103, 113; as multimedia art, 103; as comedy, 106–7; as tragedy, 106–7; synchronism in, 107–8; design of, 107–8, 113; structure of, 107, 116, 135; interiority of, 108; hero of, 108; Mighty Angel in, 108–9; providence in, 112, 123–24; resurrection in, 113, 121; perspectives in, 113; pastoralism in, 115; promise of, 118; regeneration in, 119; Christ in, 120, 135; the reading of, 121–22; symbolism in, 133–34; the story of the two witnesses in, 134; angels of, 139; *See also* Prophecy; Prophets

—various books of: Daniel, xv; Gospel of John, 60–61, 62, 84; Genesis, 63, 91, 116, 139, 168, 195; Hebrews, 117–18, 122–23; Isaiah, 119; Romans, 148; Corinthians, 151

Bicheno, James, 103

Blake, William, xiii, xiv, xv, xvii, 39, 98, 101, 104–5, 121, 129, 142, 143–84, 185, 188, 199, 203; and pictorial prophecy, 103; influences on, 143, 145; his rendering of the fall, 144; his criticism of Milton, 144–45, 146, 164–65, 178, 182–83; as mythmaker, 145; and dualism, 149; his attitude toward women, 153; his class stance, 180–81

COMPOSED BY THE COMPOSING ROOM, GRAND RAPIDS, MICHIGAN
MANUFACTURED BY MALLOY LITHOGRAPHING, INC., ANN ARBOR, MICHIGAN
TEXT AND DISPLAY LINES ARE SET IN BODONI BOOK

Library of Congress Cataloging in Publication Data
Main entry under title:
Milton and the line of vision.
Includes bibliographical references and index.
1. Milton, John, 1608–1674–Criticism and interpre-
tation–Addresses, essays, lectures. 2. English litera-
ture–History and criticism–Addresses, essays, lectures.
3. American literature–20th century–History and criti-
cism–Addresses, essays, lectures. I. Wittreich, Joseph
Anthony.
PR3588.M48   821'.4   75-12215
ISBN 0-299-06910-9